The American Short Story

Also by William Peden

Life and Selected Writings of Thomas Jefferson
   (with Adrienne Koch)

Selected Writings of John Quincy Adams
   (with Adrienne Koch)

Notes on the State of Virginia

Twenty-Nine Stories

Night in Funland and Other Stories

New Writing from South Carolina
   (with George Garrett)

Short Fiction: Shape and Substance

Twilight at Monticello

The American Short Story

Continuity and Change
1940–1975

William Peden

SECOND EDITION
REVISED AND ENLARGED

Houghton Mifflin Company Boston   1975

To the memory of my mother and my father

810.93 P341 aa

c. 1

Library of Congress Cataloging in Publication Data

Peden, William Harwood, 1913-
  The American short story.

  Bibliography: p.
  Includes index.
  1. Short stories, American — History and criticism.
  2. American fiction — 20th century — History and criticism.
  1. Title.
PS374.S5P4   1975   813'.5'09   75-23089
ISBN 0-395-20720-7

Printed in the United States of America

c 10 9 8 7 6 5 4 3 2 1

Some of these comments originally appeared in
considerably different form in the *New Republic*, the
New York Times Book Review, the *Saturday Review*, the
Sewanee Review, *Story*, *Studies in Short Fiction*, and
the *Virginia Quarterly Review.* FEB   '76

WI

Foreword and Acknowledgments

THE UNCLE REMUS STORIES, Uncle Wiggily's adventures, and the tales of Thornton W. Burgess were among the first stories I distinctly remember reading or having read to me. Two or three years later I discovered Poe and Kipling, and a year or two after that it was H. G. Wells and Conrad, by which time I realized that people in fiction could be even more interesting than animals. Since then the short story has been my favorite kind of reading, particularly the American short story of the last thirty or thirty-five years, say from around 1940. The specific date is, of course, arbitrary and might just as well be 1939 or 1941 or something of the sort. But 1940 is a good round number, and, what is much more relevant, American short fiction began to change and grow in importance around the beginning of our participation in World War II. I have tried in this book to suggest some of the directions the American short story has taken since that time. I hope I have not neglected any really significant American writers whose major contributions have been made during the last thirty-five years; if I have, the oversight is the result of ignorance rather than deliberate malfeasance, but I must say that I have not tried to compete with any encyclopedia. I have tried, rather, to suggest the variety and achievement of these years in terms of the authors whom I consider the most important or the most representative or the ones I like the best . . . or, usually, some combination of the three. Some of these authors are very well known, but there are others who have never received their just due, and among them they have made what I think is the major American literary contribution of the post-World War II years.

I wrote an earlier version of this book a little over ten years ago, aided by a Guggenheim Fellowship and a sabbatical leave from the University of Missouri. I am grateful for them, and for another sabbatical, just ended. Parts of this book were written at Cumberland Lodge, in the Great Park of Windsor, one of the most beautiful and quiet places on God's earth, and I am grateful to the staff there, too, particularly Miss Ruth Norton, the program director. I am also grateful to my colleagues and students at the University of Missouri, to my department chairmen Milton Gatch and John Roberts, and to Deans Armon Yanders and Lloyd Berry and the University of Missouri Research Council. Mrs. Pat Gülmez has ransacked our libraries for dates and books, and Miss Barbara Blunt has been an indefatigable and courageous typist. Most of all, of course, I am indebted to my wife, Margaret Sayers Peden, without whose et cetera et cetera et cetera . . . The phrases have become bromides from overuse, but the gratitude is real.

WILLIAM PEDEN

Columbia, Missouri
February 1, 1975

Contents

Chapter 1

Background and Antecedents

PARADOX has characterized the development of the short story in the United States. Although it is the only major literary form of essentially American origin and the only one in which American writers have from the beginning tended to excel, for decades it was considered a subliterary genre, which until relatively recent times most critics refused to consider as important as the more traditional forms of poetry, drama, and the novel. Its development was closely associated with that of the American magazine, yet its highest achievements have been reached during the last thirty-five years, which have seen the virtual disappearance of fiction from the mass-circulation market. The economic position of the serious short story writer in America has almost invariably been precarious, although for more than a century short fiction was the stock in trade of the American family magazine. In spite of this enormous popularity in periodicals, the adult short story in book form, with only occasional exceptions, has tended to be a financial failure. Even Poe, the father of the form and the most popular magazine fiction writer of his generation, had reason to lament that he was poor in a country where to be "poor was to be despised," and in spite of his notoriety and the great success of his stories in the leading magazines of his day he had difficulty getting his stories published in book form; *Tales of the Grotesque and Arabesque* was a financial failure for which Poe received almost no return.

From Poe's time to the present day, book publishers for the most part have been reluctant to bring out collections of short stories by individual authors, particularly those without a "name" or a following, a reluctance that has occasionally resulted in a publisher's unwillingness to refer to a volume of short stories by its proper generic name, as was the case with the paperback edition of the best-selling *Tales of the South Pacific,* which was labeled "one of the greatest *novels* of the war" (the italics are mine), or Faulkner's *Knight's Gambit,* a collection of six short stories whose dust jacket heralded "a new *book* by America's foremost novelist," Faulkner's "new *book* in six sections" (again, the italics are mine), or John Knowles's *Phineas,* billed in paperback as a brilliant new *"work."*

Despite the difficulties, more and more American fiction writers continue to find the short story the most exciting, congenial, and challenging of all contemporary literary forms. Many individual collections of short stories continue to be "lost" or "marginal" books, which for the most part do not make much money or even pay their own way, but they are no longer a publishing taboo. More good American short story writers have emerged since 1940 than in any comparable span in our history; more good-to-excellent volumes of short stories have been published during these years than ever before. Whether these encouraging trends will continue in the face of inflation, the shrinking of the periodical market, and the competition of television, film, the new journalism, and nonfiction remains to be seen.

No one has been able to explain satisfactorily just why collections of short stories by individual authors "don't sell," although a lot of "experts" have discussed and analyzed the situation from all angles and perspectives. Central to the problem, it seems to me, has been the historical association between the short story and the American mass-circulation magazine, particularly after the phenomenal growth of the big "family" magazines from around the middle of the nineteenth century until the 1950s. In one major line of its development, the short story became a piece of merchandise written to conform to the tastes of a rapidly expanding middle-class reading audience. Short story standards were set by publishers, or their advertisers, who were determined to please as many buyers and subscribers as possible and to offend or alienate a minimum number of cash customers. The result was a steady deterioration of the high standards of the first generation of American short story writers, Washington Irving, Edgar Allan Poe, and Nathaniel Hawthorne. What Poe called the "namby-pamby" quality of the nineteenth-century ancestors of the mass-circulation big flats and big slicks of our own century has always been a dominant characteristic of mass-circulation magazine fiction.

Such sponsorship of competent mediocrity partially explains why the short story continued to be regarded as a second-class literary citizen. For the commuter with half an hour to kill on his way to work or the patient awaiting his turn in the dentist's chair, short stories were regarded as pleasant diversions or comfortable time-killers, but nothing to be taken seriously. In the days before World War II when a big magazine like the *Saturday Evening Post* could be bought for a nickel — how remote that sounds in 1975; one might as well be referring to Egypt under the Ptolemys — and short stories frequently appeared both in the daily and Sunday newspapers, a short story was considered something to be read casually and tossed into the wastepaper basket, certainly not good enough to pay folding money for, particularly by the individual who purchased a book only occasionally or who joined book clubs primarily for their status value. Such reader-buyer apathy and resistance made the hard-cover publication of short stories an ever more hazardous publishing enterprise: the short story writer increasingly found himself confined within an ever-tightening circle of cause and effect.

Our national admiration of bigness-as-such also accounts in part for public indifference to the short story. Historically as a people we have tended to admire size above quality wherever it is displayed: in the bosoms of go-go girls, skin-magazine fold-outs and pop-ups, or female leads in X-rated films; in our conventional best sellers, fiction or non-fiction; in the salaries of our professional athletes; and in our automobiles, except for an all-too-brief interlude during the peak of the 1974 fuel crisis.

In spite of all this, more and more Americans have gradually been "discovering" or "rediscovering" the short story. Influenced by the accessibility of paperback reprints of good collections of short stories in supermarkets, drugstores, and airports, reader-buyer resistance has slowly diminished. Readers are finding that although the short story may demand more of them than the average novel, it is likely to give more in return. Furthermore, the popularity of such collections as Bernard Malamud's *The Magic Barrel*, distributed as a major book club selection *after* it had won the National Book Award for fiction in 1959, J. D. Salinger's *Nine Stories*, John Barth's *Lost in the Funhouse*, Jorge Luis Borges' *Labyrinths* and *Ficciones*, and Kurt Vonnegut's *Welcome to the Monkey House* — the last three particularly popular among college and university students — demonstrated that the adult short story, among other factors in its favor, can be both fun to read and stimulating. As more Americans become exposed to different types of education, formal and otherwise, and the general level of literary intelligence and sophistication continues to rise, it seems likely that the short story will become increasingly enjoyed and appreciated.

Why the short story not only survived but prospered during the decline of the magazine market that cradled it, and why so many diverse and talented writers continue to find it the most challenging and appealing of literary forms, are less debatable than its failure to sell in hard-cover individual collections.

The short story in America has always been characterized by individuality, freedom, and variety. Flexibility and the capacity for change are its hallmarks, and no other literary genre is so close to the rapidly changing climate of the times in which it is written and which in turn it reflects with vigor, variety, and verve. Never has this capacity for change been more dramatically apparent than during the late sixties and early seventies: the genre has proved itself flexible enough to accommodate the sparse realities of Leonard Michaels' "The Manikin" and the more leisurely complexities of I. B. Singer's "A Crown of Feathers" or Saul Bellows' "The Old System" along with the "crots" of Richard Brautigan's *Revenge of the Lawn* or the integration of text and graphics of Donald Barthelme's "At the Tolstoy Museum" and the fictions of the "innovationists," who agree with Alain Robbe-Grillet's contention that the use of "character" and "story" in fiction is not only obsolete but dangerous.

The short story can be a vehicle for conveying the most deeply felt social convictions, as it is in Nelson Algren's "A Bottle of Milk for Mother" or James Baldwin's "Going to Meet the Man." At the other extreme, for the writer who believes that traditional realism is being replaced by film, it is an effective medium for seeking meaning in fable, parable, legend, or myth, as we find it in John Gardner's "The Song of Grendel" or John Barth's "Dunyazadiad." It can be alive with the good humor of William Saroyan's "The Fifty-Yard Dash" or, like Jean Stafford's "The Interior Castle," it can reek of the smell of the sickroom. It can be a fully plotted story of physical conflict, or a muted study in mood and atmosphere akin to lyrical poetry, or, like John Cheever's "The World of Apples," it can be a character study rich in psychological and emotional overtones in which conventional narrative and the linear-sequential unfolding of incident and plot scarcely exist. Like the new journalism it can apply fictional methods and techniques to actual events; it can be a slice of life closely related to reportage; or it can concern itself primarily with visual effects, including experiments with typography and graphics.

It can be, in short, as H. E. Bates observed, "anything the author decides it shall be."

Equally important, perhaps, is the fact that the short story, whatever its form, subject matter, and the intent of its creator, challenges the powers of the most demanding craftsmen and artists. Not without reason did Henry James refer to short fiction as "blest" and "beautiful." In a very real sense the short story writer tends to feel his way along a tightrope between success and failure. To change metaphors, he is like a surgeon performing an operation, a quarterback directing a football team. He must be in command of the situation at all times and in all places. Within the limited boundaries of the form there is little room for lapses, false moves, irrelevancies, technical blunders. The short story demands compression, economy, and an unerring sense of selectivity. The short story writer obviously cannot explore the by-paths of a situation or ponder at length the intricacy of a character. He must constantly discipline and shape his subject matter to gain his desired effect. He must be thoughtful person, literary artist, entertainer, and expert technician. The novelist can be digressive and discursive, careless here and slovenly there, yet still create a good or great novel. For the writer of short fiction, false moves or lapses are likely to result in total failure.

At the same time that the short story demands as much of the author as does any other literary genre, it continues to be the most accessible form in which the comparative beginner can develop his ability and explore the extent and nature of his talent. The time and energy required to write a satisfactory first novel can sometimes be fatal; there is no way of ascertaining how many potentially able fiction writers have been crushed by "risking everything" on a novel before they were ready for the task. A short story writer can recover, however, from the errors and disappointments that accompany the beginner's efforts. Thus it is that the genre remains the particular province of the young, the proving ground between apprenticeship and mastery.

Whether written by novice or master, the short story is particularly compatible with the temper and temperament of the present age. The fragmented nature of contemporary life makes it virtually impossible for most fiction writers to grapple with the fundamental verities that engaged the great nineteenth- and early twentieth-century masters from Dickens, Melville, and Hawthorne through Dostoevski and Tolstoi to Hardy and Conrad. Revolutions and revelations in personal ethics and public morality; undreamed-of social, economic, and geopolitical complexities; the explosion of anxiety, neurosis, tension, drug addiction; bewildering and often horrifying scientific breakthroughs; Vietnam, the race situation, pollution, Watergate, and their attendant ills and dislocations — all this has rendered almost ludicrous Browning's comfortable assumption that all's right with the world.

The short story has become the literary mirror for reflecting an age in which the new tends to be obsolete by tomorrow, in which change seems more relevant than order, and eventual destruction the only reality. Brief, elliptical, unwinking, and very much alive, the short story usually asks questions but does not suggest answers. Unlike the traditional novelists, the short story writer usually does not bring his powers to bear on the grand questions of where are we going, why are we here. Rather, he focuses his attention, swiftly and clearly, on one facet of man's experience; he illuminates briefly one dark corner or depicts one aspect of life.

It seems to me, then, that the short story writer is creating the most significant literary form of the post-World War II years. More and more, the recent and contemporary short story has begun to occupy a position similar to that of drama in the Elizabethan age, the essay during the period of Addison and Steele, romantic poetry in the early nineteenth century, and the novel from the middle of the nineteenth century through the early decades of the twentieth. Indeed, it seems possible that future historians of American literature will find in the short story, rather than in the novel or the drama and poetry, the major literary contribution of recent decades.

Chapter 2

Publishers, Publishing, and the American Short Story since 1940

THE ANTECEDENTS of the post-1940 short story have been discussed in such detail that only a brief summary is needed here. The stories of Henry James, Chekhov, Joyce, and Sherwood Anderson were its ancestors; *Dubliners* (1914) and *Winesburg, Ohio* (1919) were towering landmarks and seminal influences in its development. The "new" fiction of the twenties, begun during the restless, skeptical years following the end of World War I, was a reaction against the formularized writings of the imitators of Kipling and O. Henry; it was a breakaway from the unrealistic, contrived, and sentimentalized magazine short stories, which for the most part were unconcerned with either ideas or artistry. The remarkable group of young writers, which included Conrad Aiken, Anderson, Faulkner, Fitzgerald, Hemingway, Langston Hughes, William March, Katherine Anne Porter, and William Carlos Williams, rejected the romantic excesses, the tricks and contrivances and the assembly-line plotting employed by the majority of popular magazine authors. Like Sherwood Anderson, many of them admired simplicity and reality of form and language and content; they strove for the truth as they conceived it to be; they were increasingly motivated by what Anderson had called the "hunger to see beneath the surface of lives." Animated by a sense of the immediate, the "nowness" of life and art, they helped free the short story from the tyranny of plot, and they restored to it a dignity and integrity that, with a few notable exceptions, had been lacking since the times of Hawthorne and Poe; they paved the way for the next great period of the American short story, that of the post-World War II decades.

The mass-circulation magazines can claim little credit for either of these periods of high achievement. To the contrary. Today, with such weekly mass-circulation general or family magazines as *Collier's* and the *Saturday Evening Post* only a memory, and with the remaining family magazines fighting for their lives and publishing relatively little fiction, it is painful to recall the shallowness of most of the short fiction published in these and similar periodicals.

Technical adroitness was always one of the hallmarks of the slick story; most of the stories in the best mass-circulation magazines were the work of skilled and disciplined professionals. The big slicks and the big flats catered to the demands of a huge audience; it has been estimated that during the late forties and early fifties *Collier's,* the *Saturday Evening Post,* and *This Week* reached a combined weekly audience of upward of fifty million readers. Such periodicals rewarded their authors generously. At a time when many small magazines of high quality could pay their contributors little or nothing, the big slicks are said to have conducted recruiting raids as zealously as did the talent scouts for Hollywood and big-time football. More than one editor of a little or high-quality magazine had reason to lament the loss of one of his discoveries, and more than one critic commented that the gap between the large-circulation and small-circulation magazines was a disaster for American literature. For despite its technical skill, its external variety, and its rapid pace, the average mass-circulation magazine story was little more than an adroitly manufactured or elaborately cosmeticized refugee from the shallow and meretricious world of the pulp magazine.

The slick story masked its endless variations upon the boy-meets-girl theme beneath the camouflage of "fine writing" or the paraphernalia of costume and period; occasionally it attempted to adorn its intrinsic shabbiness with the vestments of "social awareness." Though preoccupied with the middle and upper classes or the unusual or the romantic, and though restricted by many taboos, it pretended to contemporaneity; during the World War II years, for example, hundreds of formula stories simply put their heroes into uniforms and proceeded with business as usual. But beneath the costume of the lady of quality the faltering accents of the parvenu could usually be heard. This perpetual striving to masquerade as something it was not was perhaps the most objectionable characteristic of the slick-paper story; the pulps, to their credit, at least never presumed to be more than what they actually were — assembly-line facsimiles of the real thing. There were exceptions, to be sure: *Collier's* and the *Post* and some others published occasional good stories, but the discrepancy in the ratio between them and the thousands of pieces of commercial carpentry is appalling.

Considerable difference of opinion existed as to why such magazines consistently published so much mediocre short fiction. The mediocrity has been explained and sometimes defended in realistic terms: like any other big-business operation, the mass-circulation magazines had to operate at a profit or expire. This explanation is certainly understandable, but its corollary — that for a mass-circulation magazine to operate in the black its fiction must take no chances, run no risks, offend nobody, experiment with nothing not virtually guaranteed to succeed — is open to question. More than one fiction editor of a big slick proclaimed orally — or occasionally, but only occasionally, in print — that he wished to improve the quality of his magazine's fiction but was continually under pressure by reader reaction to adhere to the level of competent mediocrity that an unsophisticated "composite reader" demanded. Any violation of a basic taboo, it has been said, produced immediate and angry reader reactions; one of the editors of *Collier's* once told me, for example, that a 1947 *Collier's* story centering on the then inviolate taboo of racial problems was followed by an immediate drop of thousands of newsstand purchases and a flood of canceled subscriptions.

At the same time certain authors placed much of the blame on their editors: after all, one has to eat, doesn't he? Other critics laid the responsibility directly on the doorstep of "someone upstairs" or singled out the big advertisers as the villain, going so far as to claim that the only real function of the mass-circulation magazines was to provide advertising space for big business, which kept the magazines alive and directly or indirectly controlled editorial policy.

Whatever the causes, the insipidity of most family magazine fiction is an unfortunate chapter in the history of American literature. In the almost complete absence of anything resembling encouragement or sponsorship from the big magazines, the American short story writer who grappled with adult concepts and problems had to find an outlet for his work elsewhere. Of the many and varied good quality weeklies, monthlies, university-sponsored quarterlies, "little" or advance-guard literary magazines, and other difficult-to-classify publications, among the most significant were the *New Yorker* and *Story*.

The first number of the *New Yorker* appeared on February 21, 1925, but it was not till some years later that the term the "*New Yorker* short story" became current. The battle for freedom of form and idea had, of course, been fought and to a large extent won before Harold Ross conceived his idea of a weekly magazine *not* designed for the "little old lady in Dubuque." The *New Yorker* did not, as has sometimes been said, produce a revolution in the contemporary short story; instead, it stimulated and helped shape the direction of a literary form that had already asserted its independence and had begun to establish its own directions. As the magazine's circulation rose from 77,500 in 1929 to 125,000 in 1934, a period that saw the deaths of several magazines with valid claims to literary excellence, its influence deepened and widened enormously; by the middle thirties, the *New Yorker* had won considerable snob appeal, as well as prestige honestly and honorably earned. Many talented writers appeared in its pages; for one thing, the *New Yorker* paid its contributors well during the Depression and its aftermath when many smaller and less prestigious magazines were reduced to token payments, or in some cases no cash payment of any sort. In the pages of the *New Yorker* appeared Kay Boyle and

John Cheever, William March and John O'Hara, Jean Stafford and
Eudora Welty, James Thurber and John Updike, Donald Barthelme
and I. B. Singer, and scores of other fiction writers, native and
foreign, whose work is so varied as to repudiate, once and for all,
the popular and long-lived misconception of a magic formula
known as the *"New Yorker* story."

Opinions concerning *New Yorker* fiction are diverse and sometimes violent; they range from a paean of unstinted praise by as
well known a critic as Arthur Mizener to James Purdy's contention
that the magazine exerted the "worst influence in America today"
[1963] or James Laughlin's statement that "if you read all their
stories every week for a year you'd begin to think that most of them
were written by the same person using different names."

Laughlin may be overstating the case, but there is truth in his
comment. A deadly uniformity, at times amounting almost to self-
imitation, has at various periods tended to characterize *New Yorker*
fiction; there have been the plotless vignettes or slice-of-life pieces
of the thirties, the urbane stories of contemporary manners by such
authors and *New Yorker* staff members as Robert M. Coates, Roger
Angell, and Edward Newhouse during the fifties and sixties, and
the imitators of the imitators of the current Borges-Barthelme
school. Less than praiseworthy, too, has been a tendency to over-
expose certain star performers, frequently by printing work considerably below their accustomed standards: John O'Hara, John
Updike, and Donald Barthelme come immediately to mind. But
this is perhaps nit-picking. The real and continuing importance of
the *New Yorker* is indisputable. Over the long haul, issue in and
issue out, it has published more good stories than any magazine in
the world.

Story, which the *London Times Literary Supplement* once labeled the
"most distinguished short story magazine in the world," was a quite
different kind of magazine. Founded in Vienna in 1931, this
small-budget, small-circulation periodical was interested in "short
stories of significance by no matter whom and coming from no
matter where." Its founders, Whit Burnett and Martha Foley,

were coeditors until 1941, when Foley left the magazine to edit the *Best American* annual anthologies after the death of Edward O'Brien, and Hallie Southgate Burnett became coeditor. Characterized by its senior editor as an attempt to "rescue the creative American short story from what looked, at that time, like possible extinction," *Story* constantly emphasized quality and originality rather than conformity or big-name appeal, and its open-door policy of no taboos of subject matter, technique, or length encouraged many unknowns who subsequently achieved literary distinction. Such diverse authors as William Saroyan, Richard Wright, Carson McCullers, Jesse Stuart, Ludwig Bemelmans, J. D. Salinger, John Knowles, and Norman Mailer were first published in *Story;* with few exceptions most of the major writers of recent vintage, American and non-American, were among its contributors prior to its demise in 1963, when it fell victim to the spiraling costs of production and distribution that had plagued it and similar magazines throughout the years. More stories from its pages were anthologized during the thirties and forties than from any other American magazine except the *New Yorker.* (In one year eight stories from *Story* were included in *The Best American Short Stories,* the same number that the *Saturday Evening Post,* with its high fees to authors and its vast circulation, contributed to the *O. Henry Memorial Award Prize Stories* from 1940 through 1963.)

Scores of other magazines have been vital factors in the growth and vigor of the short story in America. Of the monthly magazines the most important have been *Harper's* and the *Atlantic,* which for decades published superior short fiction, including work by relative newcomers or beginners; the *Atlantic's* sponsorship of "First" publications continues to be of major importance.

Esquire, since its founding in 1934, published many good-to-excellent stories, in spite of a series of fluctuating and often incomprehensible editorial changes; particularly under the recent fiction editorship of Gordon Lish, *Esquire* has been a major force in contemporary short fiction. So too, potentially at least, is *Playboy,* with its high authors' fees and vast circulation.

With few exceptions serious American short story writers since the days of Poe and Hawthorne have had reason to lament the scarcity of magazine and book publishers interested in good fiction. From an author's point of view, of course, there have never been enough outlets for his particular kind of work, and there probably never will be. But at no other time has the need for such outlets been more acute than during the last three decades. Here again we are confronted with a paradox.

Historically, as I commented earlier, short story collections by individual authors have tended to be publishing risks. But America has been producing more and more talented short story writers, so many that even the most commercially oriented publisher was almost obliged to risk an occasional short story collection as a prestige addition to his list or as a means of holding or obtaining a promising author who might subsequently produce a profitable novel. But the bad track records of most short fiction collections discourage the publisher from allocating to such a book anything but very limited advertising appropriation. The book receives little or no attention in the major book pages. Few potential purchasers are even aware of its existence. Bookstores do not stock it. Acquisition librarians ignore it. The "name" critics and talk-show personalities forget it. The book is neither a critical nor a financial success. Everyone concerned — the publisher, the editor who worked on the manuscript, the promotion people, and the author — is disappointed, vaguely unhappy about the whole business.

The lack of success is deepened by the popularity of television, which almost single-handedly brought an end to the mass-circulation magazine fiction market. Added to this is the inflation of the seventies and the subsequent and ever-increasing gap between spiraling publishing and marketing costs and the short story reading and buying public, the growing reader preference for nonfiction, the competition of film and the achievements of the new journalism, and the enormous growth of highly specialized magazines catering to very specific interest groups.

But in spite of all of these problems the short story in America not only survives but continues to prosper. The short story writer, like the poet, tends to be a more dedicated writer than the novelist or the writer of nonfiction: certainly he is not deluded into thinking of his short stories as an easy means toward recognition or the big money.

What then, in the face of the shrinking mass-circulation periodical fiction market and the difficulties of "first book" publication, difficulties accentuated during the last decade by the disappearance of several independent American book publishers, some of them with distinguished histories, overcome by inflation and fierce competition, gone forever or swallowed up by one of the gigantic combines?

Much of the burden and the responsibility will continue to rest on quarterly literary magazines, journals of ideas that occasionally publish one or two stories and a few poems, advance-guard or experimental periodicals or newspapers, and a few admirable but unfortunately short-lived experiments in book form including Scribner's *Story* 1, 2, 3, and 4; McKay's *Story: The Magazine of the Short Story in Book Form,* which also was discontinued after four issues; Putnam's *New Campus Writing* and Random House's *The Best College Writing,* both deceased; and more recently *Intro,* an annual collection of short fiction and poetry by students at American colleges and universities affiliated with the Associated Writing Programs, published successively by McCall-Bantam, the University Press of Virginia, and, since 1974, by Doubleday.

Among the most important of these magazines and periodicals are the *Virginia Quarterly Review,* particularly since the inception of its annual Emily Clark Balch Awards, in my opinion the most prestigious magazine short story award in America today; the *Sewanee Review,* the oldest distinguished American literary quarterly; and *Epoch,* among the first, if not the first, university-sponsored (Cornell) periodicals devoted exclusively to fiction and poetry. To these and a host of others, some well known, others performing their functions in virtual obscurity, writers, readers, critics, and book publishers owe a debt too large to be calculated. Such publications are hazardous undertakings: the literary landscape of the last three and a half decades is littered with their remains. Among the bleaching bones of scores of lesser or little known victims are those of *Accent*, the *New Mexico Quarterly*, and the *Kenyon Review*.

Closely related to this type of magazine are the two annual anthologies of superior stories originally published in American magazines and periodicals, *The Best American Short Stories* and the *O. Henry Memorial Award Prize Stories*. The first *Best* collection was published in 1916 under the editorship of Edward J. O'Brien. Growing out of O'Brien's dedicated belief "in the democratic future of the American short story," the annual *Best* collections have more than justified the editor's hopes that these anthologies "may do something toward disengaging the honest good from the meretricious mass of writing with which it is mingled." An enthusiastic and indefatigable editor, as well as a sound critic, O'Brien continued editing these anthologies until his death in 1941. Since then the series has been edited without interruption by Martha Foley, assisted for several years by the late David Burnett.

In 1918 several members of the Society of Arts and Sciences of New York, many of whom had been associated with O. Henry during his Manhattan days, met to establish a "memorial to the author who had transmuted realistic New York into romantic Bagdad-by-the-Subway." Out of this meeting grew the *O. Henry Memorial Award Prize Stories*, the first collection of which, edited by Blanche Colton Williams, was published in 1921. Like O'Brien, Williams sought "originality, excellence in characterization, skill in organization of plot, [and] power in moving emotions," and like him she was a knowledgeable and dedicated editor. She was followed, successively and successfully, by Harry Hansen (1933–40), Herschel Brickell (1941–52), Paul Engle (1955–59 — no volumes were published in 1953 and 1954 following Brickell's death), Mary Stegner (1960), Richard Poirier (1961–64), Poirier and William Abrahams (1965–68), and Abrahams since 1968.

The short story is both the most personal and most varied of contemporary literary forms, and to cull a handful of superior pieces from the annual quagmire of American periodical fiction is a staggering task. Inevitably some favorites of one author, editor, critic, or informed reader are likely to leave another editor cold or at best indifferent; in face of the formidable problems involved in preparing such collections, certain selections or omissions evoked considerable disagreement and controversy. Foley, for example, at one time seemed to me to favor stories and authors from the metropolitan New York area; Brickell, on the other hand, was partial to Southern writers. Paul Engle's first *O. Henry* anthology, in 1954, contained so many selections by writers associated with the State University of Iowa as to raise a howl or two from some critics and readers, and Richard Poirier's first *O. Henry,* 1961, seemed slightly arcane. More difficult for the layman to understand, perhaps, is the frequency with which one editor was unimpressed with the other's selections: first- , second- , and third-prize *O. Henry* winners were often not included in the *Best* anthologies. Despite the differences of opinion, over the years the editors performed their difficult tasks with admirable awareness and dignity. It is impossible to overestimate the role played by these collections in stimulating the development of the American short story.

Walt Whitman's often-quoted statement that for a country to have great poets it must also have great audiences needs to be amended to read that to have great writers of any genre there must first of all be great publishers to present that which is good of its kind, new, meaningful, vital. As editorial, publication, and distribution costs continue to rise, the marginal literary forms become threatened and the role of the small-circulation literary magazine and the book publisher willing to publish first collections of stories assumes greater and greater importance. Some book publishers — Doubleday, Farrar, Straus & Giroux, and Houghton Mifflin, for example — have done this with less reluctance than many of their peers, and, it is to be hoped, will continue to do so.

One auspicious sign for the future of the short story is the growing importance and prestige of the university presses, an importance underscored by the increasing number of university press books that have been recent National Book Award nominees or prize-winners. For years university presses stimulated and encouraged American poetry but almost without exception were even more hesitant than the commercial presses to publish books of short stories. Recently this reluctance has been diminishing. In 1968 the Louisiana State University Press inaugurated an annual series of short story collections that has included William Peden's *Night in Funland,* David Madden's *The Shadow Knows,* and Hollis Summers' *How They Chose the Dead.* The second book published by the University of Missouri Press was *The White Hound* (1959), a collection by Ward Dorrance and the late Thomas Mabry; Missouri currently includes in its annual "Breakthrough" series one or two "first" collections, among them Ann Jones's *Hope Should Always* and David Huddle's *A Dream with No Stump Roots in It.* The University of Illinois Press has similarly published books of short stories by professionals, like *In the Hands of Our Enemies* by Daniel Curley, and talented newcomers, including *The Murphy Stories* by Mark Costello and *And If Defeated Allege Fraud* by Paul Friedman; in April 1975 the same press launched the projected annual simultaneous publication of four collections with books by Philip F. O'Connor, Gordon Weaver, Stephen Minot, and John Stewart. In 1970 the State University of Iowa began its own annual series, accompanied by an award of $1,000, with Cyrus Colter's *The Beach Umbrella.*

With these and similar university press projects there is hope for the future.

Chapter 3

The Period in Retrospect: World War II to Watergate

IT IS DIFFICULT and hazardous to generalize about a period that includes such diverse short story writers as Nelson Algren, Louis Auchincloss, James Baldwin, John Barth, Donald Barthelme, Saul Bellow, Paul Bowles, Ray Bradbury, Hortense Calisher, Truman Capote, John Cheever, William Goyen, Nancy Hale, Shirley Jackson, Robert Lowry, Carson McCullers, Mary McCarthy, Bernard Malamud, Leonard Michaels, Flannery O'Connor, John O'Hara, Grace Paley, James Purdy, Philip Roth, J. D. Salinger, I. B. Singer, Irwin Shaw, Jean Stafford, Wallace Stegner, Jesse Stuart, Peter Taylor, Jerome Weidman, Eudora Welty, Tennessee Williams, and John Updike. At least one conclusion is inescapable: since the early forties, the American short story has come completely of age.

During the last three and a half decades more American short story writers have been creating more skillfully, more artistically, more meaningfully, than ever before in our national history. It is no exaggeration to suggest that there have been dozens of American fiction writers since 1940 who, technically speaking, are much better novelists than James Fenimore Cooper ever was; and there are scores who can write better short stories — again speaking of technical achievement — than Hawthorne and Poe occasionally did. Even our very young writers — the Truman Capote of *A Tree of Night,* for example, published when the author was only twenty-five, or Philip Roth whose National Book Award-winning *Goodbye, Columbus* came out when he was twenty-six, or John Updike whose first collection of short stories, *The Same Door,* was published when he was twenty-seven — display dazzling virtuosity and adroitness. Comparison of any of the *Best* or *O. Henry* annual collections of American short stories since 1940 with those of the twenties, is like comparing a crystal receiving set of the twenties with one of today's transistors.

The reasons underlying this marked increase in technical skill and artistic achievement are many, disparate, and often difficult to assess. Unquestionably, however, the influence of the American college and university is a dominant factor. A half century ago young writers like Jack London, Richard Harding Davis, Stephen Crane, and O. Henry served their apprenticeships and developed their talents while they worked as journalists; today the college· classroom or the faculty study has for the most part replaced Hawthorne's "solitary chamber" and the newsroom as incubators for creative growth and development. Even most of our smaller and less experimental educational institutions now offer some work in "creative writing" or boast of a writer-in-residence, and many young writers begin to produce seriously while they are undergraduates, are first published in college or university literary magazines, and with increasing frequency combine the dual roles of writer and teacher. Long considered a pariah, gate crasher, or at best a parvenu, the teacher of creative writing or the writer-in-residence has not only been accepted within the framework of the American college or university but has become a standard member of almost every English department, large or small, distinguished or mediocre; he has, as a matter a fact, become a necessity, a drawing card, at a time of dwindling enrollments in the traditional language and literature courses.

The older generation of such writer-teachers included the likes of Robert Frost, William Faulkner, and Katherine Anne Porter; for the most part they were visitors occupying honorary positions or advisory chairs and, in fact, did comparatively little if any formal teaching. However important their roles, they were for the most part outside the movement to which they brought honor and dignity. Today's writer-teachers are full-fledged members of their academic communities and their duties extend beyond the "teaching of writing." (The phrase is unfortunate: obviously no one can *teach* anyone to write — or to paint or to compose music or to run the mile in four minutes or throw the discus two hundred feet — and few, if any, respectable writer-teachers make any such claim. The instructor conducting a class in the writing of poetry or the short story, however, *can* offer editorial advice; he can aid in stimulating whatever talent his students may possess; he can help shorten the apprenticeship period and foster a climate of mutual respect and encouragement; he can weed out the utterly untalented but earnest student whose energies should be directed elsewhere. Only the occasional fraud or deadbeat within the profession presumes to offer his students more than this.)

The roster of writer-teachers is impressive and remarkably diverse; it includes or has included — some of them, alas, are dead — John Barth, Saul Bellow, R. V. Cassill, Walter VanTilburg Clark, Paul Engle, George Garrett, Caroline Gordon, Andrew Lytle, Bernard Malamud, Mary McCarthy, Joyce Carol Oates, Philip Roth, Mark Schorer, Allan Seager, Jean Stafford, Wallace Stegner, Alan Swallow, Hudson Strode, Allen Tate, Kurt Vonnegut, Robert Penn Warren. The presence of these and many, many other able teacher-writers suggests that for the next few years at least their influence will be basically good. It remains to be seen, however, whether this situation will eventually have a positive or a negative effect on American literature. The movement, if it can be called such, already shows signs of provincialism and commercialism; today some universities sponsor so-called "writers' conferences," which have little more to do with writing than a homecoming football weekend has to do with higher education. Similarly, the directors of some university-sponsored resident training programs seem more interested in luring big-name writers to their campuses than in hiring experienced teachers, and are more intent on publicity than in attending to the business of teaching and learning. Such activities subject even the less flamboyant university writing programs to suspicion and, eventually, ridicule. Criticisms of academic writing programs and the writer-as-teacher are becoming more frequent; characteristic was E. M. Forster's petulant comment that a certain writer's short stories are "completely free from the slickness that comes from attending courses in Creative Literature."

At one time or another most of the shortcomings of contemporary fiction have been laid at the doorstep of the writer-teacher. These defects include the painful artiness of a considerable amount of the smaller or advance-guard magazine fiction; preoccupation with technique at the expense of substance and story; the love of the crutch of symbolism and the contact lenses of multiple meanings; the pretentiousness that often stalks like Madeline Usher through the pages of some little magazines; the fondness for obscurity, dilettantism, and overintellectuality; and, perhaps most damning of all, what has been called an increasing tendency toward uniformity of subject matter and method.

Whatever the pros and cons, writing programs in American colleges and universities are here to stay — at least for a while. And whatever their drawbacks, the universities seem to provide the most satisfactory emotional and economic climate for the serious writer who is not blessed with a private income or a wealthy spouse or patron. Whether he aids or endangers his own creative career or the young talent entrusted to him is more debatable than is the assumption that some of the technical skill that characterizes today's serious short fiction can be attributed to his presence and example.

If technical skill, artistic virtuosity, and mechanical adroitness were the major factors in the production of significant fiction, the years since 1940 would be golden ones indeed. The palpable achievement of the recent American short story demonstrates for the thousandth time, however, that technique is a means to an end, not an end in itself. Technique not employed in the service of some end larger and greater than itself usually becomes futile, meaningless, decadent, or destructive. The indispensable element in a short story (or in any work of art, though the generalization is peculiarly applicable to the short story, in which superficial social awareness and technical skill and experimentation sometimes masquerade as more important components than they really are) is the presence of a consciousness larger than that of any of the characters of a particular story, an illumination above and beyond plot, setting, theme, and incident. This is the ultimate, the indispensable, dimension of fiction. It is this that gives meaning to the marriage of character and incident that constitutes the heart of the short story. Something seldom or never part of an author's deliberate attempt, it is his way of seeing the world, his way of distilling his experience as a person in a world of constantly shifting values, ideas, and mores. It is this largeness of vision that makes possible some kind of moral identification between the author and the adult reader, and makes the reading of a piece of fiction a rewarding human experience. Without it any story, no matter how skillfully or cunningly contrived, is little more than a momentary diversion or an achievement in technical virtuosity. Oversimplifying a complex problem, one might say that to be a significant author a writer must first of all be a significant person, must know deeply, feel deeply, be aware deeply. This is partly what makes Hawthorne and Melville and Twain and Anderson and Faulkner great writers; this may help explain why the fiction of Eudora Welty and I. B. Singer is more significant than that of Mickey Spillane or Harold Robbins.

Illumination — awareness of the significance of the human experience even on the threshold of annihilation — is the product of many factors: the writer's belief in himself and in the worthiness of his art, his respect for the world he is in the process of creating and for its inhabitants, his need to communicate his individual view of the world, whether that view be essentially tragic or comic, skeptical or optimistic, exalted or debased. Henry James's much-quoted and debatable comment that the "figures in any picture, the agents in any drama, are interesting only in proportion as they feel their respective situations" can be extended to suggest that the events in a work of fiction tend to be meaningful to a reader in proportion to their meaningfulness to the participants of the story and, by further extension, in proportion to their meaningfulness to their creator. This involves, in a special kind of way, "old-fashioned" concepts of loyalty and commitment, of belief in the significance of the universal human experience and dilemma, and of rapport between author, his fictional world, and his audience. For the reader to become involved in a work of fiction, to care, to share, to be moved, the creator must be at once involved but detached, committed but withdrawn, identified with his materials yet above and beyond them. It is the sense of commitment that provides a common denominator between the very different worlds of Flannery O'Connor and Bernard Malamud, of John Cheever and Grace Paley, paradoxically enough during a period characterized on the one hand by heightened emphasis upon the usual and the unexceptional, and on the other by the emergence of the grotesqueries of the black humorists and the innovations of a new breed of writers who broke almost completely from traditional fictional techniques, aims, and methods, at their most extreme rejecting not only plot and character but narrative as well, fusing graphics and language, experimenting with typography and form.

It is a truism, of course, that the arts reflect the age in which they are created. Although literary fashions sometimes change with as little apparent reason as do changes in apparel or hair styles, they are for the most part caused by — and reflect and, in turn, directly or indirectly influence — changes in the contemporary social, moral, political, geopolitical, and ethical climate. Of no artistic form is this more true than the short story, the most strictly contemporary, the most sensitive to change, of all the literary genres of the twentieth century.

The towering, inescapable, overwhelming realities of the last thirty-some years have been the War and the Bomb, and Vietnam and its aftermath. The revelations of human and national depravity, for example, that resulted in the civilian exterminations at Dachau and Buchenwald, or the less publicized but no less hideous massacres of military personnel at Katyn Wood or Salamaua and dozens of similar burying grounds, forced even the traditionally minded and optimistic adult mentality to question the ultimate goodness of man and society. The bomb, similarly, necessitated his reconsidering, if only on occasion, the basic Christian-democratic concept of the significance of individual effort, the importance of individual destiny, and the idea that human beings can control or even influence the direction of history and their individual roles in it. But what perhaps will prove to be even more destructive were the events of the postwar years, which saw no peace: Vietnam, Watts, burnings in the streets and the assassination of the Kennedys and Martin Luther King, Watergate and its aftermath, and so on through the horrors of the last few years. All of this diminished, at least for the present generation, any reasonable hopes of restoring or even revitalizing the assumed order and stability and wholeness of the past. Matthew Arnold's brave adjuration to let Reason and the Will of God prevail became as anachronistic, as bitterly comical, as the Tennysonian concept of man as the "heir of all the ages, in the foremost files of time."

In a generation over which hovered the enormous shadows of suffering, injustice, the disregard for personal dignity, the waste of resources and life itself, and the gnawing awareness of the threat of individual destruction along with the possibility of the annihilation of the past as well as the present, the man in the street or on the farm was beginning to find that in rejecting the medieval devil he was becoming the victim of his many contemporary equivalents: atavistic tyrannies and archetypal woes; tensions, drugs, allergies, insomnia; air pollution, the fuel crisis, inflation, and dwindling or corrupted natural resources; even the presence of radioactive materials in the water his children drank and cancer-causing agents in the food they ate. Life and business, in short, went on pretty much as usual except for the fact that even the most somnambulistic descendants of Babbitt were occasionally aware of the dry, mirthless chuckle in the cosmic corner, or could vaguely anticipate their own obituaries in the headlines announcing the newest member of the Nuclear Fission Club or the crashing of the time barrier.

It is little wonder, then, that seriousness of purpose and somberness of tone are as characteristic of much recent short fiction as are artistry and technical skill.   Long before Pearl Harbor, of course, the trend toward subdued, unsensational realism had commenced; long before Hiroshima twentieth-century short story writers shared with Verga, Chekhov, Joyce, and Anderson the realization that in the lives of "ordinary" or "unexceptional" people they could find an unending source of fictional material and themes.   The melodrama, sensationalism, romanticism, improbability, and technical contrivances of the past had long since been questioned, found wanting, and for the most part rejected.   Both the subject matter and methods of the pre-1920s short story had become unpalatable in the face of current newspaper headlines and television newscasts.

A book like James Michener's *Tales of the South Pacific* owed much of its success and popularity to the use of "faraway places with strange-sounding names": but by and large such settings appeared as infrequently as Poe's torture chambers, Bret Harte's boom towns of the Old West or Jack London's Klondike gold camps.   An occasional collection of science-fiction or relatively old-fashioned suspense or surprise-ending stories like Roald Dahl's *Someone Like You* or *Kiss, Kiss* enjoyed considerable popularity, but for the most part the concern was with the familiar, the everyday, the unspectacular, and with the complexities underlying apparently "normal" situations.   As Verga had depicted the drama, the tensions, and the conflicts in the lives of the people he had observed in his corner of Sicily in the 1860s, as Joyce had written of his Dublin of the 1900s and Anderson of his Winesburg, writers like John Cheever, Peter Taylor, Jesse Stuart, or Hortense Calisher examined, evaluated, and created their own segment of mid-twentieth-century America, finding in it all the subject matter, all the conflict, they desired. The traditional contests of man against nature or the fall from grace of the superman were replaced by incidents in the life of the nonhero, the little man with problems important to himself if to no one else.   At the same time the emphasis shifted from the external to the subjective, from results to causes, from the depicting of exterior events to the probing of inner tensions. In another direction Eudora Welty in *The Golden Apples* or John Cheever in "Goodbye, My Brother," "The Swimmer" and "Metamorphoses" united conventional materials with myth, and by the late sixties the tendency became almost a movement in itself, highlighted by such fictions as John Barth's National Book Award-winning *Chimera* or John Gardner's *The King's Indian.* These were the years when once again it was fashionable to announce the death of realistic or naturalistic fiction in general and the linear, sequential short story in particular. Fiction was being usurped by film and the new journalism, it was often announced; the major writers were being attracted to nonfiction or the new journalism. Black humor, fantasy, fable, parable, and "innovative" fictions — nonstories, antistories, neonarratives, and surfiction — crowded the pages of magazines from the *New Yorker* to the advance-guard quarterlies. Jorge Luis Borges became the major influence on the short fiction of the sixties and early seventies, with Donald Barthelme his widely imitated disciple.

Regardless of such differences in method, subject, and indeed concept of what fiction really was and was not, most of the writers of the last decades believed that somewhere along the way the American dream of progress, decency, and order had gone awry. For all their differences in background, environment, and social behavior, the grotesques of James Purdy and Jean Stafford are kin not far removed from John O'Hara's suburbanites or Hortense Calisher's New Yorkers. Wanderers in a world in which the fragmentation of the present is in bleak contrast to the wholeness of the past, they are beset with loneliness, fright, sadness, or moral fatigue. "Life was essentially a matter of being done in, let down, and swindled," think some of the characters of Jean Stafford's "In the Zoo," a concept expressed again and again in many of the stories of the period.

But the fictional world of recent decades is not primarily nihilistic or meaningless, in spite of the predominance of bewilderment, frustration, and *angst* in the continuing search for meaning in a society in which self-realization and self-justification often seem increasingly difficult or impossible. To the contrary, author after author, story after story, reflect a slow if often grudging maturation. Life, after all, much of the fiction of the period suggests, does go on. The artist, in the face of great enormities, is compelled to shout or whisper his defiance, to himself or to his peers rather than to the large mass audience earlier fiction writers hoped to reach. In some quarters the act of writing fiction — it seems to me there is a definite parallel here with the sonneteers and song writers of the Elizabethan period — was in the process of becoming something good and desirable per se, an act of gamesmanship, of play, of delight rather than of *angst,* highly personal and aggressively unconcerned with the tastes or the demands of a mass audience.

The almost compulsive need to create and in creating reach out and touch, if only briefly, another human being animates what might otherwise be a series of clinical case histories subtitled *The Disasters of Mankind in the Second Half of the Twentieth Century* or a succession of dazzling experiments in innovative techniques. On the threshold of possible destruction the American writer has been forced into a kind of maturation that most European and Latin writers and intellectuals have for generations taken for granted; loneliness and isolation are as inherent in the human situation as are their opposites.

In brief, American short fiction since around 1940 has come of age emotionally and intellectually as well as artistically and technically. If he could not believe that tomorrow would be better, the writer was able, in many cases reluctantly, to find a kind of solace in the hope that perhaps tomorrow might not be too much worse. Human relationships are more important than philosophical speculations, much of the fiction of the period reasserts, and love is more vital than nuclear physics, in spite of, perhaps to a degree because of, the threat of catastrophe. More than one writer turned his back on the great terrors of the forties and fifties, and began once again to cultivate his own garden and accept the realization that though things were bad, very bad, one could find cause for limited rejoicing in small private pleasures. Many stories of the period are animated by compassion and tempered by the regret that the dream and the reality are so dissimilar. Othello's "the pity of it, Iago" is more suggestive of the tone and mood of this short fiction than his curse of "goats and monkeys!" The heroine of John Cheever's "The Season of Divorce" does not feel rage or hatred or defiance; it is her vague, undefinable sadness that might serve as emblem for many recent American short stories:

> Why do I cry? Why do I cry? . . . I cry because I saw an old woman cuffing a little boy on Third Avenue . . . I can't get it out of my mind . . . I cry because my father died when I was twelve and because my mother married a man I detested . . . I cry because I had to wear an ugly dress . . . to a party twenty years ago, and I didn't have a good time. I cry because of some unkindness that I can't remember. I cry because I'm tired — because I'm tired and I can't sleep.

Chapter 4

Metropolis, Village, and Suburbia: The Short Fiction of Manners

THE SATIRIC DELINEATION of the everyday life of familiar segments of contemporary society, which furnished subject matter and theme for generations of English fiction writers from Fanny Burney to Thackeray and Anthony Powell, has no significant counterpart in nineteenth-century American literature. Though Henry James and others found in the contemporary scene the major source of their short fiction, it was not until later than many of our best short story writers turned their talents to the quietly perceptive, occasionally humorous, and almost always satiric depiction of contemporary manners and mores.

Much of the most important recent American short fiction has been in this province of the usual and the unexceptional. John Cheever, John O'Hara, Peter Taylor, and John Updike seem to me among the most representative of the many talented and perceptive writers who have for the most part concerned themselves with incidents in the lives of ordinary men and women in familiar or immediately recognizable situations, and have created a contemporary fiction of manners characterized by skill, urbanity, and insight.

Of these chroniclers of the unexceptional, perhaps the most distinguished is John Cheever (1912–), born in Quincy, Massachusetts, educated at Thayer Academy in South Braintree, and currently living in New England. Cheever's first collection, *The Way Some People Live,* was published in 1943 when the author was in the army; it contains thirty stories and narrative sketches, the majority of which had originally been published in the *New Yorker,* where with very few exceptions most of his subsequent stories have appeared. Many of these early stories are brief fictional anecdotes or narrative sketches about a few moments or hours in the lives of a character or a group. Typical are "Summer Theatre," in which a group of amateur prima donnas displays higher than average pre-opening-night jitters; "Problem No. 4," in which a draftee training in South Carolina concentrates more on his wife back in New York than on his lieutenant's earnest adjurations concerning a security mission; "The Law of the Jungle," with its effective contrast between older and younger generations in pre-World War II New York; and "The Peril in the Streets," essentially a monologue delivered by an unhappy drunk in the presence of a bartender and a draftee. Longer, somewhat more ambitious stories include "Of Love: A Testimony," a restrained and melancholy description of a love affair doomed to failure.

Though some of the stories in *The Way Some People Live* border on the trivial, the collection on the whole is an impressive one, and indicates the direction the author's subsequent stories were to take. Cheever writes in a relaxed, seemingly casual but thoroughly disciplined manner; his general mood is a compound of skepticism, compassion, and wry humor; he is concerned with the complexities, tensions, and disappointments of life in a strictly contemporary world of little men and women, unheroic, unspectacular, unexceptional. Loneliness, perhaps the dominant mood of the short fiction of the forties, fifties, and early sixties, permeates the collection. The lament of the draft-dodging, divorced alcoholic of "The Peril in the Streets" is characteristic:

I know you hate me. It doesn't make any difference to me. I'm lonely. I'm persecuted. But I don't care. I've been lonely all my life. I know what pain is. I can take it. You think you know what pain is, but you don't. Have *you* ever seen a seagull with a broken wing? Have *you* ever seen a wild animal gnaw its leg off to get out of a steel trap? Have you —

The Enormous Radio and Other Stories was published ten years later, in 1953. It is unquestionably one of the major collections of the

period. Gone are the occasional triviality and the sometimes studied informality of the earlier stories. With only isolated exceptions,
Cheever has gained complete control of his medium; he is at all
times and in all places on top of his materials. The *Enormous Radio*
stories concern individuals similar to the people of his first collection, though they are often older and more mature — university
graduates, World War II alumni, young businessmen on the way
up or slightly older ones on the way down, and their anxious,
frequently harried women. The scene is contemporary, usually in
or around New York City. Cheever's subject matter continues to
be the usual, but his treatment of it is far from commonplace. He is
concerned with the loneliness that festers beneath the façade of
apparently "happy" or "successful" individuals; he suggests the potential terror or violence inherent in the metropolitan apartment
dweller's condition. Beneath the often placid, impeccably drawn
surfaces of his stories there is a reservoir of excitement or unrest
that is capable of erupting into violence; his well-mannered characters walk a tightrope that at any moment may break; the vast,
shining city masks cruelty, injustice, and evil.

The frequently anthologized title story is typical centering as it
does on so ordinary a subject as a young husband's purchase of a
radio as a gift to his wife. Judged by any conventional standards,
Jim and Irene Westcott are "nice" people "who seem to strike that
satisfactory average of income, endeavor, and respectability that is
reached by the statistical reports in college alumni bulletins." Married nine years and the parents of two pleasant children, they live
in an apartment house near Sutton Place, attend the theater and
concerts regularly, and hope to be able to live in Westchester eventually; as Irene says, "We've always been good and decent and
loving to one another."

All goes well until, in the middle of a Mozart quintet, strange
sounds and voices intrude; the radio has begun to penetrate the
bland exterior of the apartment house, and Irene distinguishes
discordant sounds, doorbells ringing, telephones being dialed, electric razors and Waring mixers going about their daily business.

Irene is amused at first, but then the radio begins to reveal harsh and shocking details of the lives of the apartment dwellers: "demonstrations of indigestion, carnal love, abysmal vanity . . . and despair." These and subsequent revelations cause Irene to re-examine her neighbors: in the elevator she attempts to identify the secrets masked behind their "handsome, impassive faces"; at lunch with an old friend, she wonders what horrors she is hiding. Listening to the radio becomes an obsession that causes her to re-examine herself as she has been re-examining her neighbors; her search for her real self ends in disaster. Her once-amiable husband is "sick to death" of her apprehensions, and the story ends with another series of revelations:

> "Why are you so Christly all of a sudden?" [Jim shouts] "What's turned you overnight into a convent girl? You stole your mother's jewelry before they probated her will. You never gave your sister a cent of that money that was intended for her — not even when she needed it . . . and where was all your piety and your virtue when you went to that abortionist? I'll never forget how cool you were. You packed your bag and went off to have that child murdered as if you were going to Nassau."

With such characters, Cheever's sad modern comedy is played out to its inconclusive finale. Most of the people of *The Enormous Radio* stories are decent, respectable, fundamentally likable. Sometimes they win a temporary victory, like Ralph and Alice Whittemore of "The Pot of Gold"; only rarely do they become malignant, like Joan Harris of "Torch Song," a "big, handsome girl" who leaves the Middle West to become a New York model. A modern vampire, Joan thrives on sickness and disaster, and well merits the cry of the man she helps destroy: "What kind of an obscenity are you that you can smell sickness and death the way you do?" For the most part the characters exist between these extremes, frightened and to all intents and purposes terribly alone, lost in a metropolitan no man's land from which most of the traditional guideposts have been removed; among the most memorable are the characters in "The Season of Divorce," "The Summer Farmer," "The Superintendent," and, perhaps the best story Cheever has yet written, "Goodbye, My Brother."

Four of Cheever's pieces, written after the publication of *The Enormous Radio,* are included in *Stories: Jean Stafford, John Cheever, Daniel Fuchs, William Maxwell* (1956). Except for "The Bus to St. James," with its account of the corrosive effect of big city mores and tensions, these stories display an extension of subject matter and theme and a considerably more leisurely technique than most of their predecessors. My own personal favorite, and I think the best of these stories, is "The Day the Pig Fell Into the Well," a warmhearted and robust re-creation of the Nudd family at Whitebeach Camp in the Adirondacks. The story possesses a variety of character and incident more usually associated with the novella or the novel than with the short story; over this "chronicle of small disasters" hovers a kind of Indian summer warmth, as Cheever portrays the American equivalent of the English middle class with Galsworthian compassion and dislike, affection and irony. Almost as good are "The National Pastime," part essay, part short story, a nostalgic re-creation of a New England boyhood, and the prize-winning "The Country Husband," one of the best of Cheever's excursions into the suburbia, which was to furnish subject and theme for his next collection, *The Housebreaker of Shady Hill* (1958).

The title piece of the Shady Hill stories, with its mingling of humor, effective characterization, serious commentary, and suspense, is characteristic of the collection as a whole. Johnny Hake has a lot to be thankful for: he has a pretty wife, four loving children, a high-paying job in Manhattan, and lives in fashionable Shady Hill ("a banlieue and open to criticism by city planners, adventurers, and lyric poets, but if you work in the city and have children to raise, I can't think of a better place"). On summer nights, sitting in the garden with the children and looking into his wife's dress as she bends over to salt the barbecuing steaks, Johnny is "thrilled." But no man in John Cheever's suburbia is happy for long. Johnny loses his job, and Shady Hill is expensive. One night, after a party, he breaks into his odious host's home and steals nine hundred dollars. The moral bottom drops out of Johnny Hake's world — "I never knew that a man could be so miserable and that the mind could open up so many chambers and fill them with self-reproach!" Like the Westcotts of "The Enormous Radio," Johnny has opened a Pandora's box. His own wrongdoing makes him painfully aware of the evil and corruption around him. He seeks a scapegoat — his father, his mother, things as they are, Shady Hill — knowing all the time that he is deluding himself. Eventually he finds a solution that, if pat and overcontrived, illustrates the seriousness of purpose that characterizes much of Cheever's writing: "There were ways out of my trouble," he concludes, "if I cared to make use of them. I was not trapped. I was here on earth because I chose to be . . . It is not, as somebody once wrote, the smell of corn bread that calls us back from death; it is the lights and signs of love and friendship."

Except for the sadistic organization man of the merciless "The Five-forty-eight," most of Cheever's nonheroes are essentially amiable men: one-time track star Cash Bentley, forty, who provides the climax for many a Saturday night Shady Hill party by hurdling sofas, tables, and firescreen; Francis Weed, who becomes infatuated with the Weeds' babysitter but eventually, at the advice of a psychiatrist, finds solace through woodwork; Will Pym, whose only sin was marrying a flirtatious woman considerably younger than himself; and Charles Flint, "fugitive from the suburbs of all large cities" whose plea, written in his journal aboard ship, suggests the real villain of Cheever's world, Shady Hill itself, with its culture vultures, its inane activity, its joyless parties and meaningless love skirmishes, its pretentiousness and unending striving for status.

> God preserve me . . . from women who dress like *toreros* to go to the supermarket, and from cowhide dispatch cases, and from flannels and gabardines. Preserve me from word games and adulterers, from basset hounds and swimming pools and frozen canapés and Bloody Marys and smugness and syringa bushes and P.T.A. meetings.

Like Johnny Hake or Charles Flint, some of these unheroic protagonists win a partial victory through love or by demonstrating a kind of courage or integrity; very rarely are they destroyed, like Cash Bentley. Most of the time they see things through; they muddle along, a little balder, a bit more short of breath, somewhat sadder today than they were yesterday. Sorrow and disappointment pervade the book: sadness for the loss of youth and love, for the gradual dimming of the dreams of the past, and for the nagging awareness of entrapment in an often comfortable present built upon an extremely flimsy moral foundation. Usually this is implicit within the narrative framework of character and incident; only rarely does Cheever indulge in commentary like that of the misunderstood child of "The Sorrows of Gin": "the pitiful corruption of the adult world; how crude and frail it was, like a piece of worn burlap, patched with stupidities and mistakes, useless and ugly."

Cheever's fourth collection, *Some People, Places, and Things That Will Not Appear in My Next Novel* (1961), contains "The Death of Justina" and "Boy in Rome," which are among his best work; and even the slightest pieces in the book display Cheever's hallmarks, urbanity, wit, intelligence, and technical dexterity. As a whole, however, the book is a letdown, fatigued and written in an over-casual manner — at times almost a parody — of Cheever's earlier work. "A Miscellany of Characters That Will Not Appear" is a moving manifesto and declaration of intent, as much essay as short story. Among the clichés and bromides of character and incident that Cheever wishes to see eliminated from fiction — his own and that of his contemporaries — are "all scornful descriptions of American landscapes with ruined tenements, automobile dumps, polluted rivers . . . diseased elm trees . . . unclean motels, candle-lit tearooms, and streams paved with beer cans," all explicit descriptions of sexual commerce, all lushes, all parts for Marlon Brando, all homosexuals, all fake artistry. Cheever's exhortation, in spite of its levity of manner, is admirable; it would have more significance if it were not embedded in a collection that is the must uneven of Cheever's books, markedly inferior to *The Enormous Radio* and *The Housebreaker of Shady Hill,* and in some ways less impressive than *The Way Some People Live.*

On the other hand, his fifth collection of short stories, *The Brigadier and the Golf Widow,* published in 1964, only three years after

The Way Some People Live, is perhaps Cheever's best. Over the years, Cheever's narrative method loosened up considerably, became more varied, more flexible: he is as adept in a brief anecdotal episode involving a son's last meeting with his divorced father ("Reunion") as he is in relatively traditional narratives of people and incidents (the title story or "The Woman Without a Country" and several others), or pieces like "The Seaside Houses" or "Just One More Time," which are essentially fictional essays in which narrative hardly exists. In the setting, too — past or present, actual or filtered through the narrator's memories — we find considerable variety; it ranges from such familiar Cheever territory as Manhattan ("Reunion") to suburbia (in "Metamorphoses," Bullet Park, the scene of his novel of the same name) to the small New England village of St. Botolph's ("The Angel of the Bridge").

Several of these stories are as good as any that Cheever has ever written: the title story with its expert delineation of a country-club militarist — "Bomb Cuba! Bomb Berlin! Let's throw a little nuclear hardware at them" — and the "other woman," for whom, as for so many of the author's female characters, adultery is replacing bridge as the favorite national pastime; "The Swimmer," one of the most conceptually interesting stories in the Cheever canon; though this story of Neddy Merrill's plan to "reach his home by water" hovers somewhat uneasily between realism and metaphor, it is nonetheless unforgettable; "The Angel on the Bridge," memorable as much in the deft creation of the narrator's ice-skating-in-Rockefeller-Plaza mother, his brother, and the young hitchhiker he encounters as it is in the portrayal of the central character, who suddenly develops an obsessive fear of bridges; "The Seaside Houses," a marvelous evocation of the influence of rented houses on those who own them and those who rent them, beautifully executed, with not a false word or jarring note until what seems to me an ending in which Cheever suddenly loses his touch; and "The Music Lesson," too delicious to be summarized, perhaps the collection's most interesting variation of the tensions-of-marriage syndrome with which he has often concerned himself.

At the conclusion of "Clementina" the central character contemplates some of the recent events in her life: ". . . remembering the cold on her skin and the whiteness of the snow and the stealth of the wolves, she wondered why the good God had opened up so many choices and made life so strange and diverse." The last words can be applied to the author himself. With over a hundred successful stories behind him, Cheever has lost none of his zest, none of his wonderment in celebrating what he has termed "a world that lies spread out around us like a bewildering and stupendous dream."

The same can be said about Cheever's 1974 National Book Award fiction nominee, *The World of Apples.* "The Jewels of the Cabots," a saga in miniature of life in St. Botolph's, is Cheever at his best, beautifully controlled, illuminated throughout by the effective juxtaposition of the trivial and the significant, the tragic and the comic. In the midst of the narrator's reminiscences of minor childhood experiences or recollections of love, adultery, and murder, we tend to remember most distinctly such asides and gratuitous comments as "when the ship sinks I will try to reach the life raft with an overhand and drown stylishly, whereas if I had used a Lower-Class sidestroke I would have lived forever."

Then there is the title story, a far remove from the world of St. Botolph's, a masterly portrait of an aging but very vigorous American poet in Italy. Or, in more familiar Cheever country, "The Fourth Alarm," full of suburban *angst* and strain, growing out of a wife's sudden decision to perform in an off-Broadway skin show, or "The Geometry of Love," in which the engineer protagonist is destroyed by the failure of his marriage.

The narrator of "The Jewels of the Cabots" comments that "Children die, beautiful women are mangled in automobile accidents, cruise ships founder, and men die lingering deaths in mines and submarines, but you will find none of this in my accounts." The statement is applicable to the body of Cheever's short stories. He is concerned with large contemporary and universal problems — hypocrisy, individual and societal idiocy, the absurdity of sham and pretentiousness, the need for love and understanding — but his approach to them is sophisticated, low-keyed, subtle. One of the most entertaining storytellers and one of the most perceptive and urbane commentators on the contemporary scene, Cheever is a wry observer of manners and customs, more saddened than amused by the foibles he depicts with such understanding and grace. And in spite of the failures of so many of his characters and the disruptions in their personal and professional lives, the overall effect, particularly of his more recent work, is anything but somber. In its entirety it is animated by the sense of wonder implicit in Clementina's previously quoted comment and in the author's statement in an interview a few years ago:

> I know almost no pleasure greater than having a piece of fiction draw together disparate incidents so that they relate to one another and confirm that feeling that life itself is a creative process, that one thing is put purposefully upon another, that what is lost in one encounter is replenished in the next, and that we possess some power to make sense of what takes place.

Collected Stories by Peter Taylor (1917–) was published in 1969. In addition to five uncollected stories the volume contains twenty-one stories from his four individual volumes, *A Long Fourth and Other Stories* (1948), *The Widows of Thornton* (1954), *Happy Families Are All Alike* (1959), and *Miss Leonora When Last Seen* (1963), which includes several pieces that had appeared in the three preceding collections. All of Taylor's stories are about family relationships in what he has termed the "quiet lives" of the responsible upper-middle class in or from Tennessee, which, he has said, "was (and is) the center of the universe" to his family; with few exceptions, it is the center of his fictional world. Change is the major factor in this world — the change from an agrarian to an urban society and the resulting conflicts between tradition and the present, between old patterns of thought and conduct and the stresses and pressures of contemporary life.

Contemporary urban Tennessee furnishes both subject matter and theme for the seven stories of the "Long Fourth," all of which take place in or near Nashville and Memphis. All, except for "Allegiance," are leisurely in narrative method, exploring the nuances of a situation and the people involved in it with almost Jamesian thoroughness. All but "Rain in the Heart" are about the deterioration of family relationships; centering on unspectacular revelations and crises of contemporary living; and all of them are concerned with the attrition of old loyalties, the breakdown of old patterns of conduct, and the collapse of old values.

The title story is characteristic. "A Long Fourth" describes Harriett Wilson, a pretty Nashville woman "just past fifty," and the members of her family and household — her amiable doctor-husband, "Sweetheart," Helena and Kate, their two unmarried daughters, her son, whom she idolizes, and two Negro servants, Mattie and her ill-smelling nephew BT. Around Son's return to Nashville from New York prior to being drafted, Taylor creates a moving series of quiet and not-so-quiet character revelations. The well-bred, proud, and genteel Mrs. Wilson explodes into violent rage when Mattie unthinkingly compares BT's intention to work in an airplane factory with Son's going into the army: "Between the moments when she even pictured Mattie's being tied and flogged or thought of Mama's uncle who shot all his niggers before he would free them . . . she would actually consider the virtue of her own wrath." Helena and Kate are shown to be potential alcoholics, constantly nagging each other, incapable of giving or receiving love. Son is courteous, affable, but completely aloof and as far removed from his family as though he had been living on another planet, and his racial ideas — "The people in the South cannot expect to progress with the rest of the nation until they've forgotten their color line" — are as incomprehensible to the Wilsons as they would be to Mattie and BT.

In *The Widows of Thornton* Taylor continues to contrast old and new, order and change, wholeness and fragmentation. He has stated:

My idea was to write a group of stories dealing with the histories of four or five families from a country town [Thornton, Tennessee] who had

migrated . . . to various cities of the South and the Midwest . . . I wanted
to present these families — both Negro and white — living a modern
urban life while continuing to be aware of their old identities and relationships.

Nowhere is this awareness of "old identities and relationships" in
the midst of contemporary change made more explicit than in
"Their Losses," a quiet study of contrasts exemplified by three
women: two spinsters, Miss Patty and Miss Ellen, and a worldly
married woman, Cornelia Werner.

Miss Patty, who is accompanying her senile aunt to Thornton,
lives in and worships the past; she laments the fading away of the
small towns between Grand Junction and Memphis, which to her
are symbols of a "prosperous and civilized existence," and mourns
the vanished glory of her family: "My people," she tells her companions, "happened to be very much *of* the world . . . Not of *this*
world, but of *a* world that we have seen disappear. In mourning
my family, I mourn that world's disappearance." At the other
extreme is Mrs. Cornelia Weatherby Werner, like Miss Bean a
native of Thornton, who had left home to marry a Memphis Jew.
Cornelia hates her mother, recently deceased, who had made her
life in Thornton miserable, yet she is an alien in Memphis: " 'It's
a wretched place!' she exclaims. 'It's the most completely snob-
bish place in the world . . . They can't forgive you for being from
the country — they hate the country so, and they can't forgive your
being a Jew!' " Somewhere between the two is Miss Ellen Watkins,
who is bringing home the body of her mother for burial. A former
classmate of Cornelia's, Miss Ellen lacks the pride and arrogance of
Miss Patty and the vigor and daring of Cornelia; she has existed in
a kind of sweet vacuum, with a widowed mother, a sister who has
developed melancholia, and two quiet, home-loving older brothers
who had made "little stir in the world, content to live there in the
house with Mother and Nora and me after Father was gone."

Among these three women, each in her own way suggestive of
the wasted life, no rapport exists; their reunion, if it can be called
that, has as little significance to them as Miss Ellen's comments

concerning scrambled eggs, which Miss Patty deliberately ignores
and Cornelia hardly hears. As the train approaches Memphis,
each goes her own way, each equally lonely and adrift, each isolated
in her pride, acquiescence, or rebellion.

Most of the people of *The Widows of Thornton* are similarly unable
to escape or forget the past, or to live very comfortably in the
present. Perhaps the best story in the collection, "A Wife of Nashville," presents two of Taylor's most memorable characters, Helen
Ruth Lovell and her Negro servant girl, Jess McGhee. When Jess
suddenly leaves the Lovell household after years of devoted service, Mr. Lovell and the three grown Lovell sons are bewildered.
Only Mrs. Lovell can understand Jess's reasons, which in both
subtle and obvious ways grow out of a sense of loneliness and
isolation that Mrs. Lovell herself experiences. Few authors have
charted with greater understanding the gulf between mistress and
servant, between white and Negro; at the same time "A Wife of
Nashville" presents with both compassion and irony two kinds of
loneliness that create an enduring kinship between mistress and
servant.

The setting of Taylor's third collection, *Happy Families Are All
Alike,* includes, in addition to Thornton, Chatham — a middle-
sized city "not thoroughly Middle Western and yet not thoroughly
Southern either" — and Paris, but the author's interests and preoccupations are the same as those displayed in his two previous volumes — the contrasts between past and present, relationships between the races, and family connections and relationships. "A
Friend and Protector," like "A Wife of Nashville," explores the
relationships among members of a responsible Tennessee family
and a Negro servant and paints with a violence rare in Taylor's
work the interacting influences of the Negro-white relationship.
The narrator of the story, an intelligent, highly aware young man,
finally realizes that the story of black Jesse's life and its ruin is also
the story of his aunt's "pathetically unruined life, and my uncle's
too, and even my own," that in a very real way the members of his
family have caused Jesse's destruction because unknowingly they
were so dissatisfied with the "pale *un*ruin" of their own lives.

The grimness beneath the surfaces of so many of Taylor's people is also present, and accentuated, in some of the *Miss Leonora When Last Seen* stories and in the previously uncollected pieces. It is found in "At the Drugstore." Home from Tennessee with his "pretty wife and two little sons" for a brief family reunion, Matt Donelson goes to the drugstore to buy some shaving cream. He remembers the nasty tricks his Country Day classmates used to play on the old druggist, tricks Matt did not participate in because he "had always been a little timid, a little too well brought up, to have any part in them." He grossly patronizes the druggist, is rude to the man's son, and is finally in effect ordered out of the store. On the way home he is appalled at his behavior — why, he reflects, he "even had his right fist tightened and was ready to fight . . . if necessary to protect the old druggist." This, of course, is a complete perversion of the actual truth; by the time he reaches home Matt knows that "he had gone to the drugstore on purpose . . . he had planned the whole adventure . . . It had been intended to satisfy some passing and unnamed need." At breakfast, smug and self-satisfied, he plays the role of happy and benevolent paterfamilias. He is a vain and weak man: his "triumph" is a defeat, an ironic reversal of the truth.

Matt's character is like those of the husband and wife of "The Heat," one of the previously uncollected stories, which involves a few hours in the life of a member of a state legislature waiting in a hotel room prior to attending the Governor's Ball that evening. As the slow moments tick by, we learn a great deal about the man lying on the bed — and of his wife — enough to prepare us for the pitiless revelations that lay bare the emptiness of their lives together. In "Dean of Men," one of the author's most recent stories, there is a similar slow stripping away of protective veneers of the professor-protagonist. Far from the noble educator he conceives himself to be, the dean is a self-righteous betrayer of others and an unwitting self-betrayer, a stranger to himself and to the son to whom he addresses his long, embarrassing, and painful soliloquy of self-justification.

Within his self-imposed boundaries — limitations or weaknesses, some readers may find them — Taylor works quietly, surely, and effectively. The success of his fiction is, to a large degree, the triumph of moderation, intelligence, and sound craftsmanship. He is traditional, even conventional, in method, whether he is examining the heart of a family relationship, his most characteristic mode, or compressing in a few sharply etched minutes the essentials of a situation and the people involved in it. In prose distinguished by simplicity and purity, he goes to the heart of personal and group relationships: why do human beings act as they do, how does one's past affect his present, what are the relationships between an individual's responsibility to himself, to his family, to the specific segment of society in which he finds himself? Such situations Peter Taylor explores with insight and understanding; few of his contemporaries limn the nuances of such relationships more successfully, more meaningfully.

The old Roman of contemporary fiction writers, John O'Hara (1905–1970) had two separate careers as a short story writer. During a long decade between the middle thirties and forties O'Hara was probably the most prolific important writer of short fiction in American literary history; within this period he published five collections of short stories: *The Doctor's Son and Other Stories* (1935), *Files on Parade* (1939), *Pal Joey* (1940), *Pipe Night* (1945), and *Hellbox* (1947). This body of work has been so frequently commented upon as to seem to belong to another era; O'Hara's social awareness, his "toughness," his shrewd observation of manners and mores, his remarkable ear for dialogue, and his unwinking recording of "the way things were then" are almost legendary. After *Hellbox,* O'Hara abandoned the short story for another long decade until 1960 when at the age of fifty-five he discovered with delight that "in spite of aches in spine and tendons, I had an apparently inexhaustible urge to express an unlimited supply of short story ideas." The fruits of this urge were several king-sized collections: *Assembly* (1960), *The Cape Cod Lighter* (1962), *The Hat on the Bed* (1963), and *The Horse Knows the Way* (1964) in which O'Hara announced his temporary retirement from short story writing, a very short-lived retirement. *Waiting for Winter* came out in 1966, followed by *And Other Stories* in 1969, and the posthumous *The Time Element* (1972); *The O'Hara Generation,* an anthology of stories originally published between 1935 and 1946, was also published in 1972.

These latest stories are among the best of O'Hara's work and display the same qualities that characterize his earlier short fiction: the penetrating and skeptical analysis of contemporary life, which is Thackerayan in its delineation of individual, group, and societal stupidity, and what a recent critic has labeled society's "dull implacable hostility"; the remarkable observation of speech, dress, gestures, actions, and the thousand and one details that make his stories seem more realistic than the columns of the newspapers of the period; and his technical facility, which is reminiscent of a George Blanda or a Henry Aaron or a Pablo Casals, of someone who has so thoroughly mastered his trade or art that even when his reflexes have slowed down he can outperform most of his younger contemporaries. Although very few would agree with his claim that "No one writes them better than I do," most of his readers would acknowledge that O'Hara was a seasoned professional; he constantly strove to learn more, accomplish more. If you are an author, he once commented, and not "just a writer, you keep learning all the time."

Central to the effectiveness of most of his stories is O'Hara's remarkable knowledge of his people. He knows them inside and out, knows what they do and what they think; he seems, indeed, to have known them all their lives. His preoccupation with pretentiousness, hypocrisy, arrogance, cruelty, and stupidity is as intense as it was during the thirties and early forties, when he was frequently criticized for showing no pity for his characters, or for writing with what seemed like intense dislike for the world he was in the process of creating. His vision, to be sure, was limited, but not quite as restricted as some commentators have indicated.

In certain stories, such as "Claude Emerson, Reporter" or "The

First Day," O'Hara's revelations of human failure are tempered with tolerance and even affection, but in the main his characters are cut from flawed cloth. They emerge strangely diminished, marvelous in their verisimilitude, but reduced and somehow drained both of their humanity and of their stature as human beings. It is far from accurate to say, as some of O'Hara's detractors do, that if you've read a few of his stories you've read them all, but his interest in the same or similar character types and situations, and his delineation of what is essentially one aspect of human experience, are his most conspicuous limitations. In spite of his very large talent and unflagging energy, his world becomes blurred in retrospect, and its people merge into an indistinguishable mass.

Lawyer and engineer, war-rich contractor and businessman, country-club drifter, adulterer, pandering husband, wealthy homosexual, deadbeat, pimp, whore, newspaperman on the way down or saloon owner on the way up, O'Hara's nonheroes possess in common the fact that they have made a mess of their lives or are on the verge of doing so. The breakdown of human relationships is his favorite theme; failure, loneliness, and boredom appear and reappear in his stories. He depicts unsparingly a continuing war between the individual and society; between the middle-aged, who constitute many of his characters and are frequently created with a depth and understanding largely absent from his earlier stories, and the young; between husband and wife and lover, if the joyless participants in O'Hara's skirmishes of the sexes can be called lovers; between parent and child. Occasionally this warfare is climaxed by physical violence, including homicide or suicide, as it is in "In a Grove," "The Sharks," "Andrea," and "Justice"; for the most part, however, the endings of these stories are as studiously unresolved as they were in the author's earlier fiction.

O'Hara's segment of the world, like Thackeray's, is neither a moral place nor a merry one; it is crowded, noisy, full of eating and drinking, making love and betraying love, laughing, cheating, fighting, and conniving. Thackeray's parting comments upon his *Vanity Fair* might well serve for O'Hara's: "Ah, Vanitas, Vanitatum!

Which of us is happy in this world? Which of us has his desire? or, having it, is satisfied? — Come, children, let us shut up the box and the puppets, for our play is played out."

There is a regrettable tendency to conclude that "anyone that prolific can't really be very good." One should be wary of such easy generalizations; after all, Shakespeare *did* write thirty-seven — or was it thirty-six or thirty-eight? — plays. But the statement is applicable: O'Hara's productivity was prodigious. His publishers announce with not unjustifiable pride, in the introduction to *The O'Hara Generation,* that in addition to his many other activities, O'Hara produced almost a hundred stories during a five-year period, and he once told me, a few years before his death, that at that time he *never* spent more than one morning on a story: his stories, as he was to say in an introduction to another collection, "came out of the author's typewriter . . . *zip-zip!* just like that . . ." In spite of his enormous energy, his insatiable curiosity and shrewdness, and his almost uncanny ability to reproduce the details of the American past and immediate present — customs, manners, speech patterns — there is something depressing about the monotony of the vast O'Hara wasteland. It is all there, O'Hara's vision of the life of his time, but it has about it the inert quality of a newspaper morgue.

John Updike (1932–) is so talented as to be alarming, so versatile and prolific as to evoke amazement. Still in his early forties, he is the author of six novels, including the National Book Award-winning *The Centaur;* three volumes of verse; four juveniles; a closet drama; a collection of miscellaneous prose pieces; and five collections of short stories: *The Same Door* (1959), *Pigeon Feathers* (1962), *The Music School* (1966), *Bech: A Book* (1970), and *Museums and Women* (1972), along with *Olinger Stories* (1964), a selection from his first two collections.

Many of Updike's earliest stories are set in the small town of Olinger, Pennsylvania, the fictional name for Shillington, where he was born and raised; in or around New York City, where he began his professional career with the *New Yorker;* and in New England, where he has lived for years. The settings of the short fiction of his three later collections range from these locales to England to Russia to Charlotte Amalie as he became a peripatetic State Department-sponsored citizen of the universe. From the beginning he has had a marvelous eye and ear, an unquenchable desire to explore what is new, sensitivity, a retentive memory, a hungry concern for the drama beneath the surface of ordinary incidents and characters. Even his least consequential stories exhibit enormous technical skill and artistry: the "perfect marriage," as has frequently been observed, of "ambition to performance."

Very smooth, very relaxed, most of these early fictions are concerned with problems, reflections, and minor revelations in the lives of sensitive and/or egotistical adolescents and young people — intellectuals, pseudointellectuals, married couples, youthful parents — and center on such unexceptional situations as two former classmates having lunch together, a young schoolteacher's difficulty with his Shakespeare class, a young married couple's return from Boston to New York with their two infant children, a quiet evening visit of an émigré professor with two of his former students.

The larger sorrows or tragedies of life are quite naturally absent from such stories. Updike's characters live moderately comfortable lives. Depression and war exist for them, if at all, only as vague memories, as remote from their actual experience as the Black Plague or the Napoleonic conquests. They live in reasonably well-furnished apartments with reasonably well-stocked bookshelves, record cabinets, and pantries. They seem to know a good sherry from a poor one, and are as likely as not to read Proust or Gide before retiring.

Despite the absence of any larger catastrophes, however, most of Updike's characters are far from happy. They are introspective and easily disturbed, by matters extending from the inconsequential to the significant. They love each other and are good parents, but the early morning yammering of their children or the sticking of the electric toaster will sometimes set their teeth fearfully on edge. They are susceptible to insomnia; they have hard-to-shake-off colds; because of their allergies they must watch their diets; they suffer from fears of inadequacy, of being conspicuous, of being outmanned or threatened in one way or another. Doing anything in public for the first time, "carving a roast, taking communion, buying a tuxedo," makes one young man's chest "feel fragile and thin"; a young wife sees "homosexuals everywhere"; one young husband and father wishes "there were such a thing as enchantment, and he could draw, with a stick, a circle of safety" around his wife and child; another, told by a doctor that he has fungus of the eyelids, immediately thinks of how beautiful his eyelashes were in his adolescence and visualizes "his face with the lids bald and the lashes lying scattered on his cheeks like insect legs"; still another, denied his marital pleasures, is pleased the following morning to see that his wife looks "ugly . . . Wan breakfast light bleaches you blotchily, drains the goodness from your thickness, makes the bathrobe a limp stained tube flapping disconsolately, exposing sallow décolletage. The skin between your breasts a sad yellow. I feast with the coffee on your drabness."

At their best, and taken singly, these stories are a triumph of the art of the usual; Updike possesses a genius for recording, as it were, the flicker of the eyelid that becomes an epiphany, and his small apartments, automobiles stuck in the snow, and mildly frustrating Sunday afternoons, which make his characters reflect that "this was the sort of day when you sow and not reap," are sharply observed and brilliantly recorded. At their least successful, or taken in large, sustained doses, however, they seem trivial rather than significant: characteristic is "Flight," in which a young married writer, Allen Dow, returns to his home in Pennsylvania. "At the age of seventeen," Allen tells us, "I was poorly dressed and funny-looking, and went around thinking about myself in the third person." Here begins a seemingly interminable series of reminiscences, about his mother, about *her* mother and his father and *her* father and her grandfather, and how and where his mother was

educated and how she had to go to work in a department store
selling cheap fabrics at $14.00 a week, and how he, Allen Dow,
made out with the girls when he was in high school, particularly
when at the age of seventeen he was chosen, along with three girls,
to represent his high school in a debate at another high school a
hundred miles away from Olinger, and how he and Molly Bing-
aman, one of the girl debaters, made it ("her lipstick smeared in
little unflattering flecks into the skin around her mouth; it was as if
I had been given a face to eat"), and how he finally breaks from his
mother by having a series of almost consummated sexual encounters with Molly, after the last of which he "went to the all-night
diner just beyond the Olinger town line and ate three hamburgers,
ordering them one at a time, and drank two glasses of milk."

All I can say is that by this time it is of little concern to me
whether Allen Dow ate three hamburgers that night, ordering
them one at a time, and drank two glasses of milk, or ate two
hamburgers and drank three glasses of milk, ordering *them* one at a
time.

A similar preoccupation with the unexceptional characterizes
most of the stories in *The Music School* and *Museums and Women*. As
his young married couples approach maturity or middle age, their
youthful petulance and irritability deepen into despair or disenchantment, or manifest themselves in hostility or paranoia.
They are lonely, dissatisfied with their wives or mistresses, at odds
with their children, their jobs, their society. The opening line of
"In Football Season," the first story of *The Music School* — "Do you
remember a fragrance girls acquire in autumn? . . . so faint and
flirtatious on those afternoon walks through the dry leaves . . .
banked a thousandfold and . . . heavy as the perfume of a flower
shop on the dark slope of the stadium . . . " — is almost like the
prelude to an elegy, an elegy with infinite variations upon the
same themes, repeated in story after story. "Now I peek into windows and open doors and do not find that air of permission. It has
fled the world. Girls walk by me carrying their invisible bouquets
from fields still steeped in grace, and I look up in the manner of
one who follows with his eyes the passage of a hearse . . ."

There is a similar tone in the title story of *Museums and Women:* the protagonist, reflecting upon some of the women in his life — mother, wife, discarded love object — concludes "it appeared to me that now I was condemned, in my search for the radiance that had faded behind me, to enter more and more museums, and to be a little less exalted by each new entrance, and a little more quickly disenchanted by the familiar contents beyond."

All of Updike's unhappy people do not, like the voice in Dylan Thomas' poem, sing in their chains in such tempered tones. The natural course of love, one character comments, is "passion, consummation, contentment, boredom, betrayal." "We are all pilgrims, faltering toward divorce," echoes another; still another, after recovering from a broken affair, "discovered himself so healed that his wound ached to be reopened." Like Richard Maples, the most unpleasant of all Updike's antiheroes, who appears and reappears with his wife and four children in several of *The Music School* and *Museums and Women* pieces, Updike's characters have "been married too long." They approach middle age ungracefully, angrily, or pitifully. They suffer from maladies real or imagined: about to donate blood for the first time, Richard almost funks out; in Rome, his feet ache hideously and he has unbearable stomach pains while visiting the Forum; on the day he is to accompany his wife on a Boston protest march, he has a terrible cold; having had his aching teeth capped, he gets drunk and smashes up a new car; eventually, persevering in his hideous marriage and wallowing like a medieval madman in his own excrement, he revels in his cuckoldry: you "whore," my "virgin bride," he cries to his wife. "Tell me everybody!" ("You honestly *are* hateful," Joan tells him in the first of the Maples stories. "It's not just a pose.")

At their best, stories like these are a devastating commentary on various aspects of contemporary manners; at their least successful, as they are in what seem to me more than a few trivial pieces like "The Orphaned Swimming Pool," the less said the better.

But then there is Henry Bech, author of "one good book and three others, the good one having come first," whom we first meet in "The Bulgarian Poetess" in *The Music School,* and subsequently in *Bech: A Book,* which seems to me Updike's major collection of short fiction and perhaps his best book to date.

For Bech — prurient, perceptive, pursued, paranoid, passionate, and I might add permanent Henry Bech — is a comic masterpiece (and if there is any other factor that weakens so many of Updike's flawlessly put together stories it is the lack of a saving sense of humor). Bech is a compound, as he comments in his foreword to "Dear John," of "some gentlemanly Norman Mailer" and of "gallant, glamorous Bellow, the King of the Leprechauns," with a "childhood . . . out of Alex Portnoy and . . . [an] ancestral past out of I. B. Singer," together with a "whiff of Malamud" and "something Waspish, theological, scared, and insulatingly ironical that derives . . . from you."

Whatever his ancestry, literary or otherwise, Bech *towers.* Bech in Russia for a month of cultural exchange at the expense of the State Department; Bech in Rumania sporting an astrakhan hat he has purchased in Moscow; Bech in Bulgaria, falling in undeclared love with the Bulgarian poetess; Bech smoking pot for the first time and switching mistresses; Bech overwhelmed by *angst* at a girls' college in Virginia; Bech swinging and having a hasty love affair and being undone by a double-talking journalist in London; Bech entering the heaven of literary lions — these are superb stories. This horny, hairy, middle-aged, likable, outrageous, unforgivable, self-searching, ponderous, light-footed spin-off from the suffering, self-contemplative Bellow-Malamud-Roth-et al.-Jewish-intellectual protagonist soars far beyond the level of caricature; with Bech, Updike has created a character so real that it is difficult to believe he did not always exist . . . and, in effect, he always has, at least in American life and literature.

John Updike has had his ups and downs, from the almost hysterical acclaim that greeted his earliest books, the subsequent fall from grace with *The Centaur* and *Couples,* and the rather dismal failure of *Buchanan Dying,* along with the unsought and sometimes dubious distinction of having become a favorite subject for term papers and doctoral dissertations. As with O'Hara, there is a temptation — one that must stubbornly be resisted until it is demonstrably valid — to think that anyone as prolific as Updike cannot really be too good. Despite the occasional shallowness, the rhetorical flourishes, the repetitiveness and what to me seems the imitativeness of the "Other Modes" sequence of *Museum and Women,* he is still the most talented and exciting short story writer under fifty in America today. His many good-to-excellent stories plus *Bech* in toto are a notable achievement.

Of all fictional types, the story of manners is the form with which the average reader can most readily identify. It has, as we have seen, its generic weaknesses: it can lapse into preoccupation with the trivial; it can become mannered, repetitious, self-imitative, or effete. Beneath its customary subdued mood and restrained manner, however, the successful story of manners is concerned with the recurring truths of the human heart and with the day-to-day changes in contemporary society. It is capable of reminding the reader of the drama in the lives of average people. It can reveal the extraordinary that is present in the ordinary, the universal that exists in the specific. Out of unspectacular events in the lives of "ordinary" people, the writer of manners suggests universal truths, creates universal images, and ponders universal enigmas.

Many other significant modern American short story writers have concerned themselves wholly or primarily with this type of fiction, so many as to make detailed discussion impossible here. Some, like J. D. Salinger or James Thurber, have already been recognized as contemporary classics; others, including Louis Auchincloss and Mary McCarthy, are better known as novelists even though they may not have done their best work in the longer form; still others have been for the most part ignored or lost in the mass of recent articles and books devoted to their more spectacular or controversial contemporaries. In the following pages of this chapter I comment briefly on a baker's dozen such authors, because some seem to me among the best and most representative of their era; because some are among my own personal favorites; or for both reasons. All of them merit full-length study, evaluation, and re-evaluation. I have also included a checklist of other writers, a few of them well known, many of them not, whose work falls within the provenance of this chapter.

Roger Angell in *The Stone Arbor* (1960) has produced a virtual gallery of types associated with the fiction of the *New Yorker,* where the author works and where all these stories were originally published between 1946 and 1960. The persons include a well-paid and harried businessman — "I am selfish and tired, and vicariousness is what I crave"; a handsome divorcée who works on fashion accounts for a big advertising agency — "thin, rather tall, with good legs and a straight back"; a perceptive broker who had been a public relations officer during the war; a highly paid television executive. Except for their names, they would immediately find a place for themselves in most of John Cheever's stories. Like so many Cheeverites, they work within a boomerang's throw of Madison Avenue. They dress well, eat well, talk well, travel well, but beneath their urbane exteriors they are frightened or bored, nostalgic or sad. Almost everything worries them — though theirs is a well-mannered, stiff-upper-lip worry — whether it be fear of nuclear destruction or concern with how best to take advantage of the low tariff on French wines. About these essentially traditional characters, situations, and attitudes, Angell writes intelligent, perceptive, and urbane stories. His fiction is as well-tailored as are most of his characters, whose lives, narrated with skill and grace, dribble off into studiously unresolved endings.

The many stories of Louis Auchincloss (1917–), collected in *The Injustice Collectors* (1950), *The Romantic Egoists* (1954), *Powers of Attorney* (1963), *Tales of Manhattan* (1967), *Second Chance: Tales of Two Generations* (1970), and *The Partners* (1974), are almost exclusively concerned with what used to be called the American upper class: lawyers, leaders of society, patrons of the arts, financiers. For a writer so prolific — he has also written novels, literary criticism, and autobiographical studies — who is also a practicing lawyer, Auchincloss maintains an admirable level: he is entertainer, craftsman, and urbane commentator on the contemporary scene, whether it be the world of a distinguished law firm, a Manhattan art gallery, or the fashionable summer places of Long Island or New England. If at times his stories seem slightly bland and a bit too leisurely in terms of what they accomplish, they are invariably amusing, perceptive, witty. My own personal favorite — and I think still his best book of short fiction — is *The Injustice Collectors,* eight stories of characters who in one way or another are self-destructors, unable or unwilling to exist without creating situations that invite mistreatment or disappointment. The best of these is "Greg's Peg," a memorable portrait of Gregory Bakewell, an amiable and awkward misfit, pushing thirty and unmarried. In his efforts to become *accepted,* he manufactures a new personality, becomes a summer colony character and an alcoholic buffoon; in a climactic scene he is tossed into a swimming pool. No longer one of Anchor Harbor's social lions, he quits his familiar haunts and subsequently dies of a heart attack. Auchincloss' extremely skillful "observer-observed" technique, which reveals bit by bit the complicated character of the narrator (in his own way more of a misfit than "Poor Greg") is characteristic of the author's thoroughly disciplined technical skill and artistry.

Warren Beck's four collections of short stories — *The Blue Sash* (1940), *The First Fish* (1947), *The Far Whistle* (1951), *The Rest Is Silence* (1963) — are intelligent and thoroughly adult. Though Beck's work is varied in method and tone, among his favorite subjects is that of the moral responsibility of adults in situations more often than not unreasonable and unfathomable. "Detour in the Dark," from what seems to me his best book, *The Far Whistle,* is characteristic. An understanding father and his young son are forced to spend the night in a dilapidated, decrepit town. Throughout the long hours of tension the father tries to shield the son from the corruption and moral decay that have destroyed the heart of the community. In the morning they are able to leave, and the experiences of the night seem to the child like the vague memory of a bad dream. The father, however, is sure that the victory is a temporary one. Life, he believes, is a process of attrition and loss, and a child's innocence will eventually be eroded by shame and despair. Meanwhile, the father concludes, he will preserve for the child, as long as he is able to, as much security and safety as possible. Child and adult, the author suggests, are alike the expendable hostages of a dark and unsettled era, an idea restated in many of these carefully wrought stories, including the poignant and powerful title story of *The Rest Is Silence.*

Most of the stories of Hortense Calisher (1911–), collected in *In the Absence of Angels* (1963), *Tale for the Mirror* (1962), and *Extreme Magic* (1963), concern New Yorkers; an occasional later story takes place in Europe, but she is at her best with her American pieces. Several of these are about incidents in the life of Hester Elkin, who appears as child, adolescent, and young adult; among the best are "A Box of Ginger" and "The Watchers" from *In the Absence of Angels,* "Time, Gentlemen" and "The Coreopsis Kid" from *Tale for the Mirror,* and "The Gulf Between" from *Extreme Magic.* Hester's milieu is the comfortable one of Manhattan apartment dwellers in the first quarter of the twentieth century, a bustling, active world of a large Jewish family with many cousins, uncles, and aunts "so close-knit that all its branches lived within round-the-corner call of each other." Hester's Virginia-born father, who had immigrated to New York in the early 1880s, is the center of this small universe, which Calisher recalls with affection and re-creates in detail, its sights and sounds, its smells, the clothes its inhabitants wore and the food they ate and the experiences they encountered, from the death of a grandmother to the ritualistic breakfast routine of Hester's father or a child's observation of Armistice Day in New York. All this is effectively rendered, simple without lapsing into the trivial, warm-hearted without being sentimentalized.

Many of Calisher's stories are set at a far remove from this sheltered world. They take place in a society in which the concept of order, harmony, and happiness has been blurred almost beyond recognition. In them, the loss of love, the failure of marriage, the inability of human beings to communicate with each other are central themes. The narrator of the title story of her first collection, for example, concludes that "in the absence of angels and arbiters from a world of light, men and women must take their place": these stories indicate that men and women are poor substitutes.

The failures of Calisher's people are not just the defeats of specific human relationships, but the failures of traditional social and personal values in a world so fragmented and beset by stress and tension that the values have become either unrecognizable or unattainable. The young intellectual of "The Woman Who Was Everybody" is aware that she is one of the "rejected"; she tries to escape the "gray encroaching smutch of averageness" by a meaningless affair with a young technician, but knows that after the "desperate wrenches, the muffled clingings of love-making," she will still be alone and unwanted. The senator's wife of "The Night Club in the Woods" tries to buy a romantic past that never actually existed. The young man who has "moved up" from Fourteenth Street to Sutton Place yearns for the past, when love illuminated a relationship that has lost its meaning. The husband and wife of "Saturday Night" have become "strangers . . . too far apart even for conflict . . . sharing the terrible binding familiarities of the joint board, the joint child . . . and the graceless despair of the common bed." The widower of the novella "Extreme Magic" is isolated after the death of his wife and children. The protagonist of another novella — a form in which Calisher excels — is similarly separated from the world of accustomed relationships and responses by hereditary baldness ("The Railway Police").

Calisher narrates these stories of human failure and fallibility with grace and insight; the grayness of her people's lives is lightened by her pervading compassion. The main character of "If You Don't Want to Live I Can't Help You," from her most recent collec-

tion, is typical. After a trying day, which includes a visit to her
death-and-failure-obsessed nephew and her participation in commencement exercises during which she is honored for her academic achievement, Professor Mary Ponthus reflects: "I'm of the
breed that hopes. May this one [a student] want to live. *Maybe this
one wants to live.* And when you see that, that's the crux of it. We
are all in the dark together, but those are the ones that humanize
the dark."

Most of the stories in the three collections of Robert M. Coates
(1897–) — *All the Year Round* (1943), *The Hour after Westerly* (1957),
and *The Man Just Ahead of You* (1964) — were orginally published in
the *New Yorker*; the best of the traditionally plotted ones, like almost
any good short fiction, do not really begin until the last line. "The
Hour after Westerly," for example, outlines the predicament of a
man who, while driving home, somehow loses an hour — and part
of his memory as well. Attempting later to retrace the events
of that fateful day, he is often on the verge of some revelation;
he is confronted by elusive recollections of romance or excitement that may have occurred during his lapse of memory. But
the mystery is never solved, the revelation never disclosed. Only
dimly aware of a sense of loss and sorrow, he returns to the tread-
mill of his prosaic life with a wife who is "always getting the wrong
meanings."

The plight of the New York business man of "Return" is similar:
what happens to him *after* he has been lured down from his precarious perch atop the water tower where he has sought solitude?
What happens to the husband and wife of "Memento" *after* the
slightly tipsy husband has hit and killed a farmer's dog? What
happens to the narrator of "The Captive" *after* the attractive Mrs.
DeCassiris' "beeper" stops? These are the unanswered questions
that hover above and around these engrossing stories.

Coates is similarly effective in the kind of blend of fiction and
nonfiction that long before the advent of the new journalism was
associated with the *New Yorker,* where he has been a staff member
for many years. A good example is "The Man Just Ahead of You."

It is he, the narrator of the piece comments, who causes all the trouble; the man just ahead of you who has criticized the elevator boy or been ugly to the waitress and has caused *them* to be ugly to *you*, to look the other way when you enter your favorite restaurant, or pretend not to see you when you get into the elevator: "things like these, I always say, they can take the heart out of a man." So it is in "The Law," a commentary on the law of averages, evoked by a sudden, unexplained exodus over New York's Triborough Bridge; beneath the author's humorous exposition one is suddenly aware of a partially glimpsed vision of impending disaster.

Though his most characteristic stories are set in or around New York City, Coates is equally skillful in "The Need," "Storms of Childhood," "The Reward," and other stories in which he recalls people and incidents from New England to the Cripple Creek district of Colorado. Whatever his form and method, he is always the seasoned professional, disciplined, perceptive, and very adroit; perhaps even more important, he is never never dull, even in his slightest fictions.

The most successful stories of Elizabeth Enright (1909–1968) also grow out of ordinary situations involving intelligent individuals; almost without exception her best work is that in which the drama exists in the minds and hearts of her characters and does not depend for effect upon unusual circumstances, tricks, or artifice. The title story of her second collection, *The Moment Before the Rain* (1955), for example, merely re-creates a few moments in the lives of an elderly man napping on a veranda and an elderly lady who watches him, yet during this brief interval the woman relives the high points of her life and the reader shares them with her — the early married years, her children and the "shrill twilight voices of the Past," her love affair that caution maimed and time killed, her acceptance of the belief that time takes away everything eventually, including love, and her realization that, no matter what she did with her life, things would have ended the same way, with "an old man napping and an old woman watching him."

Enright has been similarly successful in capturing the essence of childhood — she began her career as a writer and illustrator of children's books, one of which won a Newbery Award in 1939 — from her depiction of the fearful dream world of a child whose parents have been killed in an accident to her fine story of a wandering day in the life of a neglected child, "The Playground." Among other things, the child watches a couple making love and rescues her companion from drowning; when she returns home at dusk her reply to her mother's "What happened today?" is a laconic "Swam. Played. Nothing much."

Ways of Loving (1974) is the first collection of short fiction by Brendan Gill (1914–); as one might expect from the National Book Award-winning novelist and *New Yorker* drama editor, these sketches, short stories, and novellas are the works of a skilled and seasoned professional. Some of the best of them concern the old or the elderly, whom he draws with a blend of compassion, irony, and tart humor: a well-meaning widowed father who plays havoc with his daughter's personal life; an independent aging doctor; a withdrawn mother and daughter whose annual party is the event around which their year and their world revolve.

Then there are some very nice pieces involving members of the Catholic clergy, again impeccably constructed, again permeated with ironic understanding: an elderly nun who "loved God, but . . . who also loved life"; or a young priest who experiences an unusual kind of epiphany on the Fourth of July.

And there is a delicious little tour de force (which in spirit and tone reminds me, without being imitative, of Saki's small gem, "The Story-Teller") about the reversal of father-son storytelling roles ("Well, once upon a time," the irritated child begins, "in a deep, deep forest, there lived a boy named Christopher Robin . . . And he loved to kill people. He took a gun and shot his nurse — bang! and his bear — bang! and his mother — bang! — and . . .").

Most of all I like "Fat Girl," reminiscent of Dorothy Parker's "Big Blonde," in which Gill has created two marvelous characters, an amoral secretary, insatiable eater, and sex-object, and her idio-syncratic employer.

In addition to several novels and books of nonfiction, Nancy Hale (1908–) has published seven collections of short fiction (the first, *Earliest Dreams* [1936]; the most recent, *The Pattern of Perfection* [1960]). Intelligent, highly civilized, and gracious even when she is shedding her victim's blood, Nancy Hale is an urbane and witty commentator on the changing American social scene. Her charac-ters fight no battles to reform society or change the world. Their problems are essentially personal — how to live with or without their current spouses, how to dull the edge of inner hunger, how to adjust to a society indifferent to older standards of conduct or too hurried to allow time for contemplation and civilized personal rela-tions. She creates with gentle malice the antagonism between a faded Virginia matriarch and her Yankee daughter-in-law in "The Pattern of Perfection," dissects a neurotic but likable coed and her unresponsive teacher in "The Secret Garden," and in "The Fox" presents a seriocomic commentary on life among the Piedmont hunt-club gentry, highlighted by the character of a heavy-drinking, hard-riding, slow-thinking native son who reads only Gibbon and is convinced that intellectuality and morbidity are synonymous.

Nancy Hale is equally skillful in her narrative sketches and semi-autobiographical vignettes and reminiscences. Around such simple situations as a child's first day at school, a mother's reading to an ill child, or a visit to a university commencement, she can create moving characters and moods. That she can perform these feats of legerdemain is as much as tribute to her sensitive appraisal of people and places as it is to her thoroughly disciplined and flexible artistry.

Quotation marks are needed when one speaks of the two collec-tions of "short stories" by Mary McCarthy (1912–), *The Company She Keeps* (1942) and *Cast A Cold Eye* (1950). They are admittedly auto-biographical — "Luckily, I am writing a memoir and not a work of fiction," she says in one of her best pieces — and in each volume relatively traditional short stories are outnumbered by autobiographical essays and reminiscences, two of which she later included in her *Memories of a Catholic Girlhood* (1957). The best known and I think the most superior of these pieces is "Yonder Peasant, Who Is He?" It concerns McCarthy's experiences as a six-year-old following the death of her mother and father during the influenza epidemic of 1918. "The Rogue" and "C.Y.E." tell of her experiences in a Catholic boarding school for girls. All three are among her best work.

With only two or three exceptions, McCarthy's other "stories" apparently grow in similar fashion out of what the unnamed "she" of "Weeds" describes as events that had "passed . . . out of experience into memory." They are about incidents in the life of an emancipated young or youngish woman who recalls nostalgically the "feeling of uniqueness and identity, a feeling she had once had when, at twenty, she had come to New York and had her first article accepted by a liberal weekly, but which had slowly been rubbed away by four years of being on the inside of the world that had looked magic from Portland, Oregon." As Margaret Sargent or I, you, she, or the girl, she dominates most of McCarthy's stories: as a young married woman having an affair and contemplating divorce as something "deeply pleasurable in the same way being . . . engaged . . . had been" ("Cruel and Barbarous Treatment"); as a divorcée going to bed with the man in the Brooks Brothers shirt; as a patient on an analyst's couch in "Ghostly Father, I Confess." Shrewd, perceptive, intelligent, supercilious, arrogant, uncertain beneath her cockiness, coldly analytical, always the insider viewing outsiders with disdain yet simultaneously "always wanting something exciting and romantic to happen," Margaret is the new woman, a women's libber two decades before the term came into everyday speech. "I am myn owene woman," she tells one of her conquests, quoting from Chaucer's *Troilus and Cressida*. "Myn owene woman, wel at ease."

McCarthy's fiction has often been criticized as cold. It is, but if her peripatetic heroine casts a cold eye on her fellow mortals, the same cold eye is frequently viewing *her;* Margaret the observer is also Margaret observed. Unwinkingly, unsparingly. And this gives a dimension and depth to what otherwise would tend to be rather not much more than expert reportage. Rereading these stories after a passage of many years, I am impressed with the clarity of vision (albeit a narrowly focused one), the relaxed yet thoroughly disciplined prose, the evocation of a time when the Margaret Sargents of our society went to work for ten dollars a week and people made love in Pullman cars. The major weakness of the stories, it seems to me, is overdiscursiveness; with only occasional exceptions, most of them seem too long for what they accomplish.

The most important of the three collections of short stories by Edward Newhouse (1911–) is *Many Are Called* (1951). All of the adjectives used to praise the fiction of such *New Yorker* authors as Roger Angell, Robert M. Coates, John Cheever, and John Updike automatically come to mind when one first reads Newhouse; his work is timely, entertaining, resourceful, disciplined, witty, and urbane. *Many Are Called* contains forty-two stories originally published between 1939 and 1950, all but three of them in the *New Yorker,* where Newhouse was a staff member for many years. Like so many of his associates, Newhouse is a writer of indisputably creative gifts who is at the same time a fine reporter with a very good eye and ear; few recent collections of short fiction re-create more skillfully than his the essence of a particular segment of American life. The *Many Are Called* pieces display an almost camera-and-tape-recorder ability to reproduce the vernacular of the period, from the conversation of a group of combat air force personnel to the habitués of Jake's Third Avenue saloon; they reflect with similar accuracy the mood, the temper, the feel of the times, from the war and the uneasy peace to the lethal potentiality of modern automobiles. What seems to me the only major weakness in these stories is the scarcity of really memorable and sharply individualized characters; Newhouse's people, in retrospect, fade away into the society from which their creator has selected them.

*

Tillie Olsen's literary career is as unusual as her fictions themselves. Four short stories written and published during the fifties in *New Campus Writing, Prairie Schooner, Pacific Spectator,* and *New World Writing,* and collected in *Tell Me a Riddle* (1961) when she was already a mature woman (her short novel, *Yonnadio,* begun in 1932 when she was in her teens, was not published until 1974): four stories, each a classic, and the collection itself a permanent addition to the literature of the American short story.

Though a far remove from most of the character types and situations of the short fiction of manners previously commented on, Olsen's stories share with them the concern with the dilemmas of existence, the hopes, consolations, disappointments, and tragedies of day-to-day living and dying. Olsen unblinkingly confronts the most universal problem of the artist — that of suggesting the meaning that underlies the appearance, of embodying the ultimate reality that exists beyond the actions and thoughts of her characters. And she creates these characters with a feeling and understanding so deep as to be often literally painful, with at times an almost miraculous rendering of the rhythms of thought and speech patterns, with expert economy, with effective counterpointing of past and present, with judicious use of traditional and innovative narrative methods and technical devices.

"I Stand Here Ironing" is a mother's thoughts and recollections of her daughter ("She was a child seldom smiled at . . . of anxious, not proud, love. We were poor . . . I was a young mother, a distracted mother. There were the other children, pushing up, demanding . . . There were years she did not want me to touch her. She kept too much in herself, her life was such she had to keep too much in herself. My wisdom came too late . . . She is a child of her age, of depression, of war, of fear.")

In "Hey Sailor, What Ship?" we meet a middle-aged adventurer on shore leave with his memories to forget and "his hopeless hopes to be murdered." "O Yes" presents a twelve-year-old girl, becoming gradually and painfully aware of the dark forest that is the world of adults. But the classic piece is the title story, an account, at times almost unbearable, of the death by cancer of the matriarch.

It is a difficult and painful thing to be a human being, Olsen's stories tell us, but her characters are never completely alone, are not utterly lost. Thus the old grandfather of "Tell Me a Riddle" can answer his dying wife's lament of "Lost, how much have I lost" with the cry that *"There was joy too."* It is this beating, throbbing denial of denial itself that animates these moving and eloquent stories. In spite of loneliness and fear and pain and betrayal, in the words of another of Tillie Olsen's memorable characters, "There is still left enough to live by."

Almost without exception, the best stories of J. F. Powers (1917–) are concerned with pastors, curates, and parishioners of the Catholic Church; although never a seminarian to the best of my knowledge, he writes of the clergy with remarkable familiarity and understanding. His stories are highly individualistic and highly disciplined; they illustrate the triumph of skill and insight over such unspectacular materials as Father Udovic's reaction to a strange letter that turns up in the collection plate, Father Fabre's efforts to obtain a table for his room, or a curate's dislike for his superior's cats.

Powers is so accomplished that the casual reader is likely to be unimpressed by his admirable control of all the elements in each of his stories, by his happy integration of incident and setting, characters and idea. Perhaps the main source of his success is a thoroughly adult vision, which enables him to create characters who are good without approaching perfection, who are capable of doing evil without *being* evil, who are laughable without becoming ridiculous, or slightly unbalanced without needing to be institutionalized. Perhaps it is his remarkable sense of selectivity; his ability to isolate the significant from that which is merely interesting; his ability to select the inevitably right word, thought, detail, gesture, or incident. Perhaps it is his ability to suggest constantly the universal in the specific without recourse to the didactic or the pretentiously symbolic. Characteristic is a detail like Father Philbert's

holding a crucifix over Father Malt's cat and then beating the animal in "Death of a Favorite" in *The Presence of Grace* (1956). Similar
juxtapositions of opposites are frequently seen in Powers' first collection, *Prince of Darkness* (1947), and in his National Book Award-
winning novel, *Morte d'Urban* (1962), several chapters of which
were originally published as short stories.

Powers has succeeded in creating his corner of the universe, with
its dedicated individuals and its crass opportunists, its winners and
losers. Beneath the good humor and tolerance that characterize
his treatment of character, he presents brief but chilling glimpses
into a way of life in which the trivial becomes confused with the
momentous, in which the desire to serve mankind can result in
service of self or in envy, greed, and even cruelty. He has created,
in short, a special section of the world that is very similar to the
world outside the monastic walls.

Among the best of the many short stories of Mark Van Doren
(1894–1972) — he produced five collections, from *The Witch of Ramoth* (1950) to his *Collected Stories* (1962) — are those either about
childhood or about an adult's memories of childhood. "Dollar
Bill" is the nostalgic recollection of a fussy middle-aged man who,
before retiring to the snug enclosed world of a Pullman berth,
unsuccessfully attempts to obtain some food to make his temporary
happy isolation more complete. Lying, hungry, in the darkness, he
remembers his childhood, a trip to a fair, his yearning for a nickel
hamburger he could not afford. "Grandison and Son" explores
knowingly the gulf between a son and a loving father whose desires
for the boy's success become almost obsessive; "A Wild Wet Place"
similarly points up the contrast between old age and youth, particularly in a moving scene between a grandmother and her grand-
daughter. "Abide with Me" is a subdued character study of a New
Yorker's return to his native Midwest to be at his dying mother's
bedside; "The Streamliner" movingly recreates the emotions of
another man's return to his homeplace. Equally good are "One of
the Garretsons," in which a child at a family reunion discovers that

one of his vaunted relatives is insane; and "In What Far Country," a man's recollections of childhood incidents involving a brother later killed in the war. In all of these, Van Doren writes with admirable clarity, insight, and grace.

He is equally adept in several stories in a darker vein. "You never knew by looking at people, you never knew a thing," one of Van Doren's characters comments in words that suggest the theme of several of the best of these. "If Lizzie Tells" brilliantly and at times breathtakingly creates the emotional and guilt-ridden tumult of an outwardly prosaic businessman with an obsession for fondling young girls; at the same time he passionately desires to protect them from men like himself. "The Uncertain Glory" presents another respectable and amiable middle-aged man, who indulges in wildly erotic fancies involving a young woman he sees on the train; simultaneously, he worries constantly about his wife and boys back in New York. And "The Watchman," a sympathetic portrayal of a benevolent youthful voyeur, is one of the very good stories of recent years.

Other representative collections of stories of manners, or collections containing stories of contemporary manners — too many to be commented on individually — are: Ludwig Bemelmans' *I Love You, I Love You, I Love You* (1942) and *Hotel Bemelmans* (1946); Sally Benson's *Women and Children First* (1946); Gina Berriault's *The Mistress and Other Stories* (1965); Sallie Bingham's *The Touching Hand and Six Short Stories* (1967) and *The Way It Is Now* (1972); Kay Boyle's *Thirty Stories* (1956); Maeve Brennan's *In and Out of Never-Never Land* (1969); *22 Stories* (1969); and *Christmas Eve* (1974); Eleanor Clark's *Dr. Heart: A Novella and Other Stories* (1975); Laurie Colwin's *Passion and Affect* (1974); Evan S. Connell, Jr.'s *The Anatomy Lesson and Other Stories* (1957) and *At the Crossroads* (1964); James Gould Cozzens' *Children and Others* (1964); Elizabeth Cullinan's *The Time of Adam* (1972); Olivia Davis' *The Scent of Apples* (1972); Peter De Vries' *No, But I Saw the Moon* (1952); George P. Elliott's *Among the Dangs* (1961) and *An Hour of Last Things* (1968); Irving Faust's *Roar*

Lion Roar and Other Stories (1965); George Garrett's numerous collections, particularly *Cold Ground Was My Bed Last Night* (1964); Martha Gellhorn's *Two by Two* (1958); Shirley Ann Grau's *The Wind Shifting West* (1973); Joanne Greenberg's *Summering* (1966); Marianne Hauser's *A Lesson In Music* (1964); Robert Hemenway's *The Girl Who Sang with the Beatles and Other Stories* (1970); Helen Hudson's *The Listener and Other Stories* (1968); Ward Just's *The Congressman Who Loved Flaubert and Other Washington Stories* (1973); John Knowles's *Phineas* (1968); Frances Gray Patton's *The Finer Things in Life* (1951); William Maxwell's *The Old Man at the Crossing and Other Tales* (1966); William Peden's *Night in Funland and Other Stories* (1968); Dawn Powell's *Sunday, Monday, and Always* (1952); Gilbert Rogin's *The Fencing Master and Other Stories* (1965) and *What Happens Next* (1971); Mark Schorer's *The State of Mind* (1947); Budd Schulberg's *Some Faces in the Crowd* (1953); Allan Seager's *The Old Man of the Mountain and Other Stories* (1950); Wallace Stegner's *The Women on the Wall* (1949) and *The City of the Living* (1965); Francis Steegmuller's *French Follies and Other Follies* (1946) and *Stories and True Stories* (1972); Hollis Summers' *How They Chose the Dead* (1973); Harvey Swados' *Nights in the Gardens of Brooklyn* (1960) and *A Story for Teddy — and Others* (1965); James Thurber's *The Thurber Carnival* (1945); Gordon Weaver's *The Entombed Man of Thule* (1973); Edmund Wilson's *Memoirs of Hecate County* (1946); Richard Yates's *Eleven Kinds of Loneliness* (1962); Samuel Yellen's *The Passionate Shepherd* (1957).

Chapter 5

"A Mad World, My Masters"*

MENTAL AND PHYSICAL illness or abnormality have fascinated the creative imagination since the beginning of written literature. Prose fiction has become increasingly subjective during the last hundred years, more introspective than extroverted, more concerned with exploring inner causes than with chronicling external events. Historically, this tendency is seen with the Brontës in *Jane Eyre* and *Wuthering Heights* or, with Dickens, in *The Mystery of Edwin Drood,* though the turning point, of course, came decades after, with the work of Conrad, James, and Joyce. But it was not until the middle decades of the twentieth century that the explosion occurred in the fictional depiction of the borderland between the so-called normal and the abnormal, between sanity and madness, between customary behavior and the exceptional. As the understanding and treatment of mental and emotional disorders moved slowly out of the dungeons created by ignorance, fear, and superstition, more and more fiction writers described with understanding and compassion the twilight half-world of the mentally ill. Emotional violence, the desolation of the human spirit, madness, man's capacity for self-destruction, loneliness, Oedipal fears, and atavistic tyrannies more frequently became the subject of fiction. By the end of the fifties, the couch of the psychiatrist threatened to replace the six-shooter of the Western lawman as stock property of fiction, motion pictures, television, and cartoons. A contemporary

* A little-known play by Thomas Middleton (1608).

mythology came into being, complete with its hierarchy of good
guys versus the bad guys (the kindly or the paranoid psychiatrist,
the sadistic nurse or her compassionate counterpart, the patient
who is less disturbed than his analyst). The mentally ill and the
emotionally maimed came to be important subjects of the American short story since 1940.

A similar preoccupation with the grotesque, the abnormal, and
the bizarre is one of the major concerns of the recent American
short story. Characters like Jean Stafford's horrifyingly fat girl,
Tennessee Williams' gigantic and cannibalistic black masseur, Flannery O'Connor's wooden-legged Joy Hopewell, and Carson
McCullers' malignant hump-backed dwarf people many of the
most memorable stories of the past two decades. The grotesque —
what was labeled new American Gothic — has been an important
element in prose fiction almost from its start; the line of descent
from "Monk" Lewis to Charles Dickens to William Faulkner to the
black humorists of the sixties is more direct than some literary
historians have indicated. Like Dickens and Faulkner, the writers
of the past fifteen years have tended to employ physical abnormality, exaggeration, and caricature to suggest the inner nature of
a character or to indicate the essence of an individual who em-
bodies universal or societal traits and qualities. Beneath their eccentricities and abnormalities, the people of such diverse authors as
James Purdy and Jean Stafford and Tennessee Williams are arche-
types rather than mere freaks or biological mistakes, and so are
suggestive of the disorders of our times.

The stories of James Purdy (1923–) in *Color of Darkness* (1957)
and *Children Is All* (1962) usually concern people who are either
emotional or physiological grotesques or both. Lonely, lost, isolated, unloved, or undesirable, they are confined within private
hells that are sometimes of their own making and sometimes
created by forces over which they can exercise little if any control.
In the controversial *63: Dream Palace*, nineteen-year-old Fenton
Riddleway and his younger, half-demented brother, Claire, are

living in a moldering rattrap of a decaying house on Manhattan's
Sixty-third Street. Fenton becomes involved with a neurotic novelist and an assorted group of homosexuals, derelicts, and oddballs,
including the alcoholic and ambiguous "great-woman." Claire,
meanwhile, is dying. In his confused, amoral fashion, Fenton loves
his brother and has tried to help him since the death of their
mother. In his mind, love and hate are inextricably mingled —
"just as he had wished Mama dead, so that he felt the agent of her
death, so now he wanted Claire to be dead, and despite the fact that
the only two people in the world he had loved were Mama and
Claire." If they were "safe from trouble," Fenton would be kind to
Claire, but trouble is their destiny, and trouble always makes Fenton "mean." One night, after an almost intolerable scene involving
a production of *Othello* by the group of homosexuals with whom
Fenton has been associating, Fenton comes home drunk and murders Claire. He refuses to allow himself to accept the fact that his
brother is dead, but after several harrowing days and nights he
knows that Claire must have a "service, a funeral"; he must be put
in a "sheltered place." Fenton gets an old chest from the attic, not a
"fragrant cedar chest" such as he had desired, but an "old white
box with broken hinges . . . whose inside lid was covered with a
filthy cloth." Finally — Cain having killed Abel, and out of love
rather than hate — he nerves himself for the task at hand:

> It took him all night to get himself ready to carry Claire up, as though
> once he had put him in the chest, he was really at last dead forever. For
> part of the night he found that he had fallen asleep over Claire's body,
> and at the very end before he carried him upstairs and deposited him,
> he forced himself to kiss the dead stained lips he had stopped and said,
> "Up we go then, motherfucker."

Here, as in most of the *Color of Darkness* stories, Purdy has
created a somber world of shocking paradox and violent contrasts,
in which love and hate are so closely related as to be indistinguishable, in which traditional personal or societal relationships are confused or altered almost beyond recognition.

It is like the world of the sick child of "Why Can't They Tell You

Why?" who moons over the picture of his father, killed during the war. His mother, an "ugly pale woman . . . [with] a faint smell from her like that of an uncovered cistern," threatens to send him to the "mental hospital with the bars . . . where they sent Aunt Grace." But the child cannot tear himself away from the pictures — "They're Daddy," he screams — until the mother, in a frenzy of rage and stupidity, attempts to force the boy to destroy them. Unsuccessful, the mother seizes some of the pictures and hurls them into the fire. She turns to get the remainder but, even in her thick-witted mind, she is appalled. Her son no longer looks like a human but "in his small unmended night shirt like some crippled and dying animal running hopelessly from its pain." She takes a step toward him but "the final sight of him made her stop. He had crouched on the floor, and, bending his stomach over the boxes, hissed at her, so that she stopped short, not seeing any way to get at him, seeing no way to bring him back, while from his mouth black thick strings of something slipped out, as though he had spewed out the heart of his grief."

Another lonely child, in the title story, slowly retreats into a limbo of hate and misunderstanding. In a shocking scene the child viciously kicks and shouts obscenities at his kindly but inadequate father who, at the story's end, lies helpless and confused on the floor, writhing with a physical agony less searing than the emotional shock and damage occasioned by his son's attack. In "The Cutting Edge," the artist-son of unimaginative but reasonably well-intentioned parents shaves his beard before returning to the mother and father whom he finally "hates" and "despises" for "what both of you have done to yourselves." "Everything had come to the end" for the well-meaning man who is fired from his job because he is suspected — rightly or wrongly we are never told — of being a homosexual. The wife of a paraplegic, shut off from her war-casualty husband, is tempted to strike him across the face when he is suffering most, and is obsessed with the desire to buy a raven whose refrain is "George is dead." A husband strikes his wife at a party because she hates his name; later, outside, he knocks her down and she lies quite casually before erupting into terrible screams. "My God . . . I am in awful pain," she screams and the story ends flatly, as do so many of Purdy's fictions, with her almost laconic statement: "Can't you see I'm bleeding?"

These and similar characters from *Color of Darkness* are overwhelmed by sickness and despair. It is impossible to contemplate them without a shudder of revulsion as well as pity. The stories are not for the squeamish or the orthodox. Yet Purdy is ruthlessly and unsparingly honest in creating a world bereft of traditional values, and nowhere does he depict the morbid, the sensational or the decadent for their own sakes alone.

The stories in *Children Is All,* published five years after *Color of Darkness,* seem, at first reading, to lack the fierce and shocking impact of Purdy's earlier short fiction. "Everything Under the Sun" presents two lost and lonely youthful deviates reminiscent of Fenton and Claire Riddleway, and the prose poem "Sermon" takes the reader to the realm of a faceless, voiceless, and doomed audience. Such stories owe much of their power to Purdy's effective use of the bizarre and the grotesque, as does the nightmarish short play, "Cracks," which is highlighted by another of the author's portrayals of an unforgettable child. The settings of the *Children Is All* stories, however, and the situations out of which most of the stories evolve, are more immediately recognizable than those of *Color of Darkness.*

In "Home by Dark," for example, a grandfather and his grandson sit quietly at dusk, talking of the boy's dead parents and doing nothing more spectacular than searching for the child's tooth, which has dropped into the grass. But as the twilight silently, deeply descends, the exterior dark is counterpointed by an inner illumination — paradoxically, an illumination of darkness — as a slow tide of grief overwhelms the old man who "pushes the boy's head tight against his breast so he would not hear the sounds that came out now like a confused and trackless torrent, making ridiculous the quiet of evening."

The revelation of nameless fear or grief or revulsion is similarly unspectacular in "The Lesson," in which an aggressively masculine swimming instructor attracts and repels a teen-aged swimmer, who finally cries out: "Go away, please . . . Don't lean over me, please, and let the water fall from you on me. Please, please, go back into the pool. I don't want you close now. Go back into the pool."

In the same subdued manner, one of the most effective of the *Children Is All* stories, "The Encore," is built around a quietly desperate scene involving the chasm between a well-meaning but uneducated mother and her unpopular intellectual son. "Mrs. Benson" is an equally quiet though less effective character delineation of a mother and daughter chatting in a Paris café. "Daddy Wolf," on the other hand, is more typically early Purdy. This is a wild, weird monologue of an unbalanced, semiliterate man who pours out his problems and fears to an advice-to-the-troubled commentator: he's afraid of rats; his wife has left him because she heard that the V.D. rate was going up. In less skilled hands, such a story might end in caricature or burlesque. As it is, "Daddy Wolf" is an impressive tour de force, memorable both for its characterization and for its lyrically nightmarish quality. In somewhat similar fashion, "Goodnight, Sweetheart" hovers near the abyss of the ludicrous, but avoids the abyss and is a moving picture of terrible loneliness. Miss Miranda, an elderly schoolteacher somewhat reminiscent of Sherwood Anderson's Kate Swift or Alice Hindman, walks naked to the home of the young bachelor she had taught some years before and finally persuades him to join her in the bed. Nothing, of course, happens. They are, in reality, miles and miles apart even while they lie "close to one another, and they both muttered to themselves in the darkness as if they were separated by different rooms . . ."

Loneliness, the inability to communicate, and the slow withdrawal into the private hells of the unwanted appear in both the *Color of Darkness* and the *Children Is All* stories, which are like stones suddenly glimpsed in swiftly moving streams and transmuted into something strange, wonderful, and unusual.

It is as prose poet of the abnormal, the unbalanced, and the grotesque that Purdy has achieved his highest successes. There is nothing grotesque, however, about his narrative method. Except for long pieces like *63: Dream Palace* or the monologues of "Daddy Wolf" or "The Sermon," his stories are almost classical in their simplicity, in their time span (most of them occur within a few minutes or at the most an hour or two of elapsed chronological time), in their simplicity of setting, and their limited dramatis personae. Purdy writes without pretentiousness or exhibitionism, and relies largely on the use of external scene and a relaxed, almost laconic dialogue reminiscent of Hemingway's and O'Hara's without being in any way imitative. Quite the contrary, Purdy is as individualistic as a blue unicorn and at his best can do more with a whisper than most fiction writers do with a shout, as Dame Edith Sitwell observed.

Beneath the simple exterior of his stories, beneath such disarmingly superficial devices as the talk about food in, for example, "About Jessie Mae," the reader is allowed brief glimpses into a world in which the familiar suddenly becomes strange and terrible, as though one walking through a well-known terrain were to find himself without warning at the edge of a void alive with sights and sounds only partly recognizable. Purdy's is a strange, highly individual talent. His awareness of the murky depths of human cruelty or indifference is as startling as his recognition of their opposites. He is preoccupied with the recurring themes of loneliness and isolation, and with the paradoxes he sees inherent in the human situation — love-hate, beauty-ugliness, compassion-cruelty. Out of these paradoxes and these themes, Purdy has created a fictional world uniquely his own.

The best short stories of Tennessee Williams (1914–) are in his first two collections, *One Arm* (1948) and *Hard Candy* (1954). Quite apart from their significance in being the first or early versions of characters and situations eventually developed into full-length plays — as is the case with "Portrait of a Girl in Glass" and *The Glass Menagerie*, "The Yellow Bird" and *Summer and Smoke*, "Three Players of a Summer Game" and *Cat on a Hot Tin Roof* and "Night of the Iguana" and the play of the same name — Williams' stories are important in their own right and at their best are a permanent addition to the "sick" fiction of the post–1940 decades.

The region inhabited by Williams' characters is wide yet at the same time as limited and circumscribed as Poe's, which in some ways it resembles. His stories are filled with what one Williams character speaks of as the "sense of the enormous grotesquerie of the world." They are permeated, too, with an air of profound melancholy, and iridescent with a faded beauty and corruption that recalls statesman John Randolph's irreverent simile of a rotting mackerel in the moonlight, which "shines and stinks, and stinks and shines." Similar character types reappear throughout Williams' stories: disillusioned or frustrated artists and intellectuals, sex-starved virgins or nymphomaniacs, faded gentlewomen and hypocritical clergymen, homosexuals and alcoholics, destructive women and likable adolescents. Recurring motifs include decay, disease, abnormality, and above all *loss,* loss through the inexorable process of time and the consequent fall from grace, a fall more often physiological than spiritual.

With almost no exceptions, Williams' people are adrift, unloved, and unwanted. Heredity often plays an important part in their alienation from "normal" or "approved" standards of conduct; their deterioration is hastened or precipitated further by ironies of circumstance over which they have no control; they are exploited by their friends or family, or slowly and often passively strangled by their own weaknesses and fear. "To love is to lose," Williams once wrote, and in one way or another his characters are losers, not winners. To alter his statement to "To live is to lose" would suggest the common chord of much of his short fiction.

Perhaps the most memorable and the most moving of these stories is "Portrait of a Girl in Glass," about shy and introverted Laura, the "petals" of whose mind had simply closed with fear, who could make no "positive motion toward the world but stood at the edge of the water, so to speak, with feet that anticipated too much cold to move"; she was to become the most appealing character in what still seems to me Williams' most moving play, *The Glass Menagerie.*

Characteristic, too, of this group of quiet, unsensational stories is one of Williams' earliest, the first published under his own name, "The Field of Blue Children," an account of a transitory love affair between a young poet, Homer Stallcup, and an undergraduate sorority girl with minor literary aspirations. Homer, an "outsider," is encouraged by Myra, an "insider." They come together for a moment of love in a field of blue flowers, and later drift apart. Myra marries an unexciting fraternity boy and slips into a humdrum marriage, and Homer simply fades out of her life.

Yet the memory of the incident in the field of blue flowers persists. Myra seldom feels "restless anymore" and abandons her verse writing; her "life seemed to be perfectly full without it." But she is impelled, one late spring evening several years after her marriage, to return to the scene of her first encounter with love.

> The field was exactly as she had remembered it. She walked quickly out among the flowers; then suddenly fell to her knees among them, sobbing. She cried for a long time . . . and then she rose to her feet and carefully brushed off her skirt and stockings. Now she felt perfectly calm and in possession of herself once more. She went back to the car. She knew that she would never do such a ridiculous thing as this again, for now she had left the last of her troublesome youth behind her.

With its muted lyricism and its slowly diminishing cadences — "The whole field was covered with dancing blue flowers. There was a wind scudding through them and they broke before it in pale blue waves, sending up a soft whispering sound like the infinitely diminished crying of small children at play" — the story reminds us that if Williams achieved fame as a playwright he began his career as a poet.

Equally memorable and drawn with similar understanding and compassion are the brother and sister of the presumably autobiographical story of adolescence and death, "The Resemblance Between a Violin Case and a Coffin," which is a moving study of the loss of innocence and youth and beauty. Almost as impressive are Williams' characterizations of the awkward college students in "The Important Thing," and the actor-protagonist of "The Vine," who is finally forced to accept the fact that he is washed up. His confrontation with the truth — all defenses broken, all illusions stripped from him — is one of the high marks in Williams' fiction.

Perhaps the best of all of Williams' fictional creations is Brick Pollitt of "Three Players of a Summer Game." Delta planter, one-time famous Sewanee athlete, and dedicated alcoholic, Brick is eventually emasculated, spiritually and emotionally if not physically, by Margaret, one of the most destructive of Williams' predatory contemporary vampires ("It was as though she had her lips fastened to some invisible wound in his body through which drained out of him and flowed into her the assurance and vitality that he had owned before marriage"). By the end of the story Brick is a ruin, driven through the streets in a Pierce Arrow by Margaret, "clothed and barbered with his usual immaculacy, so that he looked from some distance like the president of a good social fraternity in a gentleman's college of the South," but no longer a man, indeed no longer a human, but a babbling and goggling wreck "sheepishly grinning and nodding," while Margaret gaily blows the "car's silver trumpet at every intersection," waving and calling to everybody "as if she were running for office," and Brick "nodded and grinned with senseless amiability behind her. It was exactly the way that some ancient conqueror, such as Caesar or Alexander the Great or Hannibal, might have led in chains through a captive city the prince of a state newly conquered."

Though he is unforgettably individualized, Brick Pollitt, like so many of Williams' people, is an effectively functioning symbol, in this case of waste, the waste of human grace and beauty and dignity. Waste and the attritions of time are twin villains in Williams' view of the world. "Physical beauty," the narrator of "Three Players of a Summer Game," comments, is "of all human attributes the most incontinently used and wasted, as if whoever made it despised it, since it is made so often only to be disgraced by painful degrees and drawn through the streets in chains."

These are Williams' great betrayers: waste and time together. They degrade and befoul, and are unconquerable.

A second group of Williams' short fiction pieces centers on characters who are pathological or societal outcasts and rejects. Here again Williams is concerned with the loss of beauty and grace and with the attritions of time, along with an almost obsessive preoccupation with homosexuality, decay, and degradation. The best of these stories is "One Arm," set in the vicinity of New Orleans, which Williams knew so well and utilizes so effectively. Oliver Winemiller, apparently no kin to the Alma Winemiller of *Summer and Smoke,* had been light heavyweight boxing champion of the Pacific Fleet but has lost his arm in an automobile accident. His degeneration and deterioration are rapid: Oliver becomes a male hustler, a notorious homosexual, and finally murders a wealthy man who had paid him to act in a blue movie. In jail, awaiting execution, Oliver finally feels the passion and desire that he had for so many years aroused in others. But it is, of course, too late, and Oliver goes to the electric chair lost and broken, incomplete and unfulfilled, with "all his debts unpaid." Even in death, however, there is about Oliver something of the heroic, the beautiful. Unclaimed, his body becomes a cadaver in the medical school. The dissectors are "somewhat abashed by the body under their knives. It seemed intended for some more august purpose, to stand in a gallery of antique sculpture, touched only by light through stillness and contemplation, for it had the nobility of some broken Apollo that no one was likely to carve so purely again."

There is similar pathos but very little nobility in the unhappy lives of most of Williams' other rejects. One can feel sorry for Edith Jelkes, the sex-starved spinster of "The Night of the Iguana," whom we are introduced to in Acapulco, where she is recuperating after having suffered "a sort of nervous breakdown" at the Mississippi Episcopal school at which she had taught art. Like many of Williams' genteel no-longer-young ladies with a penchant for disaster, Edith is the victim of hereditary taints, and to that extent is only partially responsible for her actions. Her dubious sexual triumph over a homosexual writer, however, is hardly cause of unlimited rejoicing. The writer himself, moreover, and his male companion, both of whom alternately attract and repel Edith, are fundamentally flat characters who fail to arouse either sympathy or dislike.

And it is difficult to sympathize with the two derelicts of "Two on a Party," one of the loneliest, saddest couples in recent literature. Billy is a one-time English instructor and Hollywood hackwriter who is currently a self-destroying egoist; Cora is a kindly lush with "none of that desire to manage and dominate which is a typically American perversion of the female nature." Each of these whores is sympathetically observed and as convincing as a thunderstorm, and the terrible emptiness of their lives "on the road" is chillingly portrayed.

Like "Two on a Party," Williams' fantasies are memorable in their presentation of decay and disintegration, and are alive with that "Sense of the Awful," which Williams has called the "desperate black root of nearly all significant modern art." For the most part, however, the fantasies seem the least successful of his short fiction; in them the depiction of what one Williams character calls the "mad pilgrimage of the flesh" frequently approaches caricature or burlesque.

Probably the most successful and the best known of these symbolic excursions into the province of the grotesque, the Gothic, and the hallucinated is "Desire and the Black Masseur." From his childhood Anthony Burns "had betrayed an instinct for being included in things that swallowed him up." Unloved, unlovable, a leaf in the stream of life, Burns "loved to sit in the back rows of the movies where the darkness absorbed him gently . . . like a particle of food dissolving in a big hot mouth." One day he goes to a Turkish bath, where he is administered to by a gigantic black masseur. He is attracted to the Negro and eventually "adores" the giant. In return the giant "loves" him, tortures him, and eventually devours him, flesh and splintered bones. As he drops the bones, "left over from Burns' atonement," into a lake, the black masseur thinks: "It is perfect . . . it is now completed." Perfection and atonement, the story tells us, have gradually evolved out of the antitheses of love and hate, torture and delight. Meanwhile the Negro, like some strange being above and beyond earthly passions, moves on to another city where he waits in a "white-curtained place, serenely conscious of fate bringing . . . another, to suffer atonement as it had been suffered by Burns."

Without raising the question of the author's purpose, or lack of it, "Desire and the Black Masseur" fails because Williams makes no effort to bridge the gap between the specific framework of character, incident, time, and place, and the allegorical, symbolic, or mythic. Though powerful in its Poe-like totality of effect of horror and madness, the story tends to fall apart as a self-contained piece of fiction. It is not fiction that suggests the universal in terms of the specific; it is undigested and indigestable allegory. The same is true of "The Poet," the protagonist of which distills a liquor that makes the world change color, leads a life of benevolent anarchy, and retreats into silence with an "incubus in his bosom, whose fierce little purplish knot of a head was butting against his ribs and whose limbs were kicking and squirming with convulsions."

Williams' success as a playwright has obscured the real significance of the best of the *One Arm* and *Hard Candy* stories; his later work in short fiction, however, diminishes rather than adds to his reputation. The title novella of his third collection, *The Knightly Quest* (1966), has interesting possibilities: a contemporary fable, it centers on the return of Gewinner Pearce to his "home place" after years of travel with a tutor companion. The once-quiet town has become the site of a top-secret project; the family mansion has been desecrated by the erection of The Laughing Boy drive-in across the way. This modern fable revolves around these contrasts and in terms of Gewinner's family and the proprietor of The Laughing Boy. The climax is Gewinner's being launched into space, where he and the "radiant young navigator" can "swap . . . stories about the knightly quest as both have known it in their different ways." The novella has some good moments, but for the most part hobbles between farce, slapstick, burlesque, parody, bedroom-and-bathroom-and-night-prowling sexuality, along with some asides concerning the need for paranoia to insure felicity in the modern world and an editorial on Don Quixote and Sancho Panza and *their* quest. The writing is uneven, the characters are for the most part unbelievable or unconvincing, the workmanship careless throughout.

"Mama's Old Stucco House" and "Grand" are much better. The first is a slight but moving piece involving a homosexual alcoholic failure of an artist, and includes a memorable characterization of a dying black servant and her daughter, both masterfully drawn. "Grand" is a pleasantly warm-hearted character piece about the narrator's grandmother.

"Man Bring Up This Road" is a thin variation of a favorite Williams subject: a predatory old female patroness of the arts and her cannibalistic treatment of a middle-aged poet.

Eight Mortal Ladies Possessed (1974) is also largely a disappointment. "Happy August the Tenth" is good Williams: the portrayal of two upper-class ladies, a New Yorker and a Virginian ("middle age was not approaching on stealthy little cat feet . . . but was bursting upon them") belongs with the author's best work. A similar case might be made for "Oriflamme," a moving characterization reminiscent of those of several of the bewildered helpless women in the plays, and "Completed" is redeemed from triviality by a hasty but effective portrait of a black servant.

The remaining stories are less successful. Williams' characterizations of sex-ridden females are emetic rather than cathartic: a century-old principessa who dreams of her fifth husband's prowess in bed and gets her jollies in a very peculiar fashion ("The Inventory of Fontana Bella"); an ugly and aging American poetess addicted, among other unpleasant personal habits, to lallocropia and an Italian lover ("Sabbatha and Solitude"); and a nymphomaniac liberated by the death of an aged grandmother ("Miss Coynte of Greene"). Gone is the compassion that gave meaning to the twisted lives of so many of Williams' earlier misfits, grotesques, and freaks; in its place is a continuing kind of ugliness, something close to glee in the depiction of debasement, a sort of delight in such a line as this from "Sabbatha", said by the old hag's Italian lover, who has been questioned about a recent illness: "I said a fistula . . . is a perforation . . . and I got it from being gang-banged in Bangcock, ten cocks up my ass in one night" and so on.

It is saddening to see this sort of thing in the writings of one of the most talented writers of our times. But in spite of the short-comings of so many of his recent stories, Williams' contribution to the short fiction of the period is considerable. His "blasted alle-gories" — the phrase, of course, is Hawthorne's — are a searing in-dictment of the cruelty and injustice of the world as the author sees it. Even at their least successful they have about them the same pathos found in Williams' work in general. Whatever his form, method, or mood, the mad pilgrimage comes to the same dead end. Earth, sooner or later, "destroys her crooked child."

The smell of the sickroom permeates some of the most mem-orable stories of Jean Stafford (1915–), collected in *Children Are Bored on Sunday* (1953); *Stories: Jean Stafford, John Cheever, Daniel Fuch, William Maxwell* (1956); *Bad Characters* (1964); and the Pulit-zer Prize-winning *The Collected Stories of Jean Stafford* (1969).

"A Country Love Story" is characteristic. It is one of Stafford's best stories and one of the most moving recent treatments of the breakup of a marriage and the withdrawal into the world of the mentally ill. May, an intelligent, sensitive young woman married to an historian twenty years older than she, moves to a "solemn hinter-land" following Daniel's recovery from tuberculosis. Daniel retreats more deeply into his research until May gradually becomes aware that love, "the very center of their being, was choked off, over-grown, invisible." As Daniel's indifference slowly changes to hatred and cruelty, May creates an imaginary lover. Eventually she not only believes in this lover's existence, but depends "wholly on his companionship." In her mind she betrays Daniel constantly; her sin becomes frighteningly real to her, a longing and a need that allow her no peace. Finally, after Daniel has accused her openly of

"going mad," she fancies that the lover is sitting in the old-fashioned sleigh in the front yard of their country home. After a hideous
scene in which Daniel destroys the last of May's illusions, she has
nowhere to go but to the sleigh, now empty except for a black-
smith's cat, which has curled up on the seat. May now realizes that

> no change would come, and that she would never see her lover again.
> Confounded utterly, like an orphan in solitary confinement, she went
> outdoors and got into the sleigh. The blacksmith's imperturbable cat
> stretched and rearranged his position, and May sat beside him with her
> hands locked tightly in her lap, rapidly wondering over and over again
> how she would live the rest of her life.

May, alone, unloved, and lost, is typical of Stafford's
people. Sickness, loneliness, the need to communicate combined
with the inability to do so, are predicaments occurring in all her
stories. Ramona, the grossly fat young woman of "The Echo and
the Nemesis," is bedeviled by an enormous appetite. She sees herself in dreams as "nothing but an enormous mouth and a tongue,
trembling lasciviously," and seeks escape by fabricating the myth of
a beautiful twin sister who died young, but who is in reality her own
lost beauty before eating became a disease and a madness, a beauty
"dead, dead and buried under layers and layers of fat."

So it is with Pansy Vanneman, the young girl of "The Interior
Castle," who has suffered terrible head and face injuries in an
automobile accident. Living in a nightmare of pain and fear, Pansy
retreats into a "world which she had created." Confronted by relentless, unyielding pain, which advances upon her like an army
with banners, Pansy contemplates her brain, "a jewel . . . a flower
. . . always pink and always fragile, always deeply interior and inval-
uable." She begins to love not life or the hope of recovery, but her
own spirit, "enclosed within her head." She fears that the doctor
might maim it, "might leave a scratch on one of the brilliant facets
of the jewel, bruise a petal of the flower, smudge the glass where
the light burned, blot the envelopes, and that then she would die or
would go mad."

Similar, too, is charming Beatrice Trueblood of "Beatrice Trueblood's Story," who wills herself, as it were, into deafness and is separated by this physical difference, which virtually amounts to a stigma, from friendship, love, and society; or the alcoholic young mother, reminiscing about her youthful quest for education, and romance, who gazes upon the gray landscape and confesses, "I do not know whether it is forever midnight or forever noon."

Some of Stafford's characters display their eccentricities proudly; others are unaware of the *unusualness* that sets them apart from their fellows until it erupts in an act of unpremeditated violence. Ramona of "The Echo and the Nemesis" looks at the world through the wrong end of a pair of binoculars. The refugee doctor of "The Home Front" has what is almost a love affair with a cat, his "dearest friend," nearly goes into "a tailspin" at the sight of a rose in the hair of one of the boarders, and retches at the sight of a boy burning caterpillars. A Bostonian living with his mother in a rundown house wears a stock to cover a wen, smells of Necco wafers, and walks though doors backward. A ship's captain refuses to eat a roasted Negro infant, and Mrs. Baumgartner, a "delicious blonde," is beaten by her husband with a ski pole in the railroad station at Boise.

Whether she writes in the grotesque, masquelike manner of "A Modest Proposal" or with the straightforward realism of "A Summer Day," Jean Stafford is a skilled and disciplined artist who creates painstakingly in prose of admirable texture. She develops her characters slowly, often with a leisureliness reminiscent of Henry James. Never does she force her ideas upon the reader; there are few Q.E.D.'s in her fiction. Rather, she presents her characters and situations with at times a Kafkaesque ambiguity. The world of *Children Are Bored on Sunday* is a limited one into which sunlight and fresh air seldom penetrate; the odor of decay and death hovers over it. Richly colored, often stressing the incongruous, her stories are like Japanese water shells, which open silently to disgorge a phantasmagoria of brightly colored paper flowers in marked contrast to the bland, unrevealing forms in which they are contained.

*

Even before the publication of her first collection of short stories, *A Good Man Is Hard to Find* (1955), Flannery O'Connor (1925–1964) seemed to me the most gifted young writer to emerge since the publication in 1941 of Eudora Welty's *A Curtain of Green.* Her second collection, *Everything That Rises Must Converge* (1965); her *Complete Stories* (1971), which in addition to the *Good Man* and *Everything That Rises* stories contains twelve previously uncollected pieces; her "occasional prose" — essays, criticisms, lectures and notes for lectures — *Mystery and Manners* (1969); to say nothing of her two fine novels, *Wise Blood* (1952) and *The Violent Bear It Away* (1960) — all these have more than reinforced that early and by no means unique opinion. Everyone might not agree with the late Thomas Merton's statement, related by O'Connor's editor, Robert Giroux, in his Introduction to *The Complete Stories,* that he would not compare her with the likes of Hemingway or Sartre but rather with "someone like Sophocles" but I do not see how anyone could fail, with Merton, "to write her name with honor, for all the truth and all the craft with which she shows man's fall and his dishonor." Since her early death, O'Connor has become probably the most widely written about American short story writer of the last quarter-century. Articles, books, monographs, explications, commentary of all sorts, academic and otherwise, good and not so good (one is tempted to cry, "Hold, enough," and turn instead to the comment by O'Connor herself that "it is what is left over after everything explainable has been explained that makes a story worth writing and reading") have accumulated so rapidly that only a relatively few words about this marvelously gifted individualistic writer are needed here.

The setting of Flannery O'Connor's fiction is the author's native South. Central to O'Connor's effectiveness is her creation of a remarkable collection of misfits, rejects, or grotesques — young and old, black and white, vain and humble. These characters assume monstrous life, from the wooden-legged Hulga of "Good Country People" and her Bible-toting lover who wants to add her wooden leg to his collection of pornography and glass eyes, to the narcissistic Mrs. Shortley of "The Displaced Person," the violent sons of "A Circle in the Fire," Grandma Bailey of "A Good Man Is Hard to Find," shot three times by the Misfit, and the hermaphrodite of "A Temple of the Holy Ghost."

The effective juxtaposition of opposites is the source of much of Flannery O'Connor's power. Her work is a curious mixture of love and cruelty, of the comic and the serious and the tragic. In her illuminating "The Fiction Writer and His Country," O'Connor has said that "writers who see by the light of their Christian faith will have, in these times, the sharpest eyes for the grotesque, for the perverse, and for the unacceptable." The comment has confused some of her critics, who find her belief in essentially orthodox and traditional religious values incompatible with her black humor and her preoccupation with violence and abnormality. The paradoxical character of her work is less confusing, however, when one recalls the number of the lame, the halt, and the blind, the freaks, misfits, and societal rejects of the New Testament. In this light, it is possible to accept at face value O'Connor's belief that in the greatest fiction a writer's "moral sense coincides with his dramatic sense." Nor does it come as any great shock when we are told that she thinks she "would admit" to writing "what Hawthorne called 'romances' " and that she feels "more of a kinship with Hawthorne than with any other American writer."

Flannery O'Connor, in short, is basically an allegorist or fantasist rather than a realist, although her stories are so securely rooted in specific time and place as to seem as real as rain. She is in the highest sense a moralist working out of a preconceived dogma, not a journalist or a scavenger fumbling with Gothic horrors and monstrosities for their sakes. Again like Hawthorne, who shared O'Connor's fondness for the abnormal and the diseased and the bizarre, her eye is upon both this world and the next. The fault of her characters, she suggests, is primarily in themselves, not solely in their stars, though disaster is precipitated by societal and hereditary flaws. Through arrogance, overbearing confidence, stupidity, or, worst of all, pride, her people have attempted to find their own salvation — even their groping, inchoate search for love is primarily narcissistic — and in so doing have committed the cardinal sin of rejecting the redemptive function of Christianity.

The most spectacular and certainly the most prolific "serious" fiction writer to emerge since John Updike, Joyce Carol Oates (1938–) made her literary debut with *By the North Gate* (1963). She has won just about every significant American literary honor, from *Mademoiselle's* undergraduate competition to a first prize O. Henry Memorial Award and the National Book Award (for the novel *Them*), and in less than a decade she has become perhaps the most discussed and controversial short story writer in America. One wonders what new directions her prodigious energies will take this young writer: already published are several massive novels, three or four volumes of verse, a play, two books of critical essays, anthologies, innumerable uncollected pieces, a study of D. H. Lawrence's poems, and six collections of short fiction, all but one larger than its predecessor.* Her goals, certainly, are ambitious: Balzacian, Thackerayan, Tolstoian. "I am concerned with only one thing, the moral and social conditions of my generation," she has said.

Most of the fourteen *By the North Gate* pieces, including the title story, take place in rural Eden County, Oates's Yoknapatawpha-Winesburg. "Some time ago in Eden County," "Some time ago in Eden County, in the town of Rutland," "Some time ago in Eden County in the remote foothills of Oriskany," "Some time ago in Eden County the sheriff's best deputy, Rafe Murray." So begin many of these stories of violence, death, and emotional disturbance, centering on such situations as the maiming and eventual killing of an old man's dog (the title story and perhaps the best piece in the collection); the killing of a retarded girl at a church social ("Boys at a Picnic"); the death of an old man who after aiding a pregnant girl is found with his head smashed in, the baby drowned, and the girl a fugitive ("Swamps").

* A seventh, *The Poisoned Kiss and Other Stories from the Portuguese,* appeared after this study went into production.

For the most part, these early stories follow a conventional pattern of dramatic initial situation, carefully manipulated complications, and a devastating climax. Narrative pace is Oates's major strength in her creation of this sick, disturbed, violent world: the reader is swept along in a torrent of dramatic and melodramatic events that seize his attention and with few exceptions hold it till the last lines. She is frequently less successful, however, with her characters, many of whom seem quite unbelievable. In "An Encounter with the Blind," Blind Boy Robin and "Senator B. (for Bethlehem)" Arnold Hollis emerge almost as parodies of Faulkner and Flannery O'Connor grotesques, and their sinister confrontation, which leaves the Senator's heart "cold and tight within him, like the part of him that had died," is more vaudeville than horror. Also unbelievable is the Elizabeth of "Ceremonies," who interrupts her sixth- and seventh-grade history class by screaming at her teacher, "Don't you touch me! . . . Nasty old man! Nasty old thing! . . . I'll cut out your liver! I'll cut out your liver and make you eat it, you nasty old thing! . . . Filthy beast of an illiterate!" Grace, in "Pastoral Blood," is only slightly less unconvincing. The first in what was to become a crowded gallery of Oates's misused females with a propensity for madness and self-destruction, Grace rejects her middle-class family and fiancé and searches for meaning and/or death through a series of degrading encounters with a ragtag and bobtail group of male riffraff she picks up on the road; after sex, we are told, her "stomach and loins burned, and then there came an unmistakable feeling, one associated with the bathroom at home and the rest room in her grade school: she gave in to convulsive retchings and managed to vomit something, not much, into the grass."

Oates's country is sometimes even less credible than her people. Occasionally described as Southern rice farmland bordered by swamps, where a leading citizen talks of "them redneck foremen an' a mess of women an' the prickliest-faced niggers in Eden County" or a census-taker from Oriskany is taken for a verbal ride by another vaudeville team of country girl and her brother, it often seems more rural Midwestern or, if the term exists, Westeastern than Southern, and at other times it is just a vague place where wild and wondrous events take place.

Despite its limitations, *By the North Gate* is an impressive first book, remarkable in its intensity and power. If the young author's eye and ear are on occasion faulty, still she can do beautiful small things with her left hand that many more experienced writers very often cannot do with both hands. One example of many is the dog of the title story, who comes vividly to life with a few brushstrokes, bringing to mind Liam O'Flaherty's comment that any competent professional can create an effective dramatic scene, but it takes real talent to describe, say, a chicken crossing a road.

The violence of so many of the *By the North Gate* stories is intensified in Oates's *Upon the Sweeping Flood* (1966). Blood and death are everywhere. In "At the Seminary," notable primarily for what seems to me sheer excess of emotion, a young woman visits her brother at his seminary. She notices that his hands are "streaked with something" resembling "red ink or blood" and later, gazing at a pure white statue of Christ ("About his head drops of white blood had coagulated"), she begins to feel the "unmistakable relentless flow of blood in her loins." And then her brother, Peter, is "upon her. He grabbed for her throat . . . 'Damn you! damn you!' Peter said . . . and struck her, his fists pounding." In a grade-B melodrama called "The Man That Turned into a Statue," a fugitive half kills a dog, then without motivation kills a man: "A brilliant stream of blood emerges out of him." "The Death of Mrs. Sheer" is the unconvincing saga of a pair of killers named Jeremiah and Sweet Gum. The brother of "The Survival of Childhood" kills himself with a blast from a shotgun. "Norman and the Killer" contains one homicide, possibly two. "What Death with Love Should Have to Do" concerns a motorcycle freak and his girl, whose death on the last page is as meaningless as her life. Even the effective title story is weakened by a torrent of violence and heavy-handed symbolism. Driving home from his father's funeral, the protagonist ("When only a child he had shifted his faith . . . from the unreliable God of his family's tradition to the things . . . of this world") is warned of an impending hurricane. He decides to see if he can help and finds a young brother and sister threatened by the rising waters. The three escape to the roof of a house, finally take refuge on a hill, but are threatened by snakes (the setting, remember, is again *Eden* County). The man goes berserk, kills the boy, is about to assault the girl sexually, but turns to see

> a white boat . . . a half mile . . . away. Immediately his hands dropped, his mouth opened in awe. The girl still pointed, breathing carefully, and Stuart, his mind shattered by the broken sunshine upon the water, turned to the boat, raised his hands, cried out, "Save me! Save me!" He had waded out a short distance by the time the men arrived.

Similar violence, madness or the fear of madness, and the same almost obsessive ritualistic preoccupation with blood ("Oh, the ugliness of blood, its smell . . . I begin to scream . . . I am still screaming," shrieks the twelve-year-old girl of "Matter and Energy") continue to dominate Oates's third and best collection, *The Wheel of Love* (1970). In four of the twenty stories, major characters commit suicide; in a fifth, another tries but fails. Dogs are killed. People die of cancer. They have unwanted pregnancies ("I am crying because I am pregnant") or delusions of pregnancy. They escape being drowned in fountains by insane sisters, or are almost killed in car wrecks. They are frightened by germs and the smell of their own bodies or are haunted by fears of being poisoned ("Everything is poisoned, everything is polluted"). One wishes she "could take a knife and cut out an important part of my body" and another goes nearly mad from those "strange, ugly times when your body seems transparent, your skin drawn too tight."

A little of this sort of thing goes a long way and too much of it defeats its author's purposes; if there was ever an author who loses by having her works read successively rather than with an enforced period of at least a week between individual stories, it is Joyce Carol Oates. But despite the accumulation of horror, which loses its impact under the sheer weight of repetition, *Wheel of Love* is her best collection. Though so many of these stories tend to be over-written, Oates seems more effective in dealing with intellectuals or comparatively intelligent people than with some of the Eden County caricatures of her first collections. More important, she has shifted her focus from the accumulation of corpses and Gothic monstrosities to a meaningful concern with the inner terrors of her alienated and tormented people. "Region of Ice," the 1967 O. Henry first-prize winner, is a moving and memorable depiction of the relationship between a neurotic upper-middle-class Jewish student and his teacher; the boy has a terrible fear of death, indeed wills his own death; and the description of his growing obsession and its effect upon his teacher is expertly handled. So too is Oates's treatment of the love affair between a novelist-professor, one of his students, and his wife, a Pulitzer Prize-winning poetess ("Accomplished Desires"). The title story, another academic character-suicide piece, and "Bodies," about a lawyer-suicide and his neurotic affair with a neurotic artist-teacher, are similarly effective.

Marriages and Infidelities (1972) contains some of Oates's best stories, yet it is perhaps her most uneven book, the writing so self-conscious at times as to seem burlesque. Again, violence, blood, death, and madness are everywhere: a lad dies in a drainage ditch, "sucked into the pipe, carried along on that rushing, violent, filthy water, drowned and mangled inside the pipe, his face smashed in" ("The Puzzle"); a father murders his daughter ("By the River"); a popular singer dies of cancer at the age of twenty, preparing the way for a nasty scene — in a dissecting laboratory — which for unexcelled vulgarity tops anything else in the author's canon ("Happy Onion").

Added to Oates's portraits of victims is the woman-mistreated-by-men who appears and reappears. The wife of a Detroit businessman is consumed with passion, "made nervous and lean by sensuality, tendons laid bare, limbs slick with perspiration, eyes burning in their sockets," but is "redeemed" by adultery ("Extraordinary Popular Delusions"); another character, being ravished almost to death by her crude husband, cries, "I am dying. I am disappearing" ("29 Inventions"); yet another is so mistreated that "sometimes her bowels feel locked" and she contemplates suicide

("Scenes of Passion and Despair"). Sexually used and abused and misused, the women give themselves up "musically, dreamily, like a rose of rot with only a short while left to bloom, carrying the rot neatly hidden," or they find their very lives and sanity threatened by the overuse of their "rather delicate bodies." Panic rises in them after or during sex, in "long, shuddering waves"; they raise their hands "as if to ward off a blow"; their "blood racks their bodies," which cannot be soothed by the male's postcoital query of "Did I hurt you?"

The most memorable story of this group, and the one most likely to irritate admirers of James Joyce, is "The Dead," one of four "reimaginings of famous stories" by authors for whom Oates feels a kinship, which she has termed a "kind of spiritual marriage." They include "The Lady With the Pet Dog," "The Metamorphosis," and "The Turn of the Screw," which is composed in double columns. (Among her other "innovative fictions" are "Matter and Energy," "Bodies," and "I Was in Love" from *The Wheel of Love;* "Plot" and "29 Inventions" from *Marriages and Infidelities;* and "The Wheel," ". . . & Answers," and "The Girl" from *The Goddess.*) Oates does not excel in these modes. She writes perhaps the most traditional and orthodox kind of situation-to-complications-to-climax stories of any of the important younger short fiction writers, and her departures from conventional techniques seem curiously dated, more imitative than experimental, and more pretentious than effective.

"The Dead" is the saga of a young woman novelist-turned-English instructor who after two good but unsuccessful novels makes it big with a Book-of-the-Month Club selection. Ilena's subsequent private life undergoes many vicissitudes (I am tempted to call them ups and downs) involving as it does her husband, her sociology professor-lover, and one of her students, who in the Joycean spin-off plays Michael Furey to the story's Gretta Conroy. This strenuous love-literary-academic life "taunts" Ilena's sanity, and she resorts to pills, faintings, and traumas to the extent that when she takes yet another male chauvinist lover, this time while she is conducting two hasty seminars at the University of Buffalo, her body becomes "dead, dormant" and can no longer "respond to his most tender caresses." The story ends not in the Gresham Hotel of Joyce's Dublin but in a Detroit hotel; the student-lover has died, Ilena is falling apart, and, yes, the snow is falling:

> She did not answer. Against the hotel window: soft, shapeless clumps of snow. She must remember something, she must remember someone ... there was an important truth she must understand. . . . But she could not get it into focus. Her brain seemed to swoon backward in an elation of fatigue, and she heard beyond this man's hoarse, strained breathing the gentle breathing of the snow, falling shapelessly upon them all.

Like Ilena of "The Dead," the characters of Oates's fifth collection, *The Hungry Ghosts: Seven Allusive Comedies* (1974), are academics, most of them members of the English Department of Hilberry University, a small institution in southern Canada. They're a motley crew of malcontents, misfits, professional failures, injustice collectors, deadbeats, cutters, and slashers: the paranoid Shakespeare specialist of "The Birth of Tragedy" who becomes infatuated with his teaching assistant; a black dude out of Harvard with a Wellesley wife and a fondness for sideburns, fancy ascots, and white students ("Up from Slavery"); a domineering Jewish liberal who in effect devours his followers and then deserts them ("Pilgrim's Progress").

The leaden-footed excursions of these hungry ghosts (in a characteristic series of prefatory quotations from *The Battle of the Books* and *Tom Jones,* Oates adds that "A *preta* [ghost] is one who, in the ancient Buddhist cosmology, haunts the earth's surface, continually driven by hunger — that is, desire of one kind or other") through the dreary groves of Hilberry, with sidetrips to an annual professors' convention in Chicago and a poets' colloquium at an Iowa university, have their high moments. The author's eye is as sharp as ever, and her creative energy and resourcefulness are seemingly inexhaustible. But even though her characters are all-too-recognizable academic types and very suitable targets for satire, Oates's fondness for caricature becomes boring rather than relevant, and most of her allusive comedies, particularly "Rewards of

Fame" and "Angst," seem unmercifully long for what they accomplish.

Death, destruction, loneliness, frustration, despair, anger, and physical and emotional violence continue to dominate the world of Oates's most recent collection, *The Goddess and Other Women* (1974). Like its predecessors, it is an uneven book, and contains some of her best work and some of her poorest.

The range of these twenty-five stories can be suggested by the title piece and "In the Warehouse." Uncharacteristically, "The Goddess" is about nothing more dramatic than the return of a couple to a hotel where they had spent their honeymoon twenty-three years before. Their troubles begin when they leave the hotel for dinner: the once-pleasant neighborhood, like the hotel itself, has deteriorated; they are threatened by street people; they are out of sorts and uncomfortable when they return to the hotel. Problems and tensions accumulate in a manner reminiscent of Shirley Jackson at her best. The husband thinks that the black bellboy has stolen his briefcase and in a beautifully worked-up series of mounting irritations, the visit that was to be pleasurable becomes a nightmare.

At the other extreme is "In the Warehouse." "Blood, all that blood," the comfortable matron with literary aspirations — "I write stories I hope may be put on television someday" — recalls, not unhappily remembering the day twenty years ago when she had shoved her schoolgirl friend to her death:

> She falls . . . her voice a scream . . . and then her body hits the edge . . .
> She is screaming . . . She falls again . . . and now her scream is muffled . . .
> She is bleeding. A dark stain explodes out from her and pushes the
> dust along before it, everything speeded up by her violent squirming . . .
> Blood, all that blood! — it is like an animal crawling out from under
> her . . .

In a book review published in 1973, Joyce Carol Oates commented that a "reviewer does violence to any collection if he reads it straight through, as he would a novel. Only frail, meagerly developed stories profit from such an approach . . . The richer and more demanding the story, the more it forces us to participate in its imaginative drama; to read too swiftly . . . would result in exhaustion that might wrongly be attributed to the stories."

Few professional authors would dispute the statement. Individually and collectively the characters of *The Goddess* and the five volumes that preceded it are actors in a theater of cruelty that bears frightful and frightening witness to an age in which unpredictable and senseless savagery has become almost commonplace. They tell us, like the pages of almost every newspaper, that which most of us unfortunately already know: man needs salvation; individual and societal values are disintegrating; town, village, and hamlet share with the swollen and diseased cities the unenviable knowledge that violence and death lurk everywhere; human life, rather than being sacred and meaningful, can be obscene and meaningless. The intensity of Oates's concern for such matters vitalizes her stories; her work possesses significance as sociological testament to an age of exhaustion and violation, of the ambiguities of carnality and the cruelty of man-woman relationships.

Oates's assertion — frequently expressed and constantly made manifest in her stories — that "art is built around violence, around death" and that "at its base is fear" is interesting but hardly novel. More debatable is her comment that "if violence erupts in fiction, it should come first, nor should it be accidental."

Despite the seriousness of intent underlying these and similar statements, the unevenness of her short fiction suggests that she was speaking literal truth when she commented in a 1969 interview that "with a story it's one evening, if I can type that fast." For all her talent and energy, the defects of her stories are almost as conspicuous as her assets, whether one reads twenty of them in a week or one a week for twenty weeks — and I have done both. Their formularized nature and their excessive length; the imitativeness of her "innovative fictions"; the repetition of subject matter, form, even of diction; the tendency toward caricature; the lack of a saving sense of humor; and perhaps the most destructive of all, the piling up of horrors that eventually defeats its own purposes. Unlike Henry James's concept of a spacious house of fiction with its many windows, Joyce Carol Oates's house of fiction at times becomes a windowless tomb without an exit, a contemporary House of Usher, in which her people fall upon the thorns of life and bleed, bleed, bleed. As such, her statement, in her introductory essay to *The Edge of Impossibility: Tragic Forms in Literature,* is peculiarly applicable to her own work: she writes that twentieth-century "literature is never far from parody, sensing itself anticipated, overdone, exhausted."

The concern with mental and physical illness, violence, and the bizarre that dominates so much of the short fiction of Purdy, Williams, Stafford, O'Connor, and Oates also preoccupied such nineteenth-century American masters of the genre as Poe, Hawthorne, and Bierce. More recent stories like Sherwood Anderson's "Adventure," Conrad Aiken's "Silent Snow, Secret Snow," William Carlos Williams' "The Knife of the Times," Wilbur Daniel Steele's "How Beautiful with Shoes," Faulkner's "A Rose for Emily," and J. D. Salinger's "A Perfect Day for Bananafish" have become classics of the genre. The deluge of this kind of story, however, reached its crest during the last three decades, and, as was the case in the preceding chapter, such abundance forces me to comment briefly on a baker's dozen of authors whose work seems to me outstanding or indicative of significant trends or both. In addition, many of the authors discussed in Chapter 4 have also contributed to the sick, black, Gothic, or surreal fiction of the period, among them Louis Auchincloss (particularly in his first collection, *The Injustice Collectors*); Hortense Calisher (in "Heartburn," "In Greenwich There Are Many Gravelled Walks," and "Letitia Emeritus," from *In the Absence of Angels,* and "The Scream on Fifty-Seventh Street," from *Tale for the Mirror*); John Cheever (in "Torch Song," "The Cure," and "Goodbye, My Brother," all from *The Enormous Radio,* and many others); and Nancy Hale (especially in *Heaven and Hardpan Farm*). Other contributions are such different authors as R. V. Cassill (in "Larchmoor Is Not the World," from *The Father and Other Stories*); James T. Farrell (in, for example, "Success Story" and Nor-

man Allen," both from *A Dangerous Woman and Other Stories*); Leslie
Fiedler (in stories like "The Teeth" and "The Fear of Innocence" in
Pull Down Vanity and Other Stories); James Leo Herlihy's *The Sleep
of Baby Filbertson and Other Stories* and *A Story That Ends with a Scream
and Eight Others;* Howard Nemerov (in "The Guilty Shall Be Found
and Punished" and "The Web of Life" from *A Commodity of Dreams
and Other Stories*); Irwin Shaw (in "The Climate of Insomnia,"
from *Mixed Company*); I. B. Singer, who will be discussed in the next
chapter; and Edmund Wilson (in such memorable stories as "The
Princess With the Golden Hair" and "The Man Who Shot Snapping
Turtles," both from *Memoirs of Hecate County*).

Loneliness dominates Sylvia Berkman's *Blackberry Wilderness*
(1959), stories depicting with unassuming artistry and quiet understanding moments of crisis in the lives of morbidly sensitive characters. A worried American artist alone and friendless in Rome, an
acutely self-conscious short story writer, an overfastidious proof-
reader who becomes involved in an act of sudden violence — for
all their intelligence, and to a degree because of it, these people
move through life like somnambulists. Engaged in essentially meaningless activity or frightened by nameless fears, they establish
contact with other humans only briefly before their dread of "involvement" forces them to retreat. The story of their lives is the
story of unfulfilled moments, gambits refused, love denied, or the
rejection of someone's need.

"Which is delusion, which is real? — Festival or blackberry wilderness?" This is the dilemma that confronts Berkman's unhappy
people, who are often unable to distinguish between external reality and the inner world of personal visions. Like Madeleine, the
career woman of "Pippa Passes," they yearn to establish contact
with their fellows, but fear forces them to remain isolated, contemplating the world as Madeleine contemplates her fellow travelers
on a New York to Paris flight:

> Turning, she scanned the faces of the other passengers. Who escaped?
> Strip any one of them down and you'd find a hidden mutilated segment

too — a nerve center choked, a muscle stunted, a capacity blocked. That was why she and her New York . . . friends walked so warily. They were afraid because they were ashamed, and ashamed because they were scarred.

Although some of Berkman's characters, like Beatrice Ransome of the title story, find a kind of salvation through art, only occasionally do they dare, as does the discarded wife of "October Journey," to invade the realms of despair and survive to say, "This journey into alien land is over. I am ready now. I am ready to go back."

In *Victoria at Night and Other Stories* (1958), Vienna-born Uli Biegel presents thirteen finely drawn stories concerned primarily with women; men are relegated to the position of minor nuisances or necessary evils. Her characters, like many of Jean Stafford's, are exiled from the world of healthy or "normal" responses and relationships. The Victoria of the title story wanders dazedly around Manhattan until she returns to the room where she had spent the night with a nameless young man. Another of Biegel's agonizingly self-concerned young women searches desperately for "aloneness"; feeling that her lover has violated her inner identity, she throws herself beneath the wheels of a subway train. Still another, a "gnawingly bored" schoolgirl, is nauseated at the "little, little things she was forced to be concerned about" and withdraws completely from reality. At a time when many talented younger writers were combining post-Freudian interest in the psyche with the traditional concept of the short story as an art that should both delight and inform, some of Biegel's stories have about them a curiously arcane quality. Her territory is sometimes vaguely defined; her characters are abstractions rather than individuals. She seems to me most effective when she applies relatively traditional fictional methods to her subject matter, the battleground of the tormented human mind and spirit. Particularly notable are "World Without a Sun," about a painfully self-conscious Jewish girl involved in the wedding festivities of a Gentile friend, and "Snapshots," a pleasingly buoyant account of one fourteen-year-old's demolition of the father image.

In *To Whom It May Concern* (1960), Elisabeth Mann Borghese writes about a civilization sick and starving in the midst of technological plenty. In nine unusual and often bizarre stories, the daughter of the late Thomas Mann paints a nightmarish fantasy in which the individual has become an obsolescent experiment, a cipher in a world of untapped creative resources. The narrator of the title story, almost destroyed in the warfare between man and machine, offers to sell himself to the Inland Joy Development Corporation; a scientist, frozen in a daring experiment, is killed before he can record his experiences; in the best and most original story, "The Rehearsal," the members of a symphony orchestra mutilate themselves during a performance when their conductor, an ape, misses a figure on the score and runs amok.

The technique used in these stories is as unconventional as their subject matter. Borghese relies upon scenic dialogue almost as frequently as upon straight narrative; she has a predilection for artificial devices, such as long letters, and is fond of abrupt transitions and shifting points of view. Such methods, however, are unusually effective in her presentation of a society whose "new God is statistics," in which science, standardization, and technology threaten to overwhelm reason, free will, and the creative act.

At their best, as in "The Rehearsal," "Again," and "Twin's Wail," Borghese's stories succeed both as fiction and as vehicles for the most serious ideas. Sensational and melodramatic though they are — they will shock you or make your hair stand on end, some of them — they have about them the essential qualities of reasonableness and reality. And they contain characters with whom the reader can identify — be they Will and Phil, the talented Siamese twins whose fates are as closely linked as were their physical bodies, or an American dentist on a compulsive drive through a crepuscular Italian countryside.

*

Perhaps the most extreme use of strange and violent materials in recent short fiction is seen in the first collection of short stories by Paul Bowles (1911—), dedicated to his mother "who first read me the stories of Poe," *The Delicate Prey* (1950). And Poe-like they are, both in their power and uneven quality. The title story, for example, contains homicide, sodomy, emasculation, and insanity. "By the Water" presents a young North African traveler — most of the seventeen stories take place in North Africa, where the author has lived for many years — who is threatened by monsters both human and crustacean. In "A Distant Episode" a professor is captured by a tribe "in the warm country"; they remove, successively, both his tongue and his reason, and the story ends with the professor, dressed in tin, running madly through the countryside. "You Are Not I," one of two stories with an American locale, introduces a crazy girl who drops stones into the mouths of corpses.

Such immersions into a bloodbath of violence and the macabre are arresting and usually carry the impact of a savage kick in the groin. Bowles's stories are often individually powerful but collectively are likely to leave the reader with an impression akin to that produced by a visit to a chamber of horrors; after the initial shock, the blood is seen to be red paint, and the accumulated disasters often defeat the author's purpose. More impressive are two subsequent collections. *A Hundred Camels in the Courtyard* (1962) contains four stories of Moslems in North Africa, which possess in common what seems to be a perceptive understanding of life among the native inhabitants. Similarly concerned with violence, sorcery, and hashish — "a pipe of Kif before breakfast gives a man the strength of a hundred camels in the courtyard" — they have a ring of authenticity lacking in some of *The Delicate Prey* pieces. All four are included in *The Time of Friendship* (1967). Bowles is uniformly effective in these stories of North Africa and Mexico (and in "The Frozen Fields," one of the two stories with an American setting), although as a purely personal reflection I must say that I like him least in his two fables, "The Hyena" — a very Kafkaesque hyena, I might add, without the really sinister and enigmatic quality of Kafka's jackals — and "Tapiama" which evokes effectively and characteristically a dreamlike, hallucinated atmosphere. The title story is reminiscent of my favorite Bowles novel (*The Spider's House*) in its perceptive and moving portrayal of the curious relationship between a European woman and a North African youth.

The spectacular literary career of Truman Capote (1924–) began in the middle forties with the publication of two strange and eerie tales, "A Tree of Night" and "Miriam," which bear the characteristics to be found in his first collection of short fiction, published in 1949, *A Tree of Night and Other Stories*. These early stories are an effective mingling of psychological insight and the familiar materials and themes of the horror story. Gothic extravagance, madness, sensationalism, the supernatural, and the surreal permeate them, but the best of them are contemporary classics of the genre, remarkable in their totality of effect, and executed with virtuosity and technical ability.

The title story is typical. Kay, a young woman traveling alone by train, is set upon by a female dwarf with an oversized melon of a head (freaks of one sort or another appear in Capote's stories with about the same frequency as they do in Poe's) and her male companion, a cadaverous cretin (he has "queer" eyes, wears a Mickey Mouse watch, and has "anointed himself with a cheap, vile perfume"), who formerly made his living by being buried alive in carnival sideshows. As the rickety train creaks and groans its way through the Alabama night, the strange couple slowly casts a spell over Kay; she wants to "cry out and waken everyone in the coach" but is unable to do so. As she gazes, as if hypnotized, at the pale-eyed man, his face seems "to change form and recede before her like a moon-shaped rock sliding downward under a surface of water. A warm laziness relaxed her. She was dimly conscious of it when the woman took away her purse, and when she gently pulled the raincoat like a shroud over her head."

The same nightmarish quality animates several of Capote's stories, including "Miriam," in which a middle-aged woman is besieged by a strange child; the surrealistic "The Headless Hawk";

"Master Misery," with its somber conflict between the world of dreams and external reality; and "Shut a Final Door," with its compelling depiction of individual disintegration. In these stories Capote has created a universe of opposites — of daily vision contrasted with the vision of nightmare and delirium, of light and darkness, of accustomed reality as opposed to myth or romance. Capote's victims are trapped in this world, as Coleridge's Christabel is trapped, to become apathetic or helpless witnesses to their own destruction by the forces of the dark, or at the hands of devil child or wizard man, or by projections of their inner weaknesses or fears. Like Walter of "Shut a Final Door," shivering and vomiting and falling to pieces physically and emotionally in a New Orleans hotel, most of the people in these "dark" stories are "awfully alone in this world." All their acts are "acts of fear," and fear and loneliness destroy them as thoroughly as Walter is destroyed.

In marked contrast to the "nocturnal" tone of the above stories is the "daylight" mood of "My Side of the Matter" and "Jug of Silver." The same contrast exists in the now classic title novella of *Breakfast at Tiffany's* (1958) and particularly in the much-anthologized "A Christmas Memory," a sunny and warm-hearted recollection of an ingenuous seven-year-old boy and his "sixty-something" cousin.

Charles Criswell's only collection of short fiction, *Nobody Knows What the Stork Will Bring* (1958), consists of a dozen macabre tales of madness, perversion, frustration, and death; he was particularly adept in resolving such thematic material through the agency of perverse or perverted children, and has produced some memorable additions to the garden of child-horrors. In "The Linden Tree" a mad woman reconstructs her past. In the title piece a perverse child performs a chillingly indecent act upon her paralyzed grandfather. In "The Hobby" a dead father's collection of stamps and books turns out to be pornography. And "Come In, Come In," with its painfully convincing portrayal of a frustrated young woman threatened by overwhelming evil, is reminiscent of the early Capote at his best.

Criswell demonstrated considerable skill in producing swiftly paced and fascinating stories out of this kind of material. But as we have seen with some of the work of Paul Bowles or Joyce Carol Oates, for example, the accumulation of horror upon horror tends to defeat its author's purpose and more often than not demonstrates once again that success in fiction depends more on the creation of human beings than on sensational, dramatic, or "shocking" material.

Far from the City of Class (1963) and *Black Angels* (1966) by Bruce Jay Friedman (1930–) are representative of the black humor of the sixties. Like many of the authors previously discussed and such leading exponents of the theater of the absurd as Ionesco, Beckett, and Albee, the black humorists exploit the fictional possibilities inherent in the grotesque, the bizarre, the fantastic, and the sick, but for comic — if darkly comic — purposes; theirs is a literature of striking reversals and juxtapositions, perverse and unusual contrasts, outrageous symbols and situations.

"23 Pat O'Brien Movies," from Friedman's first collection, is characteristic. On a gray day in March a young man is standing on the sixteenth-story ledge of a New York hotel, planning to leap to his death in twenty minutes: "I'm twenty-nine . . . and . . . I'm tired. Six operations . . . and my stomach's the size of an aspirin box and there isn't much more can come out. I've got four kids and my wife's a bum." With him is a patrolman, veteran of many similar encounters. They talk, the young man sarcastic, the patrolman at first quiet, steady, resolute, but eventually impatient: "You get me sore . . . because you're so damned smug." He reveals that he too has a physical problem, a bad heart, but "There's just one thing. I happen to believe that life is worth living. You have a short time to live and one hell of a long time to be dead." And with that he "rolled up his sleeves very neatly, and then, with a look at the sky as though checking the weather, threw his cap off the ledge and followed it, executing, except for his legs, a perfect swan dive."

So it goes in the absurd universe of the author's alienated characters. A fortyish man addicted to television to avoid "going upstairs to [a wife] who had discovered sex in her early forties" is warned by the m.c. of a television show that "I've got six days to kill you." Eventually he smashes the set, bleeds to death, and replaces the original m.c. in a search for victims ("For Your Viewing Pleasure"). Another Friedman victim dies when his investment in stocks collapses; his doctor marries the widow; their sex life is determined by their subsequent investments ("The Investor"). The narrator of a story about an air force major whose "mind fell apart" concludes that the major was "very sane and that everyone else was crazy" ("The Man They Threw out of Jets"). A group celebrates Labor Day — and the harvest season — by betting on the number of traffic fatalities ("The Holiday Celebrators"). A psychiatric patient — he suffers from excessive cringing — kills his analyst's wife so that his subsequent confession will cure him, makes the doctor aid in the disposal of the body, and concludes: "I'm your patient and the only thing . . . that counts is how I feel" ("Mr. Prinzo's Breakthrough"). Less bizarre role reversals are effectively negotiated in "The Trip," the first of two *Far from the City of Class* stories introducing a reasonably sensitive college freshman and his loudly exhibitionistic mother ("What other mother that you know would do something like that?") out of which Friedman's best novel, *A Mother's Kisses*, developed.

After the distressingly unrelieved gloom of some of the sick writers, the humor, the relaxed style, and the stripped and economical narrative structure of Friedman's stories is like air and sunlight in a long-darkened room.

In the first collection of short stories, *Ghost and Flesh* (1952), by William Goyen (1915–), the nature of reality is depicted in terms of a never-ceasing conflict between the present and the past, between the visible and the invisible. Goyen presents this conflict with considerable variety of mood, method, and subject matter. Grandpa Samuels, in the realistic "The White Rooster," kills the young woman who is planning to kill a stray rooster that has caught his fancy; in the grotesque and masquelike "The Grasshopper's Burden," a monster of a child, seated on the King's Throne in a burning schoolhouse, strikes terror into the soul of the narrator; in the fantasy "A Shape of Light" an eccentric widower, Boney Benson, like a "skeleton-headed ghost on a purple horse", pursues a distorted vision of reality.

These and other characters are dominated or victimized by what the author seems to consider the tyrannies of the past, of tradition, of sex, and of an all-encompassing, nameless fear. They search for a means of effecting some kind of satisfactory compromise between past and present; they struggle to believe that life and death, the visible and the invisible, are factors in the continuous chain of being that is existence.

"Us humans are part ghost and part flesh," the central character of "Ghost and Flesh, Water and Dirt" concludes, "but I think maybe the ghost part is the longest lasting . . . there's a world both places, a world where there's ghosts and a world where there's flesh, and I believe the real right way is to take our worlds, of ghost or of flesh . . . as they come and take what comes in em . . . and be what each . . . wants us to be."

Ghost and Flesh is a memorable book. Like his first novel, *The House of Breath,* its very excesses indicated a real, if youthful, talent. The promise of this collection was fulfilled in his later stories, collected as *Faces of Blood Kindred* in 1960. Goyen here remains concerned with the relationship between the past and the present, between the living and the dead, but these stories are purged of the Gothic extravagances of their predecessors. Only the novella, "A Tale of Inheritance," is close kin to *Ghost and Flesh.* This remarkable fable of the bearded Lester sisters — "One time were two sisters in a faraway country of Texas . . . and they had little black beards" — is an impressive tour de force, if slightly marred by an overelaborate concern for language and technique at the expense of clarity of vision.

Many of the best stories of Charles Jackson (1903–) are concerned with the slow but steady emotional or intellectual disintegration of fundamentally decent persons who are their own worst enemies. The title story of his first collection, *The Sunnier Side* (1950), was certainly one of the best stories of that year or of recent years, although it was ignored by the editors of the *Best* and *O. Henry* volumes. Violating just about every known taboo of mass-circulation magazine fiction, and one or two others until then undiscovered, "The Sunnier Side" is part essay on the nature of short story writing and part re-creation of the lives of four "nice" girls from a fictional upstate New York small town, Arcadia, during the middle of the second decade. Narrated in retrospect by a writer who had been a small boy when the girls were teen-agers, the story is a compassionate and ironic commentary on the sad gap between the dreams of youth and the uncompromising realities of adulthood. Death, violence, or shame is the destiny of each of the four nice girls, whom the narrator, even after all the shocking revelations of their adulthood, remembers as

> Campfire Girls, paddling earnestly . . . along the bay in twin canoes . . . hair parted in the middle and hanging straight . . . on all sides, long below your shoulders, bound with a beaded bandeau . . . I can still hear your Campfire cry, "Wo-he-lo" — and the words of the song that went with it:
> "Wo-he-lo for work, Wo-he-lo for health, Wo-he-lo . . . for love . . ."

The same blending of compassion and irony, affection and disgust, characterizes Jackson's second collection, *Earthly Creatures* (1953). The central character of most of these stories is his own worst enemy. He appears in many forms, as adolescent boy, young woman, middle-aged novelist, or elderly mother. Something has gone wrong in his life or is in the process of going wrong. In an agony of self-indulgence or self-pity, he lashes out at things as they are. In story after story, he methodically goes about the business of destroying himself.

Like the schizophrenic nonhero of the best story in the collection, "The Boy Who Ran Away," Jackson's people are worthy of the love or understanding they need so desperately and seek with such futility. The narrator of "The Boy Who Ran Away," for example, hates his gawky nephew for the very traits that had made his own childhood unhappy. When the nephew breaks the gift the narrator's daughters gave him for Christmas, the awkward boy sets in progress an unhappy chain of events. The father deprives his children of their anticipated New Year's Eve pleasure and hates himself for it, yet is powerless to do more than resort to additional whiskey and his every-present Seconal. He is chained with bonds of his own forging, forever tearing at the exposed viscera of his own self-respect. In effect, he feels he has abdicated life:

> He was finished, through, done for, as finally as if God had come into the room and beckoned him with the ultimate finger. He was ridden with fear, guilt, and self-disgust . . . He was his own devil, his own black beast . . . He hated himself with an active hatred that was almost too much for a single human body to contain . . . and he did not think he could contain that hatred another hour.

Following the success and notoriety of his first novel, *The Lost Weekend* (1944), and the Ray Milland motion picture version of it, Jackson's reputation declined, although he published two good novels in addition to his short stories, *The Fall of Valor* (1946) and *The Outer Edges* (1948). Except for *The Lost Weekend*, his best work is in the short story; he is a greatly underestimated writer.

Few writers achieve notoriety with a first collection of short stories, let alone with a single story. William Saroyan did with "The Daring Young Man on the Flying Trapeze" and so did Shirley Jackson (1919–1964) with "The Lottery," which is said to have elicited more letters to the editor than any story published in the *New Yorker,* so many that it was included in a collection of her stories in press at the time, published, in 1949, as *The Lottery or, the Adventures of James Harris.* There are no buckets of blood here, no heavy rhetoric. The success of these carefully crafted stories is due as much to the author's low-keyed disciplined craftsmanship as it is to her quiet intelligence and seriousness of intent.

I know no one who can evoke more successfully the elements of fear and surprise than she, whether it be in the form of a parable-like fantasy of the good and evil inherent in tradition and in law-abiding citizens, like "The Lottery"; or whether she writes of ordinary people in an ordinary situation that gradually becomes extraordinary, as it does in "The Daemon Lover," a terrifyingly bleak depiction of a plain thirtyish woman whose anticipated wedding day becomes a nightmare of anguish and loss. Or, in one of my own personal favorites, the uncollected "The Summer People," in which another perfectly ordinary situation, involving a similarly ordinary middle-aged couple that decides to remain at their summer place after Labor Day, gradually becomes fraught with sinister overtones and ends in another kind of nightmare as "with the first sudden crash of thunder, Mr. Allison reached out and took his wife's hand. And then, while the lightning flashed outside, and the radio faded and spluttered, the two old people huddled together in their summer cottage and waited."

In a very real way, Jackson suffered from the enormous initial popularity of "The Lottery" in both its original form and subsequent adaptation for television (and from the motion picture version of one of her least important novels). Far from being the "Virginia Werewolf of seance-fiction writers," she was both impeccable craftsman and thoughtful person, whose "fierce visions" of madness and cruelty and terror — as her husband and most perceptive critic, Stanley Edgar Hyman, has written — constitute a "sensitive and faithful anatomy of our times, fitting symbols for our distressing world." Her death in her forty-sixth year was a very real loss to our literature.

To say that Carson McCullers (1917–1967) possessed a fondness for the Gothic is but to note — and superficially at that — her interest in the grotesque, the freakish, and the incongruous. "The Ballad of the Sad Café" amply underscores the generalization. Miss Amelia, a six-foot virgin bootlegger with a face "like the terrible dim faces known in dreams, sexless and white," has lived for years isolated in a decaying, boarded-up, swaybacked house in a "dreary" Southern town. Marvin Macy, her husband, is as sinister as any

Gothic hero in English or American literature; it is rumored that he carries with him the ear of a man he had once killed in a razor fight. Before the opening of the novella, Marvin and Miss Amelia had been married, a marriage never consummated, and Marvin had left town after being humiliated by Miss Amelia. A decade after this departure, a hideous dwarf, Lyman, appears on the scene —

> scarcely more than four feet tall . . . he wore a ragged, dusty coat . . . His crooked little legs seemed too thin to carry the weight of his great warped chest and the hump that sat on his shoulders. He had a very large head, with deep-set blue eyes and a sharp little mouth. His face was both soft and sassy — at the moment his pale skin was yellowed by dust and there were lavender shadows beneath his eyes.

Lyman claims to be kin to Miss Amelia, drinks her corn liquor, and very effectively courts her. But Marvin Macy returns, and with this strange, obscene triangle McCullers creates a forceful and ugly parable of love that is not love and human relations that are inhuman in their thick and clotted perversity. The "Ballad" reaches its peak in perhaps the most grotesque of all grotesque climaxes, a fantastic Ground Hog Day tournament between Miss Amelia and Marvin Macy, a wrestling match that becomes strictly no contest when Lyman enters the fray.

Though few of McCullers' people are as memorable as Miss Amelia, Macy, and Lyman, they share with these three the fact that they are failures or outcasts in a world in which traditional values are reversed or almost unrecognizable. They include a jockey who is on the skids, a music student who is losing her technique, a writer who can no longer write, a foreign correspondent who is perpetually an exile and an alien, and a once-brilliant teacher who has become a pathological liar. Empty or ungratifying or distorted love, loneliness, and decay are dominant elements in the lives of these unhappy misfits.

Like the work of the black humorists, the National Book Award-winning *Going Places* (1969) by Leonard Michaels (1933–) is marked by striking contrasts and reversals; these thirteen nervous and kaleidoscopic glimpses of life in Sin City constitute a curious kind of collage of almost manic activity where the real merges with the surreal, the comic and the tragicomic are at times indistinguishable, and vivid color and a vague grayness are first cousins.

A Turkish fellowship student rapes a coed and she kills herself. A vision of her drifts up out of the dew: "She came closer. He seized her in his arms and they rolled together on the grass until he found himself screaming through his teeth because, however much of himself he lavished on her, she was dead" ("The Manikin"). Philip and Veronica of "City Boy" are discovered making love on the living room floor by her father ("a hundred fifty-five pounds of stomping shlemiel"); Philip flees naked — he will reappear in later stories — to the nearest subway; the father has a heart attack; Philip ("no innocent shitkicker from Jersey . . . my style New York City") and Veronica take up where they had left off. A similar couple awaits the arrival of the girl's father; they fight; she almost scratches out the young man's eyes (but eventually, with a corneal transplant, he may see again); and at story's end they "totter slowly" to the municipal building to obtain a marriage license.

Characters scream often in these stories, long and piercingly. A naked man at an orgiastic party, sitting "pertly" in a bathtub, announces to the Philip-like protagonist, "I'll bet you're Zeus; I'm Danäe." The "I" of another story has a blind date; like a Chagall lover floating over the Eiffel Tower, he cries to her, she cries for him, he hears church bells, he faints, glass breaks, and finally "my arms disappeared and I was a head on legs. Running." Pots and pans fly. Fingers and toes work into a man's body like worms. A Talmudic scholar slips on an icy New York street, won't reach for his hat, dies. Beckman, the central character of the more conventional title story, drives a taxi, is hideously beaten up; Beckman, "the college graduate . . . son of good people, risking life with strangers, ruining health in a filthy machine, it literally made them sick."

Going Places is filled with grossness, obscenity, meanness — and their opposites. The overall effect of these vivid, individualistic, and — I loathe the word, but it fits here — *marvelous* stories is far from depressing. As it appears to Philip in "A Green Thought," the city at night, despite its sordidness, despite its horrors, is alive and vibrant, "full of wonders, mysteries."

The deathly sickness of modern metropolitan life that has furnished both subject matter and theme for so many fiction writers has perhaps never been more painfully and powerfully described than in *Last Exit to Brooklyn* (1964) by Hubert Selby (1928–). Frequently classified as a novel, the book consists of six related episodes; here is a dark world of freaks, queers, drug addicts, muggers, and assorted societal rejects and derelicts that makes the Nighttown sequence of *Ulysses* appear by comparison understated and sun-drenched. Typical are the lost lives of Georgette, the hip queer, who "didn't try to disguise it with marriage and man's talk" but "took pride in being a homosexual" and her/his relationship with Vinnie, the greatest event in whose life was "the glory of having known someone killed by the police" ("The Queen Is Dead").

This contemporary Inferno, a decade after its sensational publication, seems to me of more sociological than literary value. For all its brutal power, its soulless, dehumanized zombies remain strangely inert and uninteresting, and the long soliloquylike pieces, of which "And Baby Makes Three" is an example, are more boring than moving.

Most of the characters in *A Thirsty Evil* (1956) by Gore Vidal (1925–) pursue a "thirsty evil" to their ultimate destruction. Like Shakespeare's rats (the title is taken from *Measure for Measure,* that darkest of all his dark plays) that "ravin down their proper bane" when they "do drink," they die. Characteristic are the two haunted and haunting characters of "Three Stratagems": Michael, though he proclaims the existence of a fiancée, unconsciously equates marriage with his own death. Completely aware of his own decadence — "I see my eventual downfall from beloved angel to deluded monster" — he has neither the will nor the desire to resist. And Mr. Royal, the widower who is infatuated with Michael, is an ominous foreshadowing of what Michael will become, destined forever to "dangle between belief and doubt."

There is acute perception in these stories, and sensitivity and irony, but except for the effectively understated story of a brief encounter between a young man and a twelve-year-old boy in Washington's Rock Creek Park ("A Moment of Green Laurel") the collection as a whole lacks illumination; the atmosphere is as murky as a den. There is some humor in "Erlinda and Mr. Coffin," an odd piece about a refined widow who resembles some of Tennessee Williams' middle-aged ladies on the way down, but it is essentially of the boys' boarding school variety.

If some of the *Thirsty Evil* stories are less than we might expect from Vidal (although the earliest was apparently written in 1948, he had published seven novels before the collection appeared), the book is certainly more than what I once termed a rather dreary landmark in the literature of homosexuality and the doomed search for self-realization.

The reasons underlying the recent fiction writer's preoccupation with illness, violence, and the grotesque are many and varied, and have been exhaustively discussed during the last decades. The pervasive influence of Freud and others and a corresponding growing concern for the emotional complexities of the human experience; the revolt from tradition of all kinds; three major wars; unparalleled political scandals and the increasing disillusionment with big government, big business, big anything; the loss of individualism in an authority-dominated society — these and many other factors have been suggested as explanations for the ever-growing body of contemporary sick fiction. Whatever its causes, this is a literature of bizarre contrasts, opposites, and paradox, a merging of the serious and the ridiculous, the meaningful and the meaningless, the beautiful and the ugly, the good and the debased. It is concerned with the alienation of its people, with the often frantic search for identity, or the retreat into isolation or abnormality as perhaps the last defense against a society or a concept of life that seemingly has become ridiculous, senseless, destructive, or obscene. Its recurrent themes and subjects include man's capacity for self-destruction, his inability to communicate with others; violence, loneliness, human waste, abnormality, and perversion appear continually in its pages. Except for the work of the absurdists or the black humorists, it is essentially somber, a literature in which in one way or another "the earth destroys her crooked child."

Chapter 6

"Oh, These Jews — These Jews!
Their Feelings, Their Hearts!"*

THE MILITANT Marxist literature of the twenties and thirties had just about run its course before the beginning of World War II. The end of the Depression and the growing disillusionment with Russia had hastened its decline; the Soviet-Nazi nonaggression pact of 1939 and America's entry into the war marked its demise. In the face of war's wholesale death and destruction, far-reaching social disorganization, and full employment and fat paychecks at home, the Marxist concept of literature as a weapon in the battle between capitalism and the working class had become anachronistic. The naturalistic proletarian story of the thirties, with its oversimplified and distorted picture of class conflict or the exploitation of the have-nots by the haves or the delineation of specific economic, political, and social injustices faded away like the memories of the Depression. In its place the "war" story emerged, along with escape fiction of various sorts, which had little or no connection with reality as such; stories glorifying or romanticizing the American past; stories of science fiction and fantasy; stories centering on such contemporary problems — almost invariably concerned with middle-to-upper-middle-class white Anglo-Saxon Protestant types — as the breakup of a marriage. As the defeat of the Axis became inevitable, coinciding with the emergence of more revelations of Nazi persecution of the Jews and similar horrors, more and more writers concerned themselves with injustice and oppression

* Saul Bellow, "The Old System," *Mosby's Memoirs.*

of all kinds and persuasions, particularly those in connection with minority ethnic, racial, or social groups. The then-new fiction concerned with the problems of society, particularly those growing out of racial or social injustice, was a far cry from the one-dimensional propaganda stories of the thirties; it possessed artistry as well as awareness. It concerned people with problems, not just the problems themselves. It was compounded of deep feeling, understanding, and creative expertise. It existed, in short, like all literature worthy of serious consideration, as art, as entertainment, and as idea.

The major achievement of this post-World War II socially conscious short fiction has been that of an extremely diverse group of Jewish-American writers. Despite the extreme differences of viewpoint, background, and concept of what it means to be a Jew held by a Malamud or a Salinger or a Bellow or a Roth, the writers possessed in common their concern with the role of the Jew in postwar America and the postwar world.

Of this rich and varied body of short fiction by American Jews about American Jews, perhaps the most distinguished single collection is *The Magic Barrel* (1958) by Bernard Malamud (1914–). Three stories are set in Italy, the remainder in or around New York City; they range from the comic to the seriocomic to the tragic, from the commonplace to the surreal, from the accustomed to the unusual.

Malamud's best stories are concerned with intimate crises in the lives of ordinary lower- to middle-class first- or second-generation American Jews: the shoemaker whose assistant is in love with his daughter, a story warm with the family affection that is so much a part of Jewish life and literature, and compassionate in its portrayal of a worried father who dreams of a better life than he himself had had, to attain which he had "slaved and destroyed his heart with anxiety and labor" ("The First Seven Years"); the aged man of "The Mourners," who is evicted from his tenement room but keeps returning to the only place in which he can feel he belongs, until both he and the landlord are mad, a story permeated by a

profound and haunting melancholy that is at once realistic and
bizarre; a graduate student's frantic efforts to obtain an apartment
in Rome ("Behold the Key"); an obscure novelist "for whom nothing comes easy" ("The Girl of My Dreams"); and the rabbinical
student and the fish-eating rabbi of the title story, about which so
much has been written that all I can say here is that if there has
been a better story written in America, or anywhere else for that
matter, in the last quarter-century, I have not read it.

Malamud's people are brilliantly individualized; his gift for characterization is often breathtaking. At the same time — though this
is hard for a non-Jew to state with any authority — they seem to be
Jews in the generic sense. The reader is constantly aware of the
almost palpable presence of persecution and misunderstanding,
which is as much a part of Malamud's characters as the flesh of
their bodies. It makes them bellicose or anxiously placable, thick-
skinned or painfully vulnerable, a presence almost as old as history
yet as alive as memories of Buchenwald or tomorrow's news from
the Middle East.

Male or female, young or old, Malamud's people are haunted by
a sense of injustice and grief, of suffering and persecution. All of
them, one way or another, live with the awareness of past perse-
cutions, just as miserably as does Isabella, the young woman of
"The Lady of the Lake," who has tattooed on her "soft and tender
flesh a blueish line of blurred numbers," the stigma of the concentration camp in which she had been interned as a child. "I can't
marry you," she tells the young American Jew in disguise who has
gone to Europe in search of romance. "I can't marry you. We are
Jews. My past is meaningful to me. I treasure what I suffered
for." It is the same with the widow, Eva, of "Take Pity"; when the
ex-salesman, Rosen, offers to help her and her children, she refuses: "In my whole life, I never had anything. In my whole life
I always suffered. I don't expect better. This is my life."

Such atavistic identification with past grief is as much a part of
Malamud's stories as his marvelous language (he captures what
seems to be the essence of American Yiddish); his striking and vivid

contrasts; his seemingly complete understanding of his characters and their ways of life. At once fantastic and curiously noble, often not far removed from being ridiculous but at the same time endowed with courage and the ability to endure (not silently; far from it!), Malamud's people stand up and confront the onslaughts of the world as often as they retreat from them. And perhaps the most remarkable aspect of these stories, something that differentiates Malamud and many of his contemporaries from their predecessors, is a robust and genuine sense of humor. The retired Yiddish actor in Malamud's "Suppose a Wedding" refutes an academic youth who discusses tragedy in classical terms, concluding with a Yiddish proverb *Leid macht auch lachen* — "suffering also makes for laughter." So John Updike's Bech, commenting on his own work and that of his Jewish contemporaries, trying for "one more degrading time to dig into the rubbish of his 'career' and come up with the . . . truth" tells the young interviewer in "Bech Swings":

> . . . he was sustained, insofar as he was sustained, by the memory of laughter, the specifically Jewish, embattled, religious, sufficiently desperate, not quite belly laughter of his father and his father's brothers . . . that the American Jews had kept the secret of this laughter a generation longer than the Gentiles, hence their present domination of the literary world . . .

If *Idiots First* (1963) and *Pictures of Fidelman* (1969) seem somewhat less impressive than *The Magic Barrel,* it hardly need be said that the latter was a very hard act for anyone to follow and that Malamud is one of the relatively few prolific authors whose work has only occasionally suffered or deteriorated with success, awards, and adulation. The eleven stories and the scene from a play ("Suppose a Wedding") of *Idiots First* exhibit even more variety, if sometimes less depth, than their predecessors. They include "Black is My Favorite Color," about a Jew who falls in love with a black woman but is eventually degraded by the black community and deserted by the woman; a rather slight piece about two bereaved individuals who meet in a Roman cemetery and come together briefly before the woman, now pregnant, is abandoned ("Life is Better than Death"); "The Bill," more familiar Malamud territory in which, with irony and effective use of contrast, a janitor turns against the grocer who has trusted him; and two remarkable fantasies, "The Jewbird," in which Jew preys upon Jew when a frozen food salesman eventually throws out of his home a talking crow named Schwartz who is "flying but . . . also running" from the "anti-Semeets," and the title story, where a dying man struggles against the "cosmic universal law, goddamit" in an attempt to aid his idiot son. But perhaps the most memorable story in *Idiots First* is "Still Life," the first of two pieces about Arthur Fidelman (*fidelman?* fiddle-man?), the "self-confessed failure as a painter," who had made his debut in "The Last Mohican" (in *The Magic Barrel;* after coming to Rome to write a critical study of Giotto, the first chapter of his manuscript is stolen by one of Malamud's best minor characters, Shimon Susskind, a Jewish refugee from Israel). "Still Life" is a semicomic masterpiece, highlighted by another effective minor character, the beautiful and passionate and neurotic Anna-maria Oliovino, whose studio and favors and wrath Fidelman shares. "Naked Nude," in which Fidelman appears as forger, is less impressive; "A Pimp's Revenge," "Pictures of the Artist," and "Glass Blower of Venice," which with the three earlier stories make up *Pictures of Fidelman: An Exhibition*, are first-rate. Ranging from the relatively straight narrative method of the earlier stories to the psychedelic innovativeness of "Pictures of the Artist," and varying in tone from comedy to absurdity to pathos, the Fidelman sequence is a brilliant tour de force. Fidelman as heterosexual lover with hangups, Fidelman as homosexual, Fidelman as pimp, forger of paintings, potential suicide, fraud digging square holes in the ground and charging spectators ten lire, and finally Fidelman back in America, where he "worked as a craftsman in glass and loved men and women," is a remarkable achievement in any writer's canon.

Malamud's most recent collection, *Rembrandt's Hat* (1973) is equally varied. Over the years, as we have seen, he has tended to shift his focus from New York City's tenement dwellers and small storekeepers to intellectual or semi-intellectual academic and creative individuals. He has lost none of his skill and insight — quite the contrary — but he seems somehow less at home; the impact of the collection as a whole seems slightly diminished. As his people move "uptown," however, their cries are seldom muffled; they have lost none of their anguish, paranoia, uncertainty, and the capacity for suffering. Gans, of the stunning "The Silver Crown," has a father dying of cancer. He meets a semi-idiotic young woman who is advertising "Heal the Sick. Save The Dying. Make a Silver Crown" and after many misgivings pays her father, a suspicious-appearing rabbi, a substantial sum to cure his father ("We got two kinds crowns . . . One is for 401 and the other is 986"). But Gans is "easily irritated; angered by the war, atom bomb, pollution, death . . . [and] the strain of worrying about his father's illness" and at story's end, sleepless and harried by the thought that he has been swindled — or has he? — by a phony rabbi faith healer, he curses the man and his daughter and damns his father. The superb title story — like "The Silver Crown" one of Malamud's best since "The Magic Barrel" — with its compassionate yet satiric and often comic treatment of a feud between colleagues at a New York art school is similarly moving. Arkin, art historian and "hypertensive impulsive bachelor," meets his sculptor friend in the hall one day and offhandedly tells him how much he admires his hat: "It looks," he says, "like Rembrandt's hat that he wears in one of the middle-aged self-portraits, the really profound ones." They become estranged, then hostile; finally they exchange epithets of thief, and murderer. Arkin is so upset he cancels his class, suffers from tremors, sleeps badly, can scarcely eat. "What has this bastard done to me?" he cries. "What have I done to myself?" The resolution of this predicament is Malamud at his best, understanding, quizzical, compassionate.

One of my students told me recently that malamud is a variation of the Yiddish word for "teacher" and reminded me that in the Jewish tradition teachers have always been respected and trusted. And Malamud *is* a teacher. Out of ugliness and poverty and suffering and deprivation he has created a world of his own, tragic, comic, ridiculous, elevated, but constantly illuminated by the feeling of the need to teach men how to live, how to become *menschen*.

The thoughtfulness characteristic of the novels of Saul Bellow (1915–) also permeates the six stories in *Mosby's Memoirs* (1968), three of which had previously been published with the short novel *Seize the Day*.

Unlike most of Bellow's work (but like *Henderson the Rain King*) the protagonist of the title story is not a Jew but a Gentile. As much essay as conventional storytelling, "Mosby's Memoirs" concerns the recollections and musings of an intellectual refugee from a fundamentalist Missouri family, a one-time Princeton professor formerly with the OSS. Aided by a Guggenheim Fellowship, Mosby is introduced in Oaxaca, where he is planning his memoirs. His thoughts run from purely personal recollections of the war and former friends, including the man with whose wife Mosby had had an affair, to his philosophical speculations on intellectuals like Santayana, Malraux, Bertrand Russell, Sartre, and others, men whose lives had been "devoted to thought" and the life of reason, men dedicated to the salvation of mankind or offering mankind "mental aid in saving itself" but who could suddenly "turn into gruesome idiots" as had Sartre in "calling for the Russians to drop A-bombs on American bases in the Pacific." Within the span of a few hours, with Mosby drinking mescal while waiting for a guided trip to the nearby ruins, Bellow presents his reading of the role of one kind of intellectual in post-World War II society. Like the alienated Jew Tommy Wilhelm (born Adler) of *Seize the Day*, Mosby's "doom" is "to live life to the end as Mosby" — as a man of good will in a world of irreconcilable values. The story ends with Mosby in the ruins, panicking, choking, desperate for air (again like Tommy Wilhelm without, perhaps, Tommy's hoped-for redemption through love). Like the Confederate Virginian Mosby, he is a raider, swift, valiant, but engaged in a hopeless cause.

Perhaps the best of Bellow's stories is "The Old System," almost a novel-in-miniature, with a Herzog–Mr. Sammler-like persona, Dr. Braun, who recalls and ponders the meaning or lack of meaning of his life from his childhood in a family of first- and second-generation Jews in upstate New York. It is a thoughtful day for Dr. Braun, winter, the short end of December, as — victim or wise fool — he ponders the meaning of life from his recollections of a childhood sexual encounter with his cousin Tina, until at the story's end he stands by her deathbed, reflecting:

> Oh, these Jews — these Jews! Their feelings, their hearts! . . . One after another you gave over your dying. One by one they went. You went. Childhood, family, friendship, love were stifled in the grave. And these tears! . . . what did you understand? . . . *nothing!* It was only an imitation of understanding. A promise that mankind might — *might*, mind you — eventually, through its gift which might — *might* again! — be a divine gift, comprehend why it lived. Why life, why death . . . And, again, why these particular forms — these Isaacs and these Tinas? . . . These things cast outward by a great begetting spasm billions of years ago.

In a less somber vein is "A Father-to-Be," a beautifully compressed account of a few hours in the life of a research chemist in his early thirties. Rogin, like so many of the characters of the Jewish fiction writers, is easily depressed and easily elated. On his way to visit his fiancée, seeing a repulsive person on the subway, Rogin reflects that his own children might end up like that. Thoughts often "grow fertile in the subway," he thinks. "I won't be used." By the time he arrives at Joan's apartment, he is boiling inwardly and has planned to upbraid her. " 'Do you think,' . . . he was going to tell her, 'that I alone was made to carry the burden of the whole world . . . ? Do you think I'm just a natural resource, like a coal mine . . . ? Remember, that I'm a man is no reason why I should be loaded down.' " The delicious roast beef and frozen raspberries he has purchased at a delicatessen no longer interest him; he rejects Joan's anticipated offer to shampoo his hair. But she insists, forces him to the basin, "surrounding him, pouring the water gently over him until it seemed . . . it was the warm fluid of his own secret loving spirit . . . and his anger at his son-to-be disappeared." He sighs fondly at Joan and the story ends: "You always have such wonderful ideas . . . a kind of instinct, a regular gift."

The last story by J. D. Salinger (1919–), "Hapworth 16, 1924," was published in June 1965. Whatever the author's reasons for subsequent voluntary retirement and exile, his only collection of short stories, *Nine Stories* (1953)* and the novellas *Franny and Zooey* (1961) and *Raise High the Roof Beam, Carpenters* (1963), bound with its companion piece, "Seymour — An Introduction" continue to be among the most popular and the most frequently written about recent works of short fiction. The Glass family, like Faulkner's Snopeses or Compsons and Hemingway's Nick Adams and Salinger's own Holden Caulfield, have become part of our national mythology. Rereading his stories every year or so in connection with a course in modern short fiction, I am always impressed anew; after more than two decades of enormous change in our society, they have lost none of their individuality, freshness, and often poignant appeal.

"A Perfect Day for Bananafish," "Uncle Wiggily in Connecticut," and "For Esmé — with Love and Squalor" are alive with an intense sensitivity to the nuances of the human experience. Each is, in a way, a very different kind of war story, or the story of a casualty of war, humorous, warm-hearted, even frivolous in tone, but with the exception of "Esmé" is bleak and terrifying and tragic beneath the surface. It is this kind of contrast to which many of Salinger's stories owe much of their effectiveness. His war stories are discussed further in the first section of Chapter 8.

Even Salinger's minor stories — though there are those who would deny that he wrote anything but "major" works — are peo-

---

* I have been unable to obtain copies of the pirated and unauthorized *The Complete Uncollected Tales of J. D. Salinger* (1974), a two-volume set of stories originally published in *Collier's, Esquire,* the *Saturday Evening Post,* and some other magazines between 1940 and 1943, nor do I know any book reviewer who has. Salinger has brought suit against the "publishers" — known only as John Greenberg — who at the time of writing, February 1975, have refused interviews and shunned any contact with the public.

pled with brilliantly portrayed characters, some of whom may appear for a few moments only but are endowed with distinct and individual life: typical are the irritable father of the young genius in "Teddy," the harrassed window-dresser of "De Daumier-Smith's Blue Period," or even someone who never actually appears in a story, the husband of "Down at the Dinghy."

The stories move swiftly, engrossingly; in his preoccupation with Salinger's people the reader is likely to ignore or take for granted his infallible sense of narrative pace. And his dialogue, as has so frequently been observed, is at its best superb. But above all, Salinger's stories pass what seems to me the ultimate test of any work of fiction, the test of memorableness. Once having been read, they become part of one's vicarious experience. They linger in one's consciousness; they suggest far more than they actually tell; they evoke a stir of echoes that reverberate in the reader's mind: why did Sergeant X do so-and-so; why did Teddy kill himself; what will become of Ramona and Eloise and Mary Jane and all the others?

The novellas have a lot to be said for them and they have their ardent admirers, but for all their awareness, erudition, wit, and pathos they seem to me decidedly inferior to the stories. Despite its freshness and originality, all but the best of Salinger's fiction is occasionally marred by a curious kind of shadowy, lurking tendency toward cuteness and self-imitation; this bent seems more obvious in the novellas than in the shorter pieces. No one, of course, was more aware of this than the author himself. The later works unhappily justify Salinger's fears that his saga of the New York Glasses "might sooner or later . . . bog down, perhaps disappear entirely, in my own methods, locutions, and mannerisms." His retirement suggests, perhaps, that the possibility became, to him at least, a reality. There is some consolation, however, that in William Roeder's *Newsweek* interview (November 18, 1974) — only the second Salinger had granted since his rise to fame and notoriety with *Catcher in the Rye* — he is reported to have said that "of course I'm still writing." Whether these new writings will ever be made public remains — as of 1975 — to be seen.

*

In comparison with so prolific a writer as Malamud, Grace Paley (1922–) at first glance seems a comparative beginner: only two collections in approximately fifteen years, *The Little Disturbances of Man* (1959) and *Enormous Changes at the Last Minute* (1973). The first of these appeared with relatively little fanfare, but gradually won its devotees and was subsequently republished (by another publisher, something unusual in American publishing history); the second, deservedly, was a National Book Award nominee, but for the most part Paley, like so many short story writers, has worked in comparative obscurity. In her own unspectacular fashion, she is one of the very important living American practitioners of the form.

Paley writes simply, powerfully, and seemingly artlessly about first- and second-generation Jewish Americans fighting their way up, or occasionally down, from the tenements of New York, falling apart or pulling themselves together: a child selected to perform in a Christmas pageant to the dismay of her Orthodox parents ("The Loudest Voice"); the buxom, amoral, good-natured mistress of a popular actor in the Yiddish theater ("Goodbye and Good Luck"); a fourteen-year-old runaway who kills herself after being sexually savaged ("The Little Girl"); a middle-aged woman who returns to the building in which she had been raised, now a tenement in a black ghetto, and spends an enlightening and enlightened week or two with a black mother and her child ("The Long-Distance Runner"); a precocious teen-ager's infatuation with a GI who flunks his Wasserman test ("A Woman Young and Old").

Grace Paley's people come miraculously to life, sometimes with one simple brushstroke, like the grandmother of "A Subject of Childhood," who "mourned all her days for some kid who'd died . . . at the age of five" and who on her own deathbed was heard to murmur "Oh, oh, Anita, breathe a little, try to breathe, my little baby." Or they emerge slowly and gradually through the author's unerring sense of detail, the nervous, staccato dialogue, and her complete understanding of the characters. Perhaps the most memorable of these people, and certainly my own favorite, is a skeptical, frank, intelligent, hard-boiled but compassionate tenement-to-apartment dweller, Faith, who appears in several of these completely disciplined fictions: as the daughter in one of the best stories about writing a story I have ever read, "A Conversation with My Father"; in "A Subject of Childhood," as the young mother of two boys and mistress of a good-natured vegetarian who "would not hurt a fly" but "simply can't take those kids" (". . . I have raised these kids, with one hand typing behind my back to earn a living . . . We have in fact risen mightily from toilets in the hall and scavenging . . . at the Salvation Army for underwear and socks"); as the mature woman of "Living," consoling a friend with terminal cancer.

As I have commented elsewhere I find it difficult to describe Paley without sounding fulsome or resorting to clichés. In the often imitative and conforming world of the remaining large-circulation periodicals that continue to publish short fiction, she has gone her own way, done her own thing, and it is no coincidence that until fairly late in her career she published for the most part in relatively small-circulation, low-budget magazines. Whatever her subject, Grace Paley's voice, her style, her view of the world are hers and hers alone. A story of hers could not be mistaken for someone else's, any more than a Hemingway or a Joyce or a Faulkner or a Sherwood Anderson story. Here is Faith talking to her dying friend:

> Two weeks before Christmas, Ellen called me and said, "Faith, I'm dying." That week I was dying too.
> After we talked, I felt worse. I left the kids alone and ran down to the corner for a quick sip among living creatures. But Julie's and all the other bars were full of men and women gulping a hot whiskey before hustling off to make love.
> People require strengthening before the acts of life.

And a later statement Faith makes to her dying friend: "Life isn't that great, Ellen. We've had nothing but crummy days and crummy guys and no money and broke all the time and cockroaches and nothing to do on Sunday but take the kids to Central

Park and row on that lousy lake. What's so great, Ellen? What's the big loss?"

No buckets of blood here, either. But intelligence, craftsmanship, and abundant grace — lower case — in the midst of squalor; and always humor and compassion and a kind of dogged buoyancy in the face of Grace Paley's uncompromising realities.

Philip Roth's debut was spectacular: *Goodbye, Columbus* (1959), a novella and five stories, won the National Book Award when the author was in his middle twenties. Like Malamud, Bellow, and the other major Jewish writers, Roth knows his people well, and depicts them with wit, sympathy, irony, affection, impatience, and occasional dislike; like them, too, he is deeply concerned with individual, family, and societal relationships and like them he can transmute ordinary experiences and people into something both familiar and strange, something that has about it the somewhat fey, mad, hallucinated touch so characteristic of much Yiddish and Jewish fiction.

Neil Klugman, familiar to innumerable nonreaders through the film version of "Goodbye, Columbus," is typical of many of Roth's young Jews. A thoroughly mixed-up youth in an equally mixed-up society, he is vacillating, pompous, and often irritating; at the same time he is ruthlessly honest in his fashion and admirable in his efforts to find some kind of meaning and some measure of self-realization and justification in his particular corner of society ("Whenever anyone asks me where I went to school I come right out with it: Newark Colleges of Rutgers University"), an enclave troubled by memories of a frequently shabby past that is in conflict with an uncertain present.

Neil's summer affair with beautiful Radcliffe undergraduate Brenda Patimkin and her new-rich family (country-club Jews out of Newark by way of Patimkin's Kitchen and Bathroom Sinks) is an effective mingling of conventional boy-pursues-and-captures-girl and portrait-of-the-artist-as-a-young-Jew materials. The two worlds are vividly brought to life, and Neil's inner struggle is perceptively delineated: "What was it inside me that had turned pursuit and clutching into love, and then turned it inside out again? What was it that had turned winning into losing, and losing — who knows — into winning?" And the minor characters are beautiful: Brenda's basketball-playing brother with his immature memories, and the older Patimkins, who in the gray confusion of the brother's wedding morning appear to Neil "round-shouldered, burdened, child-carrying — like people fleeing a captured city."

The characters of Roth's stronger pieces are similarly beset with problems involving their own identities or their roles in a changing society. He writes with equal skill and awareness of the preadolescent boy who rushes to the top of a building and threatens to kill himself unless his dominating mother and the family rabbi accept the story of the Virgin Birth ("The Conversion of the Jews"); of a young lawyer on the edge of emotional collapse when his suburban security is threatened ("Eli the Fanatic"); of an elder Leopold Bloom type whose domestic disasters include a daughter-turned-Socialist and her affair with a folksinger, his wife's loss of beauty, a complicated love affair, *and* a heart attack ("Epstein"); and a Jewish noncom's attempt to train a group of Jewish draftees at Fort Leonard Wood, Missouri, his only story with a setting outside metropolitan New York or New Jersey ("Defender of the Faith").

Two of the three fictions in Roth's *My Life As A Man* (1974), a National Book Award nominee, have been classified as short stories although they might more aptly be termed chapters from an unfinished novel about the son of a New Jersey small businessman, Nathan Zuckerman. "Salad Days" is highlighted by Nathan's relations with sexually innovative, ingenious, and inexhaustible Sharon Shatsky, teen-aged daughter of Al "The Zipper King" Shatsky. "Courting Disaster (or, Serious in the Fifties)" is concerned with Nathan's subsequent experiences, culminating in his marriage to one of his creative-writing students, a divorced woman five years his senior who eventually commits suicide, and his involvement with her daughter. The two stories are an agonizing *mea culpa*, illuminated by Roth's characteristic effective blending of the serious and the comic. Close kin to both Neil Klugman and Alexander Portnoy, Nathan Zuckerman is simultaneously unbearable and likable, and one can only agree with his lament: "There was more than enough there for a Jewish boy to break himself upon."

   Polish-born and an American resident since 1935, Isaac Bashevis Singer (1909–) is at once one of the most distinguished and most prolific living fiction writers: he is author of more than twenty books, including six collections of short stories, from *Gimpel the Fool* (1935) to the National Book Award-winning *A Crown of Feathers* (1973). Whereas most of the leading American-born Jewish fiction writers share a concern with the role of the American Jew in contemporary American society, Singer, particularly in his earlier collections, was preoccupied with echoes of a Jewish past extending from prehistoric days when "time stands still . . . Adam remains naked, Eve lustful . . . Cain kills Abel, the flea lies with the elephant, the flood falls from heaven, the Jews knead clay in Egypt [and] Job scratches at his sore-covered body" to a European present. In his later collections, particularly *A Friend of Kafka* (1970) and *A Crown of Feathers*, he more frequently employs a contemporary American setting ("I have developed roots here," he says in the Author's Note to his most recent collection, but "just the same, my American stories deal only with Yiddish-speaking immigrants from Poland so as to ensure that I know well not only their present way of life but *their* roots — their culture, history, ways of thinking and expressing themselves.")

   Regardless of their time and place, Singer's stories are an unforgettable blending of the old and the new, order and change, the ordinary, the spectral, and the surreal; they are a compound of a wild humor, unearthliness, and verisimilitude that can be as convincing as a Baedeker; they are constantly preoccupied with the gulfs and the bridges between illusions and reality: "No doubt the world is entirely . . . imaginary . . . but it is only once removed from the true world" ("Gimpel the Fool"). Individually impressive, his stories in toto constitute a panorama of Jewish folklore, tradition, myth, and manners that on the one hand is haunted by the past, subject to the caprice of the occult, the spectral, and the demonic, and on the other alive with the sights and sounds of the late nineteenth and twentieth centuries, whether they emanate from a Warsaw soup kitchen or a cafeteria in Coney Island.

Among Singer's primarily realistic earlier stories are "The Spinoza of Market Street," with its unforgettable portrayal of Dr. Nahum Fishelson, a Warsaw philosopher, and his marriage to the derelict food vendor, Black Dobbe, and consequent redemption as a human being, a vivid depiction of the contrast between the scientific, completely rational life and the emotional, personal urges of man; "Caricature," another story of an elderly Warsaw philosopher and his wife during Hitler's rise to power; "Gimpel the Fool," the story of the baker of Frampol and his whorish wife; and "The Little Shoemaker," the family saga of Abba Shuster, the best shoemaker in Frampol.

At the other extreme are stories like "The Black Wedding" (my own personal favorite), "A Tale of Two Liars," "The Destruction of Kreshev," "The Mirror," "Taibele and Her Demon," "Jachid and Jachida," and "Blood," which range from the ghetto of Warsaw or the village of Krashnik to a region inhabited by incubi and succubi, imps, demons, and the Devil himself. These stories are vibrant with the high, singing poetry of the supernatural and the hallucinatory, piercing in their portrayal of crime and punishment, sin and redemption, and universal in their implications.

Contrast is central to the effect created by these strange and wonderful stories. Satan's comments on the depraved Schloimele (in "The Destruction of Kreshev") sum up this aspect of Singer's esthetic:

> Those who understand the complexities of human nature know that joy and pain, ugliness and beauty, love and hate, mercy and cruelty and other conflicting emotions often blend and cannot be separated from each other. Thus I am able not only to make people turn away from the Creator, but to damage their own bodies, all in the name of some imaginary cause.

This strange world simply *is*. It is real and convincing in the same way that Rousseau's jungle paintings or Chagall's *Arabische Nächte* illustrations are real and convincing. In each case, the creator's vision is so complete, so whole, so harmonious within its own juxtaposition of opposites that only the irremediably literally minded individual questions the appearance of Yadwigha's comfortable bourgeois red sofa in the middle of a leafy jungle, or rejects Chagall's bemused and beautiful gold, pink, blue, and emerald-fleshed women, or bizarre, a-worldly animals, birds, and fish. So one accepts the hallucinated bride-to-be of Singer's "The Black Wedding." Hindele *knows* that the "fancy garments" of her attendants

> hid heads grown with elf-locks, goose-feet, unhuman navels, long snouts. The sashes of the young men were snakes in reality, their sable hats were actually hedgehogs, their beards clusters of worms. The men spoke Yiddish and sang familiar songs, but the noise they made was really the bellowing of oxen, the hissing of vipers, the howling of wolves. The musicians had tails, and horns grew from their heads. The maids who attended Hindele had canine paws, hoofs of calves, snouts of pigs. The wedding jester was all beard and tongue. The . . . relatives . . . were lions, bears, boars . . . Alas, this was not a human wedding, but a Black Wedding.

Similar juxtapositions characterize Singer's stories set in America or narrated by a Polish emigré in America from "A Wedding in Brownsville" (in *Short Friday*) to more than half the twenty-four stories of *A Crown of Feathers*. The heroine of the title story becomes a pawn in a battle between supernatural forces; a chess prodigy insists on a medical examination to verify his bride's virginity; a once-beautiful and talented dancer is destroyed in the bombing of the Warsaw ghetto after a last mad, macabre dance with her son; the "cabalist of East Broadway" falls into a deadly melancholy after being forced to eat pork while hospitalized in a Colorado sanitarium; a marriage feast turns into an hallucinated nightmare.

For the most part, Singer's narrative method is conventional and traditional. Perhaps his favorite mode is the story within a story, often told by a character who is a projection of the storyteller himself. The narrator meets a friend or acquaintance who tells him a story about another friend or acquaintance. Singer's people are prodigious, insatiable, indomitable talkers; I often have the feeling that if the Big One is finally dropped, perhaps the last sound on our planet will be that of one of Singer's wonderful people, relating a tale of love, lust, betrayal, passion, demonic possession, madness, success, frustration, suicide. As is inevitable with this sort of narrative method, related events flow from past to present, time blurs, fuses, is telescoped or fantastically heightened and lengthened. Few authors can manipulate such sequences and time-wrenchings effectively. Singer can. From his earliest to his most recent fictions he is a masterly technician.

But perhaps the most remarkable element in so many of his stories is the presence — not the intrusion, but a kind of extra dimension, never obtrusive, never articulated, but always there — of the narrator himself: wise, witty, skeptical, compassionate, obsessed, emancipated, a kind of all-seeing I-Eye-Consciousness as old as the hills and as contemporary as today, a kaleidoscopic angle of vision alive with understanding and wisdom that continually illuminates his strange and often terrifying glimpses into the human condition.

Among the many other important and representative collections of stories by and about American Jews — too many to comment on individually — are Charles Angoff's *When I Was a Boy in Boston* (1947) and *Something of My Father and Other People* (1965); Burton Bernstein's *The Grove* (1961); Harold Brodkey's *First Love and Other Sorrows* (1958); Jerome Charyn's *The Man Who Grew Younger* (1967); Alfred Chester's *Behold, Goliath* (1964); Stanley Elkin's *Criers and Kibitzers* (1968) and *Searches and Seizures* (1973); Seymour Epstein's *A Penny for Charity* (1965); Leslie Fiedler's *Pull Down Vanity* (1962), *The Last Jew in America* (1966), and *Nude Croquet & Other Stories* (1971); Merrill Joan Gerber's *Stop Here, My Friend* (1965). Herbert Gold's *Love and Life* (1960) and *The Magic Will* (1971); Ivan

Gold's *Nickel Miseries* (1963); Joan Greenberg's *Summering* (1966); Norma Klein's *Love and Other Euphemisms* (1972); Arthur Kober's *Thunder Over the Bronx* (1935), *My Dear Bella* (1941), and *Bella, Bella, Kissed a Fella* (1951); Albert Maltz's *Afternoon in the Jungle: Selected Short Stories* (1970), most of which were originally published prior to 1940; Arthur Miller's *I Don't Need You Any More* (1967); Jay Neugeboren's *Corky's Brother* (1969); Hugh Nissenson's *A Pile of Stones* (1965) and *In the Reign of Peace* (1972); Howard Nemerov's *A Commodity of Dreams* (1959) and *Stories, Fables and Other Diversions* (1971); Cynthia Ozick's *The Pagan Rabbi* (1971); Norma Rosen's *Green: Eight Stories and a Novella* (1969); Leonard Q. Ross's (Leo Rosten), *The Education of H*Y*M*A*N K*A*P*L*A*N* (1939) and *The Return of H*Y*M*A*N K*A*P*L*A*N* (1959); Delmore Schwartz's *The World Is A Wedding* (1948) and *Successful Love* (1961); Jerome Weidman's several volumes, selected in *My Father Sits in the Dark* (1961); James Yaffe's *Poor Cousin Evelyn* (1951); Samuel Yellen's *The Passionate Shepherd* (1957); Sol Yurick's *Someone Like Me* (1971); Eugene Ziller's *In This World* (1960).

Chapter 7

The Black Explosion: "I Mean, with All Things Considered, the Field Is Opening Up More and More . . . Ya Know — Bein' Black and Meanin' It. We're in Vogue These Days."*

IN HIS INTRODUCTION to what seems to me still the best of many good recent anthologies of short fiction by American black writers, Langston Hughes in 1967 commented on a question frequently put to him: "Why aren't there more Negro writers?" He addressed the question primarily in contemporary economic rather than historical terms, citing the fact that at that time Hollywood and the other mass media had "not touched" the work of any of his black contemporaries and that because "most Negro writers from Chesnutt to LeRoi Jones . . . found it hard to make a literary living . . . or derive from other labor sufficient funds to sustain creative leisure, their individual output has of necessity often been limited in quantity, and sometimes in depth and quality as well."

There was a great deal of validity in the comment, though the situation has changed for the better since it was made. But because the short story writer in America — white or black or red or yellow — has always tended to be a kind of creative stepchild working for the most part in comparative obscurity and with very few financial rewards, it applies relatively little to him. More relevant — and no one of course was more aware of this than Langston Hughes — are the harsh sociological factors.

The development of a minority literature, particularly that of a persecuted minority, seems almost inevitably to follow a similar pattern. Much of the older generation of Hebrew fiction writers,

* Ed Bullins, "The Real Me," *The Hungered One.*

for example, as specialists have pointed out, was essentially didactic. It was more concerned with what it meant to be a Jew, with specific polemics and propaganda than with universalities or art per se. On the other hand, the younger generation of Israelis, writing in Hebrew, tended to be both polemicists *and* artists, Zionists *and* citizens of the world. The American-Jewish author similarly passed through, a generation or two ago, a period of acute consciousness of his *Jewishness* to an awareness of his position as a *Jewish American*. Malamud and Roth and the writers discussed in the previous chapter continue to remind us that the Jew is different and his role in America is often difficult and uncertain: Sheldon Grossbart's remark in Roth's "Defender of the Faith" is not uncharacteristic: "Because I'm a Jew . . . I *am* different. Better, maybe not. But different." But most of the best Jewish-American fiction writers, as specialists like Harold Ribalow and others have commented, are less neurotic about their Jewishness than their predecessors and are increasingly likely to write about Jewish-Gentile relations in America with compassion and understanding rather than bitterness, out of knowledge rather than ignorance — in short, to transcend the role of sociologist and polemicist and to write as Jewish-Americans rather than Jews-in-America.

So with the situation of the contemporary black writer. Though the number and quality of stories by and about American blacks increased in the years immediately following World War II, it was only within the last decade — give or take a year or two — that American blacks began creating a body of short fiction even remotely comparable to the Jewish-American stories previously discussed. Despite great improvement in the black situation during recent years, we do not need 1975 headlines from South Boston or anywhere else to be reminded of how far we must progress before the black writer in America can truly think of himself as an American black. Ten years ago James Baldwin summed up the uneasy paradox. On the one hand, "I was icily determined . . . to die and go to Hell before I would let a white man spit on me"; on the other, "I love America more than any other country in the world and, exactly for this reason, I reserve the right to criticize her perpetually." Not all his contemporaries are that optimistic: compare the violence of much of the militant nonfiction of the period, or William Melvin Kelley's dedication to the four novellas of *Dem* in 1967 — "This book is dedicated to the Black People in (not of) America" — or the hatred and despair that characterize so many of the stories of Chester A. Himes.

Writing about this over ten years ago, I said that not until the violent emotions engendered by racial inequalities and crises in America subside, and not until the contemporary American climate makes it possible for the writer to think of himself as a black American rather than a black-in-America, will he be able, as Herbert Hill observed in his introduction to another good anthology of black writing in America, "to break through the limits of parochialism into the whole range of the modern writer's preoccupations."

The short fiction of Langston Hughes (1902–1967) — from *The Ways of White Folks* (1934) to *Laughing to Keep from Crying* (1952) or *Something in Common and Other Stories* (1963), and particularly the Simple pieces (*Simple Speaks His Mind* [1950], *Simple Takes a Wife* [1952], *Simple Stakes a Claim* [1957]) is in my opinion the best and most likely to endure body of work about blacks — and whites — by an American black prior to the beginning of the new and vigorous black literature of the sixties and seventies.

Hughes's narrative method is relaxed and leisurely; he is at his best in his own combination of traditional short story, essay, and autobiographical reminiscence. He is gentle rather than violent, more good natured than bitter, but his stories are deadly serious and highly provocative beneath their smooth surfaces. "Who's Passing for Who?" concerns two very different kinds of Harlem intellectuals and their encounter with three visiting schoolteachers from Iowa; "Trouble with the Angels" depicts the situation of an all-black cast presenting a play in Washington, D.C., a play the local black population is not allowed to attend; in "Breakfast in Virginia" a pair of black soldiers are not allowed to eat in the dining car despite the fact that an understanding white offers to share his table with them; and in "Something in Common" a black and a white are thrown out of a Hong Kong bar — the black resented having been called George, they exchanged mild insults and finally attempted to fight each other — but unite against the common enemy and together return to fight for their rights. Such stories suggest as much or more about the nature of intolerance and atavistic reactions to black-white relations as the more militant and often savage work of James Baldwin, Imamu Baraka (formerly LeRoi Jones), Eldridge Cleaver, and Ed Bullins; at the same time, they constitute a plea for tolerance and understanding with which the average white is most easily able to identify.

At the opposite end of the spectrum are the short pieces of Richard Wright (1908–1960): *Uncle Tom's Children* (1940), four savagely powerful novellas; and *Eight Men* (1961), stories originally published between 1937 and 1957, along with a play and an autobiographical essay. Wright's stories of helpless or long-suffering blacks bearing the brunt of societal and individual white brutality mark the beginning of a new era in black fiction and even his least important pieces contain unforgettable scenes and characters that burn their way into the reader's consciousness; characteristic is the savage sequence of events of "Big Boy Leaves Home," climaxed by a lynching that leaves the protagonist completely lost, alienated from life, a victim of ugly racial hatred and bigotry. But for all his talent, Wright's people — misunderstood, exploited, vilely misused by whites — tend to be almost as one-dimensional as many of the stereotypes of the proletarian short fiction of the thirties. As a sad and moving testimonial to the evil of racism and its effect upon a gifted and bitterly disillusioned man, *Uncle Tom's Children* and *Eight Men* constitute a disturbing and towering and permanent landmark in the literary history of black-white relations; their influence upon the younger generation of black writers was and continues to be profound.

Except for Langston Hughes, Chester Himes (1909–) is the most prolific of the older generation of black American writers. Though he is best known for the black detectives of the successful film *Cotton Comes to Harlem,* his eighteen novels, many militant books of social criticism including *If He Hollers, Let Him Go* and *Lonely Crusade,* and innumerable articles and stories span some forty years from the beginning of his writing career during his imprisonment — for jewel theft — to his autobiography and such stories as "Prediction," written in 1969 in Alicante. (Like Wright, Hughes, Baldwin, and Bullins, he has traveled widely; since the early fifties he has lived in France and Spain.)

His writings, Himes says in his introduction to *Black on Black* (1973), a retrospective selection of his essays, short stories, and what he terms a "black 'Greek Tragedy,' " *Baby Sister,* are "admittedly chauvinistic. You will conclude if you read them that BLACK PROTEST and BLACK HETEROSEXUALITY are my chief obsessions. And you will be right."

The comment is an understatement. Almost all of Himes's short fiction bears the marks of these obsessions: his "stories" are powerful and disturbing and hate-filled polemical essays or tracts involving fictional techniques. The ultimate is "Prediction," a devastating allegory written after he had "become firmly convinced" that "the only chance Black Americans had of obtaining justice and equality in the United States was by violence." In it a black gunman hides in a cathedral, waiting for the appearance of a parade "to demonstrate the capacity of law enforcement . . . during this time of suspicion and animosity between the races." He opens fire.

> In a matter of seconds the streets were strewn with the carnage, nasty gray blobs of brains, hairy fragments of skull . . . bone splinters from jaws and facial bones, bloody, gristly bits of ears and noses, flying red and white teeth, a section of tongue; and slick and slimy with large purpling splashes and gouts of blood, squashy bits of exploded viscera, stuffed intestines bursting with half-chewed ham and cabbage and rice and gravy . . . It was the most gratifying episode of the black man's life . . . he had killed seventy-three whites . . . and had wounded an additional seventy-five.

If there is less gore in other Himes stories, there is no less hatred and indignation. His villains are not only the white establishment police and sheriff who kick and beat to death the decorated black soldier returning home for Christmas ("Christmas Gift") or fill full of bullets the narrator of "One More Way to Die"; they are the "ordinary" members of white society, epitomized by the "respectable" white man of "All He Needs Is Feet," deliberately bumping into the black man who has stepped off the sidewalk to let him and his companions pass. In one way or another, in one story after another, the society itself precipitates the chain of events leading to the destruction or humiliation of its victims.

Too oversimplified to be successful as fiction, the work of Chester Himes, like that of Richard Wright, is a shocking mirror of our times; it makes us reflect, in the words of one of the author's few compassionate whites:

"What have we done to him?"

Of the fiction produced by American blacks after the Hughes-Wright-Himes generation, *Going to Meet the Man* (1965) by James Baldwin (1924–) seems to me the most important single short story collection and its controversial title piece the most powerful story by a recent American black writer. Out of such stock characters as a Southern sheriff, his sexually unexciting wife, and his brutally mistreated black victims, Baldwin has created another hideous fable of the sixties (a story still so shocking in its impact as to evoke more than one cry of protest when I included it in an anthology designed for university students three or four years ago). As in his essays and other works of nonfiction, "Going to Meet the Man" brings more forcefully to mind than any news stories or telecasts what it must mean to be black in a white man's world, a world in which the sheriff Jesse can say with all sincerity that he was a "good man, a God-fearing man . . . who had tried to do his duty all his life," and this after recollecting the events of the day and the young black he has beaten almost to death. The whole terrible paradox of irreconcilable forces and immovable objects is suggested in this memorable scene, which in its impact is far more terrible than the much-discussed crucifixion scene that climaxes the story:

Each day, each night, he felt worn out, aching, with their smell in his nostrils and filling his lungs, as though he were drowning — drowning in niggers; and it was all to be done again when he awoke. It would never end. It would never end. Perhaps this is what the singing had meant all along. They had not been singing black folks into heaven, they had been singing white folks into hell.

One wonders how even one myopic book reviewer could say in a leading liberal national magazine that "Going to Meet the Man" has the same trivial effect as *Blues for Mister Charlie:* "It appears that what all this racial fuss stems from is the white man's inability to get it up."

The world of Ann Petry (1911–) in *Miss Muriel and Other Stories* (1971) bears somewhat the same relation to James Baldwin's as that of Langston Hughes does to Richard Wright's. The Layen family of the title story and other pieces are the only blacks in horse-and-buggy upstate New York. They are solid citizens: the Father is a pharmacist; Aunt Ellen plays Bach and Beethoven, writes articles for magazines and periodicals, and lectures at schools and colleges; another relative knows Shakespeare's sonnets and can recite "whole acts from Macbeth or Hamlet"; they are proud of their Haviland china and "sterling silver knives and forks with the rose pattern," and when talking with whites refer to each other as Mr. or Mrs. Layen. But beneath the surface, the old, old tensions and uncertainties exist. Leisurely, almost novelistic in technique, "Miss Muriel" ("Nigger, what's the matter with you? Don't you see that picture of that beautiful white woman on the front of this box? When you ask for them cigars, you say *Miss* Muriel cigars!" is a line from one of Uncle Johno's favorite anecdotes) centers on beautiful Aunt Sophronia and her two suitors, a swinging jazz musician and a white shoemaker, elderly Mr. Bemish. Although the twelve-year-old narrator tends to speak in a fashion I have seldom heard from the lips of either black or white, the piece moves rapidly despite its length and generates a considerable amount of interest, as do all Ann Petry's stories. I find it difficult to accept the child's "You don't seem to realize that you're the wrong color, Mr. Bemish" but I am convinced of the reality of her growing awareness of prejudice and the pitfalls and heartbreaks that may lie ahead.

Perhaps Petry's most interesting story conceptually is "Mother Africa." A black junk dealer in New York City receives — for reasons that strain the reader's credibility — a nude statue. At first reluctant to accept it, he becomes obsessed by it, calls it Mother Africa. His business suffers, his friends and clients are wary of him, his entire lifestyle is altered. Junkman Pygmalion has been deluded by a spurious Galatea:

> It had never occurred to him that this alive-looking statue was of a white woman . . . the hair, the straight sharp nose, the thin-lipped mouth. He'd been so busy looking at her breasts and thighs, he hadn't paid any attention to her face.

Ann Petry is most effective in some of her more economically constructed pieces. "The New Mirror," for example, is a little gem. The "I" narrator of the title story is now fifteen and is helping her father in his drugstore. Father leaves, doesn't return; the frightened family finally notifies the police: has he met with foul play? But by nightfall he returns, and with a brand-new set of false teeth. He couldn't bear the thought that the white churchgoers would see his open mouth with its naked gums and occasional tooth when he sang his solo — the "mouth of an idiot out of Shakespeare . . . the mouth of the nurse in Romeo and Juliet, the mouth of the gravediggers in Hamlet."

The literary career of Cyrus Colter (1910–) did not begin until the writer was fifty. A graduate of Ohio State, the Kent College of Law, and a practicing lawyer and Illinois Commerce Commissioner, he published his first stories in the comparative obscurity of the "littles" and with *The Beach Umbrella* (1970) won the first Iowa School of Letters Award for short fiction. Like Ann Petry's, the world of his fiction is a far remove from the jungle of James Baldwin's Harlem or Richard Wright's Depression-ridden Deep

South; almost all of Colter's stories are concerned with small crises or problems involving unexceptional people and situations. (An exception is "An Untold Story".)

The Beach Umbrella pieces are set in Chicago, ranging from the public beaches of the title story to the homes of the self-conscious black elite of "After the Ball." Colter knows and understands his people and depicts them without sentimentality, condescension, or brutality. His world and its inhabitants are clearly and sharply drawn, whether they be the sexually-awakening Verna of "A Man in the House," the pathetic Elijah of the title story with his craving for a dazzling beach umbrella, Anita of the "posh Hyde Park–Kenwood black community" ("Black for Dinner"), or the Hamlet-quoting barfly of "An Untold Story." Above all, these quietly competent stories are notable for the sincerity and straightforward intelligence of their creator.

Among the newer and younger generation of black short story writers of the middle sixties and seventies, Alice Walker (1944–), Ernest J. Gaines (1933–), Ed Bullins (1935–), and James Alan McPherson (1943–) seem both the most outstanding and the most representative. The authors are very different in background, training, and temperament, and their work suggests the variety and achievement of the black short fiction of the last decade.

In Love and Trouble: Stories of Black Women (1973) by Alice Walker (1944–) is a remarkable book that deserves to be much better known and more widely read. The range of these thirteen fictions is impressive, including as it does a two-page prose poem in which a young black girl discovers in a bed of flowers the skeleton of what had been a lynching victim; a relatively conventional story of the attraction between a student in a Deep South college for black women and her emigré professor whose wife and child had been exterminated in a Polish concentration camp; the wedding day reflections of a black Mississippi woman; the parable of an ancient black woman and her effect upon the white community she offends by attempting to attend *their* church (". . . so they gazed nakedly upon their own fear transferred; a fear of the black and the old, a terror of the unknown as well as of the deeply known"); and a series of stunning pieces that float from the world of customary human relationships to one of dark and terrible actions and visions alive with the violence and sexuality and sense of the *awful* that pervade so much black fiction since the time of Richard Wright. Of these, "Her Sweet Jerome," "Really, Doesn't Crime Pay?" and above all "The Child Who Favored Daughter" are the work of a major writer, thoroughly disciplined, thoroughly in command of the situation at all times and in all places.

Ernest J. Gaines (1933–) has written three novels, including *The Autobiography of Miss Jane Pittman,* which was made into one of the most memorable television productions of recent years. His equally memorable collection of five long stories, *Bloodlines,* was published in 1968. Gaines's strength lies in his quietly compassionate accounts of plantation blacks in his native Louisiana, where he lived until he moved to California in his teens. There he graduated from San Francisco State College and studied at Stanford on a Stegner creative writing fellowship.

"A Long Day in November," the best piece in *Bloodlines* (all five are good), is a masterly novella of a young boy, his father and mother, and their world on a Louisiana plantation. There are no technical pyrotechnics here, no violence, but in their place a steadily seen and beautifully rendered picture of family life, alive with the minutiae of day-to-day existence: going to school, moving to Gran-mon's when the mother leaves her husband because of his obsessive interest in his beat-up car, finally coming back together when the father obeys the mother's demand to choose between car and family. The novella is climaxed by two powerful scenes, which in less skilled hands would become either ludicrous or melodramatic: father destroys the car, and the appeased mother insists that her husband whip her: "You whip me . . . or I turn right round and walk on out that door." Gaines's fine sense of control, his effective use of dialogue, and the quiet reasonance of his scene-building can perhaps be suggested by the following excerpt following the whipping.

> I raise my head and look at Mama . . . Her face is all swole . . . Mama and Daddy don't talk . . . I eat my food . . .
> "What a day," Daddy says.
> Mama don't say nothing. She's just picking over her food.
> "Mad?" Daddy says.
> "No," Mama says.
> "Honey?" Daddy says.
> Mama looks at him.
> "I didn't beat you because you did us thing with Freddy Jackson, did I?"
> "No," Mama says.
> "Well, why then?" Daddy says.
> "Because I don't want you to be the laughingstock of the plantation," Mama says.
> "Who go'n laugh at me?" Daddy says.
> "Everybody," Mama says. "Mama and all. Now they don't have nothing to laugh about."
> "Honey, I don't mind if they laugh at me," Daddy says.
> "I do mind," Mama says.
> "Did I hurt you?"
> "I'm all right," she says.
> "You ain't mad no more?" Daddy says.
> "No," Mama says. "I'm not mad."

"The Sky is Gray" is almost equally effective, another triumph of the usual, this time about the boy and his mother and their visit to a dentist. Avoiding the Scylla and Charybdis of didacticism and heavy symbolism, Gaines creates another memorable picture of family and racial relationships in which both love and pride animate extremely conventional materials.

Different as the writings of Alice Walker and Ernest J. Gaines are, they share one thing in common: they are the work of mature writers who in one manner or other (and quite apart from their concern for their race) have moved from the platform of sociology to the realm of art. "What moves a writer to eloquence is less meaningful than what he makes of it," Ralph Ellison has said. In their best stories, Walker and Gaines have made that implied transition. And that makes all the difference.

Ed Bullins (1935–) is primarily known as a playwright and his controversial work has been performed in Harlem's New Lafayette Theater (where he has been writer-in-residence) and Lincoln Center's Forum. He grew up in what he has referred to as the "jungle" of North Philadelphia, which serves as setting for some of his stories and sketches originally published in relatively obscure "little" magazines and collected, in 1971, in *The Hungered One*.

Though far from an impeccable craftsman like Alice Walker, Ed Bullins, in the range of these early writings, is equally impressive. His collection includes brief commentaries spoken or narrated by a single voice, such as "Moonwriter"; essentially naturalistic stories like "DANDY or Astride the Funky Finger of Lust"; the grotesque title piece about its unnamed narrator's terrible encounter with a monstrous symbolic bird; surreal sketches like "The Saviour" or "The Reluctant Voyage," which are almost Kafkaesque in their mingling of realism and fantasy; familiar but very competent stories of racial violence like "Travel from Home"; and some very good single-episode narratives like "The Drive." In spite of their uneven quality, the overall effect of the collection is impressive. Though his subject matter had become traditional by the seventies, Bullins is his own man and speaks with his own voice. And a strong, powerful voice it is, and one that will continue to be heard.

The physical violence of much recent black fiction is for the most part absent from the stories and novellas in *Hue and Cry* (1969), by James Alan McPherson (1943–), Savannah-born, and educated in Georgia and at the Harvard Law School. McPherson's method is as conservative as his subject matter is traditional: he can nibble around the edges of a situation and explore with thoroughness the nuances of a character relationship, as he does in his title story. Reminiscent of Baldwin's "Come Out of the Wilderness," it concerns a black heroine, Margot Payne, who passes through a series of unsatisfactory and unfulfilling relations, first with Eric Carney, a well-intentioned but weak white liberal (a Quaker, "Eric had been taught all his life to look for causes," finds one in Margot, wants to marry her, but things begin to fall apart after he arranges an un-successful coming-together with Margot and his New England par-ents); then with Charles Wright, a black plodder who to Margot "represented stability at its worst" but thrives on her body and finally discards her; and finally with Eric's roommate, who is drift-ing toward homosexuality. The *hue* and cry (the collection is pref-aced by a quotation from a history of English law: "When a felony is committed, the hue and cry should be raised") ends where it began, with Margot reflecting, "But if that is all there is, what is left of life and why are we here?"

"On Trains," another effective treatment of conventional subject matter, is a swiftly paced story of racial intolerance involving a "plump and matronly" bigot who sits up all night in a day coach rather than stay in her roomette in the same car with an aged black porter; it is a good story but is weakened by an additional turn of the screw when another white passenger invites the black bar-tender to spend the night in *her* compartment. "Gold Coast" is first rate; a leisurely piece about another kind of intolerance, it concerns a black Harvard student working as a janitor in a Cambridge room-ing house and a loony superintendent, the author's most mem-orable character. "An Act of Prostitution" is a commonplace treat-ment of a trivial subject; and "Private Domain" again explores black-white/heterosexual-homosexual relationships in an unlikable cadre of intellectuals and pseudointellectuals.

Other notable and representative collections of black short fiction range from Toni Cade Bambera's *Gorilla, My Love* (1972) and Paule Marshall's *Soul Clap Hands and Sing* (1961) to William Melvin Kelley's *Dancers on the Shore* (1963), Georgia McKinley's *The Mighty Distance* (1965), the savage *Tales* (1967) of Imamu Baraka, and the posthumous stories of Henry Dumas, *Ark of Bones* (1975). Important individual stories, some of them frequently anthologized but as yet uncollected, include Frank Yerby's "Health Card," Albert Murray's "Train Whistle Guitar," subsequently developed into a novel, Ralph Ellison's "Flying Home," Eldridge Cleaver's "The Flashlight," and J. A. Williams' "Tell Martha Not to Moan." Good introductions to writers are available in several recent paperback anthologies including, in addition to a reprint of the Hughes collection cited earlier, *Black Short Story Anthology*, edited by Woodie King with an introduction by John Oliver Killems (1972); *New Black Voices: An Anthology of Contemporary Afro-American Literature*, edited by Abraham Chapman (1972); *Right On: An Anthology of Black Literature*, edited by Bradford Chambers and Rebecca Moon (1970); and *What We Must See: Young Black Story-tellers*, edited by Orde Coombs (1971).

It is one of the ironies of American literary history that with few exceptions and until relatively recently the most convincing and certainly the most sympathetic fictional portrayals of American blacks have been created by Southern whites, from Joel Chandler Harris to William Faulkner, Eudora Welty, and Flannery O'Connor to "Ellen Douglas," William Styron, Berry Morgan, and a good many others. The black literary explosion of the sixties and seventies has left many white critics in somewhat the same position as the protagonist of Alice Walker's "Her Sweet Jerome," who discovers under her bed a vast collection of revolutionary black books: "She looked with wonder at the books that were her husband's preoccupation, enraged [ed. note: substitute *amazed* or *delighted*] that the obvious was what she had never guessed before."*

* ". . . . after [Hughes and Wright] it becomes difficult to single out [black] stories which have survived the changes in the social and ethical climate in which they were produced. This scarcity of good Negro stories can perhaps be explained by the very gravity of the Negro situation in America during the postwar years, a seriousness which renders impossible the objectivity and maturity . . . necessary for the creation of literature as opposed to social commentary in fictional form." William Peden, *The American Short Story: Front Line in the National Defense of Literature*, 1964.

". . . the production of a vital Negro American literature is likely to be one of the major directions the short fiction of the next decade will take." *Ibid.*

Chapter 8

Of War and Peace and Other Matters

I. The Wars and the Short Story

WORLD WAR II was the most fully recorded disaster in the history of the world: miles of official records, tons of dispatches and news stories, truckloads of histories, biographies, and reminiscences of innumerable individuals ranging from chiefs of staff to cooks, stenographers, and mistresses of military personnel. Yet relatively few distinguished collections of short stories came out of it. To be sure, hundreds and hundreds of so-called "war" stories appeared in American magazines of the forties, the last great period of the mass-circulation family and pulp fiction magazines, but most of them were jerry-built pieces written according to a formula that satisfied a prosperous civilian populace's craving for fiction about characters and events "over there" or "overseas." This avalanche of mediocrity was little more than an opportunistic transformation of the pulp or slick fiction of the recent past. Military installations, theaters of operation, rest camps, and the like replaced the Western cattle town, the metropolitan apartment, or the athletic field. The sheriff or professional baseball player turned up in sergeant's stripes or lieutenant's bars; the golden-haired girl or the erring young housewife underwent similar transformations and emerged as WAC, WAVE, USO entertainer, or Rosie the Riveter. Almost buried in this quagmire, however, are many good stories and a small handful of notable collections. Still fewer followed Korea, and Vietnam has for the most part yet to be heard from in spite of the number of very good books of nonfiction and three or four first-rate novels about the most controversial war in American history.

The Long March by William Styron (1925-) was published in hardback in 1956 but originally appeared in *discovery* the preceding year. Classified as a novella rather than a novel, it seems to me the most important single piece of short fiction to come out of any of our three post-1940 wars. From its opening sentence — "One noon, in the blaze of a cloudless Carolina summer, what was left of eight dead boys lay strewn about the landscape, among the poison ivy and the pine needles and loblolly saplings" — to its final scene, it contains hardly a wasted syllable or a false move. Styron works surely and swiftly around a trio of conventional, indeed, stock, character types: a leather-minded, spit-and-polish career marine lieutenant colonel and two reserve officers, Lieutenant Culver ("almost thirty, he was old, and he was afraid") and a Captain Mannix ("a dark, heavy-set Jew from Brooklyn"), both combat veterans of World War II unwillingly called back to active duty in the early years of the Korean War.

About these three men and a thirty-six mile march involving the entire battalion, Styron has written a contemporary classic. Particularly notable is his characterization of Captain Mannix — "old great soft scarred bear of a man" — whose confrontation with Colonel Templeton has about it simultaneously the ring of an epic and the contemporary significance of a news bulletin. The last brief, powerful scene involving Culver, a defeated yet unvanquished Mannix ("naked . . . making his slow and agonized way down the hall"), and the unnamed Negro maid who comes miraculously to life with a few masterly brushstrokes (and by actual count only twenty-three words) is a triumph of understatement and illumination.

The best single collection of stories about World War II is *The Gallery* (1947), by John Horne Burns (1916–1953) if this powerful series of what the author terms "promenades" and "portraits" of American military personnel and Italian civilians whose lives cross in and around the Galleria Umberto in Naples during the late summer of 1944 can be called a collection of stories rather than a novel. John Burns was a major talent. He wrote with gusto, prodigality, and energy reminiscent of Thomas Wolfe's. Like Wolfe he was expert in recreating the essence of places and people; his pictures of wartime Casablanca and Algiers and Naples are unforgettable and, according to those who were there at approximately the same times, more real than any documentary ever could be. And Burns was a fine reporter with a great ear for dialogue and an attitude toward human misery compounded of skepticism, despair, and affection that reminds one, as do so many of the younger war writers, of Hemingway. But Burns was not just another talented young imitator. He was a fresh, powerful, and independent genius, and his early death, in Italy where he was working on a novel, was a disaster. *The Gallery,* as some contemporary book reviewers were quick to point out (and to overemphasize), is an uneven book. It is too sentimental toward the Italians, too repetitious in its concern with sex, too clinical in its description of, say, the one hundred and eighty hours in the life of an American sergeant confined to the venereal disease ward of a Naples hospital. All this is true, but only to a degree. *The Gallery* is a big book, big in concept and big in achievement, and as uncompromisingly realistic as a death certificate. Only rarely do its characters get bogged down in detail; the book is full of vitality and life, and rich in compassion and understanding.

If *The Gallery* is the best collection of short stories about World War II, *Tales of the South Pacific* (1947) by James Michener (1907–) is unquestionably the most popular; as best-selling book, musical drama, and motion picture it is one of the phenomena of recent entertainment history. Michener's popularity is understandable. He tells a tale well, whether it be a pleasantly gossipy anecdote about what happened to the zipper on Admiral Kester's trousers, a recollection of a conversation with the aged daughter of Fletcher Christian, or a more dramatic and traditionally plotted story like

"The Airstrip at Konora." Michener demands little of the reader; his stories are like a pleasant exchange between friends over cigars and brandy. He satisfies his readers' desire for apparently authentic information about the faraway places of romance, and gives them at the same time tidbits of information and legend or the stuff out of which legend is made. Perhaps central to his enormous popularity, however, is his flair for contemporaneity. The reader is constantly made aware that beneath the casual air, the relaxed method, and the ingratiating manner of the nice-guy narrator there are the faint pulsations of history in the making — Guadalcanal, the Coral Sea, the last great battles of the Navy Line. Tragedy and violence sometimes appear in *Tales of the South Pacific,* such as the death of Commander Hoag at the hands of a suicidal, "screaming, wild, disheveled" Japanese, "his eyes popping from his horrible head, this primitive indecent thing," but for the most part Michener paints a not unpleasant picture. His officers are "gentlemen all" and theirs is the kind of war about which a mother, daughter, wife, or fiancee might pray, if *he* has to go, let it be like this.

Next to *The Gallery, The Wolf That Fed Us* (1949) by Robert Lowry (1919–) seems to me the best short story collection directly concerned with World War II. The stories range in time from the beginning of the war to its aftermath; their settings include New York, San Francisco, El Paso, and Rome during the Allied Occupation. Collectively, they lack the total impact of *The Gallery* and the sweep and lyrical intensity of Burns's stories. But like Burns, Lowry is an expert reporter and a compassionate observer of people and places and events. At his best, as he is in "Layover in El Paso" or the title story, about American infantrymen in newly occupied Rome, Lowry captures the essence of characters at a specific time in history with an accurate understanding that more than compensates for his occasional repetition of mood and incident. The lonely wife of "Layover in El Paso," for example, is described in only two lines, and then immediately fades out of the story, never to reappear, but in those two lines she comes to life completely, both as an individual and as a type. "Who cares! says the lonely wife returning from visiting her husband for the last time before overseas duty. She holds hands with two soldiers she never saw before, and she has starry eyes and a short skirt, and helps kill a pint on the platform." In such stories the author's constant ability to suggest the universal in terms of the specific transcends reportage. Lowry's angry, sad, flea-bitten stories and their likable, often ingenuous men in and out of uniform are part of the history of our times.

Though none of the several collections of short stories by Irwin Shaw (1913–) is exclusively concerned with the war, his war stories are among his best known and most successful work. "Sailor off the Bremen" is an engrossing, if ideologically confusing, mixture of suspense, violence, and political commentary about a Nazi steward, a Communist deck officer, and two sharply contrasted American brothers. In "Gunner's Passage," perhaps Shaw's best story, three American enlisted men at an air force base in North Africa talk and think about their past experiences and what the future holds in store for them; it is a work eloquent in its simplicity and revealing in its understanding of uncomplicated men of good will in a world of violence. "Walking Wounded," a character study of the disintegration of a British officer confined to a desk job in Egypt after years of combat, was the first-prize winner in the 1944 *O. Henry Prize Stories.* "Act of Faith" is a kind of parable that contrasts racial intolerance and good will; it is the adroitly and often movingly told story of three American combat infantrymen, including a Jew who has just received from his father a terrifying letter concerning anti-Semitism in America. "The City Was in Total Darkness" pictures a successful novelist with prewar jitters, whose trip to Tijuana with a party girl is interrupted by the news that England has just declared war on Germany. "The Passion of Lance Corporal Hawkins" is a story of sadism and the persecution of the Jews, and in "Hamlets of the World" some French soldiers kill their commanding officer, whose fate suggests one aspect of the tragedy of modern France. Other Shaw stories concerned with war or its aftermath include "The Priest," "The Man with One Arm," "Medal from Jerusalem," "Preach the Dusty Roads," and "Tip on a Dead Jockey."

Although Shaw is a first-class journalist and a very skillful fiction writer, even some of his best stories, like "Act of Faith," seem overcontrived and overmanipulated when read in an emotional or sociological climate different from that in which they were written. Some later stories, collected in *Tip on a Dead Jockey* (1957), are a decided letdown, and Shaw's shortcomings — his contrivance and too-clever card-stacking — are more apparent now than they were when his fiction was concerned with the larger problems of international politics, war, and racial injustice.

J. D. Salinger's war stories are not concerned with war itself but with its effects upon participants and nonparticipants alike. "For Esmé — with Love and Squalor," "A Perfect Day for Bananafish," and "Uncle Wiggily in Connecticut" are contemporary classics. Each of these highly individualistic stories is concerned with a different kind of casualty of war: "Esmé," with its fresh and vivid characterizations of a precocious English girl whose father "was s-l-a-i-n in North Africa" and an American infantryman; "A Perfect Day," with its equally memorable portrait of the amiable and gentle Seymour Glass, the suicide who has become the dominant figure in Salinger's hierarchy of saints; and "Uncle Wiggily," with its civilian casualty, if the young mother whose lover had been killed during the war can be so designated. Each of these stories is alive with the warm-hearted sympathy and lightness of touch of Salinger at his very best, yet each beneath its surface is bleak and tragic. Few writers can manipulate these contrasts more adeptly than Salinger, just as few writers have been able to ring more successive changes on the recurring thesis, central to almost all of Salinger's work, both short and long, of the need for love and understanding, without which life becomes unbearable or meaningless — a "perfect day for bananafish," but not for human beings.

*

Of the short story collections by lesser-known writers, the best, far and away, is *Serenade to the Big Bird* (1952) by Bert Stiles (1920–1944). Somewhat reminiscent of William March's World War I classic, *Company K,* Stiles's *Serenade* is a series of terse, simple, and very moving sketches of combat and its effect on the narrator, together with the author's remembrances of the past with a "doll named August" and his hopes for the future. The death of this talented and likable young man while flying escort on a bombing raid in the autumn of 1944 was a tragedy in more ways than one.

There are other notable books about the war. The two novellas and five stories, highlighted by "Migdone" and "Deep Scout," of *A Hole in the Lead Apron* by Jesse Bier are concerned with World War II experiences in both the European and Pacific theaters of operation; *The Smoking Mountain: Stories of Postwar Germany* (1951) by Kay Boyle (1903–) is an effective blending of reportage and fiction, memorable because of the contrast between conqueror and conquered in an occupied country. Her *Thirty Stories* (1946) include several good pieces concerned with the prelude to World War II and the war itself; among them is "Defeat," the first-prize winner in the 1941 *O. Henry Memorial Award. A Role in Manila: Fifteen Tales of War, Postwar, Peace and Adventure* (1966) by Eugene Burdick (1918–1965) is a readable and knowledgeable collection by an author-journalist who died before reaching his full potential; two of the best are "Rest Camp at Maui" and "A Fine Figure of a Girl." *The Pistol* (1958) by James Jones (1921–) is a first rate novella beginning with the bombing of Pearl Harbor and following the actions of Pfc. Richard Mast through the early days of the war in the Pacific. *East by Southwest* (1944) by Christopher LaFarge (1897–1956) contains a poem and ten stories, slightly uneven but at their best moving and unpretentious, about American military personnel in a remote battle area in the South Pacific, which LaFarge covered as a correspondent for *Harper's. The Sons of Martha* (1967) by Richard McKenna (1914–1964) is based, like his novel *The Sand Pebbles,* upon his experiences during twenty-two years in the navy; it contains two very good stories, an interesting "chronicle of a walking tour" in Guam, three excerpts from an unfinished novel, and an extremely informative essay concerning the beginning of his writing career after he left the navy. *A Short Wait Between Trains* (1945) by Robert McLaughlin (1908–) comprises eighteen brief stories ranging in topic from basic training in Alabama ("Basic Soldier") to combat in New Guinea ("Unopposed Landing"); many are set in the United States and, like "Poor Everybody," are concerned with contrasts between military and civilian life. Tom Mayer's *The Weary Falcon* (1971) consists of five stories concerning the war in Vietnam by a former winner in *Story's* college contest who was a freelance correspondent in Vietnam. *A Corner of the World* (1946) by Robert Shaplen contains one short and four long stories, all preoccupied with the aftermath of war, involving Americans, Asiatics, and transplanted Europeans in the Far East.

Among the many good individual stories, some of them collected in books not primarily or solely concerned with war, some of them as yet uncollected, the following eleven are representative: Robert O. Bowen's "A Matter of Price," in *Marlow the Master and Other Stories* (1963); Laurence Critchell's "Flesh and Blood," the best "first" winner in the 1947 *O. Henry Memorial Awards;* Daniel Dodson's "The Let-Down," from *Story: The Magazine of the Short Story in Book Form,* Number One (1951); Harris Downey's "The Hunted," first-prize winner in the 1951 *O. Henry Memorial Awards;* William Faulkner's "Two Soldiers," reprinted in the 1942 *O. Henry Memorial Awards;* George Garrett's "The Old Army Game," in *Cold Ground Was My Bed Last Night* (1964); Martha Gellhorn's "Till Death Do Us Part," in *Two by Two* (1958); Ivan Gold's "Taub East," in *Nickel Miseries* (1963); Edward Loomis' "Friendship," in *Heroic Love* (1960); Robie Macauley's "The Mind Is Its Own Place," in *The End of Pity and Other Stories* (1957); Vern Sneider's "A Pail of Oysters," in *A Long Way from Home and Other Stories* (1956).

The best of these war stories are concerned more with the effects of war upon the individual participants than on acts of war in themselves; at their best, they are characterized by a depth of emotion and a need to communicate, as if to reassert the importance of the individual at a time when individuals were being engulfed or destroyed in the sweep of great events.

II. *"The Woods Are Full of Regional Writers"**

Except for Poe's stories, which usually take place in a nebulous region "out of Space" and "out of Time," the American short story has tended to be firmly rooted in specific place — whether place, setting, and background are essentially a stage where the action of a story occurred, or imply the preoccupation with locale of so many of the mid-nineteenth-century regionalists, or involve the more contemporary concept of place as a moral-sociological-cultural reality. Today, more than a century after Bret Harte's gamblers with consciences and prostitutes with hearts of gold began what was to become the craze for the local color–dialect story, regionalism has become almost a dirty word, frequently associated with parochialism, shallowness, and mediocrity. Or, as with the fictions of the "innovationists" of the mid-sixties and seventies, place and setting have been either minimized or rejected.

In the South, Flannery O'Connor commented:

> there are more amateur writers than there are rivers and streams. In almost every hamlet you'll find at least one lady writing epics in Negro dialect, and probably two or three old gentlemen who have impossible historical novels on the way. The woods are full of regional writers, and it is the great horror of every serious Southern writer that he will become one of them.

And Eudora Welty wrote:

> "Regionalism," I think, is a careless term, as well as a condescending one, because what it does is fail to differentiate between the localized raw material of life and its outcome as art. "Regional" is an outsider's term; it has no meaning for the insider who is doing the writing.

* Flannery O'Connor, "The Fiction Writer and His Country," *The Living Novel* (Granville Hicks, ed.).

The adult fiction writer of the last half-century increasingly tried to avoid the tricks and affectations of the run-of-the-mill local color story of the past with its one-dimensional actors and its hand-tinted settings labeled the Missouri Bootheel, a Mississippi plantation, or the California desert. He intentionally neglected the landscape and the details of local or sectional dialect, customs, and manners for their own sakes; instead, he attempted to suggest that which is universal in the specific, that which is archetypal in the individual in terms of heredity, environment, and things as they are.

In this sense regionalism, or what can more properly be called the sense of place, is not mere embroidery or decoration to be added to a story as one hangs ornaments on a Christmas tree; it is a basic and indispensable element, as important or in some cases more important than character, situation, or idea. It is both a seminal force and a unifying element, which can shape a work of fiction and give the fullest extent of meaning and drama and vitality to the characters and events within it. It is something, again in Eudora Welty's words, upon which "fiction depends for its life . . . as essential to good and honest writings as a logical mind."

The New South is the region that has produced the recent body of short fiction most likely to endure, stories so varied and individualistic as to render useless such academic labels as the "Southern School" of writers, and so universal in their implications as to negate the appellation of "distinctly regional literature." The reasons underlying the Southern literary renascence have been widely analyzed, commented on, and theorized about: a sense of guilt because of the institution of slavery; a sense of outrage because of the indignities the South suffered during the occupation and Reconstruction; the glorification of "the lost cause" and the way of life that died with it; the conflicts between an agrarian and a commercialized society and the impact of a new working class; a heightened awareness of disintegration and change, and the resultant search for identity and self-justification in a region of decaying loyalties, values, and life styles.

Whatever the reasons, it is not happenstance that many of the most significant recent fiction writers whose work is very closely identified with their region, their "country," are Southerners. Nor is it accident that the work of the greatest American short story writer of the past half-century, William Faulkner, is as securely rooted in place as are the stories of perhaps the greatest of nineteenth-century "regionalists" — how absurd the term becomes — Nathaniel Hawthorne.

The short fiction of Eudora Welty (1909–) — like that of Faulkner, Katherine Anne Porter, and Erskine Caldwell, who belong essentially to the period prior to that discussed in this book although all of them continued to write short fiction after 1940 — is the work of a rare and original talent. *A Curtain of Green* (1941), *The Wide Net* (1943), *The Golden Apples* (1949), *The Ponder Heart* (1954), and *The Bride of the Innisfallen and Other Stories* (1955) are permanent contributions to the literature of the American short story. Mississippi furnishes both subject and theme of most of her stories but her range and variety are remarkable, embracing gentle comedy and grim satire, the grotesque and the ordinary, the technically straightforward and the elaborately indirect, implicational, and allusive.

In her perceptive and appreciative introduction to *A Curtain of Green*, Katherine Anne Porter has commented on some of the paradoxes and contrasts of Welty's first stories, contrasts that were to reappear in almost all of her later fiction. Perhaps the most significant of these is the contrast between the simplicity of the author's narrative method and the complexity and ambiguity of her themes and moods. "A Piece of News," one of her best and more frequently anthologized stories, is representative of her work. Almost stark in its external simplicity, the story concerns a few moments in the lives of Ruby Fisher and her bootlegger husband, Clyde. A simple rural girl, Ruby returns to her cabin at the beginning of the story and reads in a newspaper an account of the shooting of a woman who is also named Ruby Fisher. She is shocked, pleased, eventually excited. She fancies herself dying, bedecked in "a brand-new nightgown, her heart . . . hurting with every beat, many times more than her toughened skin when Clyde slapped at her." When Clyde returns to the cabin she is sensuously attracted to him; she "gently" prepares his meal, standing almost tiptoe on "bare, warm feet," like a priestess performing a ritual. The coincidence of the newspaper story and her identification with the other Ruby Fisher have made her more intuitively aware of her own being than she has ever been before; the unromantic facts of her drab life have been imperceptibly changed, and Ruby at the conclusion of the story is not quite the same as Ruby at the beginning, and whether she will ever be quite the same is doubtful.

Beneath the surface simplicity of this and other such stories, Welty probes the enigma of human personality and suggests the depths of individual identity. Human "relationship," she once commented, "*is* a pervading and changing mystery." Her early — and it seems to me with only a few exceptions her best — stories are fictional explorations into the nature of this mystery. There have been scarcely any more impressive recent collections of short fiction than *A Curtain of Green*. "Petrified Man," "A Worn Path," "Death of A Travelling Salesman," "Keela, the Outcast Indian Maiden," "Old Mr. Marblehall," "Powerhouse"; so familiar, so good, so varied!

The Wide Net is almost as good: "Livvie," "At the Landing," the title story, and two or three others are among Welty's best work. *The Golden Apples,* however, in terms solely of personal preference, is something of a letdown. Though certain individual episodes are delightful, her people, including her Jovian King Mac-Lain, and the forty years of incidents and events in the author's mythical Morgana, Mississippi, become blurred and faded, and the collection, anticipating as it does so many of the flights into myth of the innovativionists of the mid-sixties, seems to me more important historically than it is for its literary and imaginative qualities per se.

Similarly the seven long and short stories of *The Bride of the Innisfallen* seem to lack the power, the intensity, and the memorableness of *A Curtain of Green* and *The Wide Net*. The variety is impressive: the Gothic War-Between-the-States piece, "The Burning"; "Ladies In the Spring," very nice Welty indeed, with its fine portrayals of the boy Dewey and Miss Hattie the post office lady praying for rain; "Kin," a conventional but effective version of the visit-to-the-old-homeplace theme; and "No Place for You, My Love," about a Yankee couple beginning — or ending — an affair at Galatoire's. But the title story and "Circe" and "Going to Naples" seem to me to lack the force and insight of her earlier work.

Not so *The Ponder Heart,* a masterpiece in miniature, a superb tour de force about Uncle Daniel Ponder, "rich as Croesus," splendid in white suit and pretty red bow tie, and Bonnie Dee, no-account little white trash he had picked up in the dime store and married. Did Uncle Daniel knowingly murder Bonnie Dee, or had he just been playing "creep-mousie" with her that fateful afternoon when the ball of fire rolled across the parlor of the old Ponder Place? Or had she dropped dead of a heart attack? The author, working with tantalizing ambiguity, does not answer these questions: she leaves the last words unsaid, the action unconsummated. Never, it seems to me, has she been more sure of herself than in this novella about the town of Clay and its leading citizen, Uncle Daniel Ponder.

The "interior world," Eudora Welty has commented, is "endlessly new, mysterious, and alluring." It is this sense of unending interest and wonderment in people that is common to her varied and often enigmatic fictions and their concern with basic and universal verities, love and loneliness, joy and sorrow, life and death.

The most undervalued good Southern short story writer I know of is the late John Bell Clayton (1906–1955), whose posthumous *The Strangers Were There* (1957) deserves to be widely read. Though he lived in California following his retirement from the Charlottesville *Progress* in 1946, Clayton's stories are as Virginian as Joyce's are Irish. They are as deeply rooted in place as Joyce's; they are as universal as Joyce's in their implications. All of them have a common setting, the small fictional city of Colonial Springs and its

surrounding country, which is very closely patterned after Charlottesville and Albemarle County where Clayton attended the University of Virginia and lived most of his life. The place and its
people are keenly observed: the white-columned mansions of the
Yankee millionaires; the foul-smelling back streets of the paregoric
drinkers and the red-lipped girls from the wrong side of the tracks;
the courthouse square with its heroic statue of General Lee; the
Negro district, Jug Hill, exploding into manic activity every Saturday night; the hills and the hollows of the hunters and the mountain men, awkward and ill at ease in town but, in their blue hills
and walking softly with dog and gun, having about them an inefface-
able dignity and strength. Clayton was passionately interested in
people, as any writer worthy of the name must be — the unsung
but not insignificant little people who are everywhere and who are
the heart and soul of a region or a way of life: people like gentle
Uncle Gene McCantland, who kills the intruder who had murdered his dog; or the violent Gatemyers and Lowhatters and their
feudin'; or Antietam Blankenship, who looked like a bird and had
his moment of greatness the day the highway froze over in Cherry
Glen.

The narrator of several of these stories, a newspaperman in
Colonial Springs, prays for "that most improbable of all miracles:
that I be permitted to see clearly." John Bell Clayton did learn
to see things clearly, to see them steadily and see them whole,
and to record them with sensitivity and insight, humor and compassion, affection and indignation. "It is my native land and I
love it," the journalist-narrator reflects after being witness to the
slaying of two Negroes by a sheriff's deputy, "but there are times
when I hate it."

For readers unfamiliar with Clayton's work, the range of his
mood and method can be suggested by such pieces as "The White
Circle," "Snowfall on Fourth Street," "The Silence of the Moun-
tains," "The Summer of the Insistent Voices," and "The Man Who
Looked Like A Bird."

*

Several of the most important recent Southern short story writers have been discussed in preceding chapters. Apart from them, some of the best writers of short fiction have come out of the Middle South, including Caroline Gordon (1895–), whose best stories, "The Captive," "The Forest of the South," "The Ice House," and "Her Quaint Honor" from *The Forest of the South* (1946) and *Old Red and Other Stories* (1963), have about them the ring of permanence. And there is Jesse Stuart (1907–), certainly the most prolific short story writer of the region, whose many, many collections — in a recent radio interview he claimed authorship of over five hundred stories — are written in a fresh, strong voice. Stuart is a good storyteller whose tales have the quality of oral narrative at its best — quick moving, vibrantly alive — and his humor, sincerity, and affectionate understanding of the Kentucky hill country and its people are a refreshing antidote to the groanings and lamentations of so many of the metropolitan Jeremiahs.

So too are the equally vigorous stories of life among the Florida Crackers, collected in *When the Whippoorwill* (1940) by Marjorie Kinnan Rawlings (1896–1953). Some appeared in an earlier novella, "Jacob's Ladder," which was printed originally in *Scribner's* magazine in 1931 and in book form several years later. Another fine writer out of Florida by way of South Carolina is George Garrett (1929–) poet, novelist, critic, and author of five collections of short fiction, *King of the Mountain* (1957), *In the Briar Patch* (1961), *Cold Ground Was My Bed Last Night* (1964), *A Wreath for Garibaldi* (1969), containing for the most part previously collected stories, and three novellas, *The Magic Striptease* (1973). Garrett's four collections of short fiction and a volume of novellas are as diversified as is his work in general; some of his best pieces, from the title story and "The Rivals" of his earliest collection to the title novella of *Cold Ground,* are set in Florida, but Garrett is equally at home in a variety of places and modes. Among other things he is a very deft humorist — see "Man Without a Figleaf" — and fantasist — as he is in "The Magic Striptease" — with an Elizabethan gusto and love of language.

Representative collections from Georgia include Donald Windham's *The Warm Country* (1962) and *Emblems of Conduct* (1963) and Mark Steadman's *McAfee Country* (1971); and the Carolinas have produced more than their share of good short stories from the work of older writers like James Boyd's *Old Pines and Other Stories* (1952) and Paul Green's *Salvation on String* (1946) and *Dog on the Sun* (1949) to more recent collections, including Frances Gray Patton's *The Finer Things in Life* (1951) and Reynolds Price's *The Names and Faces of Heroes* (1963) and *Permanent Errors* (1970). Particularly notable are the three collections of Doris Betts (1932–), *The Gentle Insurrection* (1954), *The Astronomer and Other Stories* (1965), and *Beasts of the Southern Wild* (1973), a National Book Award nominee. Rural or small-town Piedmont people undergoing relatively unexceptional experiences are the subjects of most of Betts's stories: a homely girl on a bus, a hitchhiker with a hangover, a young woman having a baby or bringing a father home from hospital to die of cancer. She writes with controlled power and insight and points out the significant in the commonplace with unsentimentalized simplicity.

Other notable work includes Robert Penn Warren's *The Circus in the Attic* (1948); James Still's *In Troublesome Creek* (1941), which could be claimed by Kentucky where it is set or by Alabama where the author was born and raised; Thomas Mabry's stories of Middle Tennessee's "Black Patch," which with Ward Dorrance's stories of Missouri's Little Dixie constitute *The White Hound* (1960); Dorrance's fine novella *A Man About the House* (1972); Andrew Lytle's *A Novel, Novella, and Four Stories* (1958); Jesse Hill Ford's *Fishes, Birds, and Sons of Men* (1967); David Madden's *The Shadow Knows* (1970); and Hollis Summers' *How They Chose the Dead* (1973). Arkansas's Thyra Samter Winslow belongs to the period preceding that covered by this study although her last short story collection, *The Sex Without Sentiment,* was not published till 1954. Story collections from the Deep South include Shelby Foote's *Jordan County* (1963), Charles East's *Where the Music Was* (1966), Cecil Dawkins' *The Quiet Enemy* (1963), Robert Canzoneri's *Barbed Wire and Other Stories*

(1970), "Ellen Douglas'" *Black Cloud, White Cloud* (1963), Shirley Ann Grau's *The Black Prince* (1954) and *The Wind Shifting West* (1973), Peter Feibleman's *Strangers and Graves* (1966), John William Corrington's *The Lonesome Traveler* (1968), and Berry Morgan's *The Mystic Adventures of Roxie Stoner* (1974).

As much Middle South as Southwest are some of the best stories of three Texas-born writers, Katherine Anne Porter and William Goyen, who have been discussed in earlier chapters, and William Humphrey, author of *The Last Husband and Other Stories* (1953) and *A Time and a Place: Stories from the Red River Country* (1965). Oliver La Farge's *A Pause in the Desert* (1957) and Fray Angelico Chavez' *From an Altar Screen* (1957) represent two quite different kinds of short fiction, each in its way admirable, from New Mexico; even more important are the stories of two other first-generation South-westerners, William Eastlake's *Portrait of an Artist with Twenty-Six Horses* (1965), perhaps the most important single collection to come out of the Southwest in recent years, and Paul Horgan's *The Peach-stone: Stories from Four Decades* (1967). Max Evans' *The One-Eyed Sky* (1963) was an impressive "first" collection.

Notable stories from the Far West or the West Coast include *The Watchful Gods* (1950) by Walter VanTilburg Clark (1909–) and the many collections of William Saroyan (1908–), among them *My Name Is Aram* (1940), *Dear Baby* (1945), and *The Assyrian and Other Stories* (1956). The best of Clark's stories, like "The Winds and Snows of Winter," are richly textured and thought-provoking, ad-mirable in their remarkable evocation of place. Saroyan has been around so long and is so prolific that one forgets the importance of his contribution to the American short story; his first and best-known collection, *The Daring Young Man on the Flying Trapeze* (1934), brought to the short story a freshness of vision, simplicity, gaiety, and sympathetic understanding of little people at a time when the genre was becoming enmired in an angry social conscious-ness or basically meaningless slice-of-life realism. In spite of whimsy, repetitiveness, and self-imitation, Saroyan's stories are part of the permanent literature of the American short story, and his "country" — particularly San Francisco, Fresno, and their environs — is as real in its way as Faulkner's Mississippi. Particularly effective is Saroyan's depiction of childhood and adolescence; stories like "The Fifty-Yard Dash," "The Parsley Garden," "The Home of the Human Race" and "Winter Vineyard Workers" are little classics, which have about them the warmth of an August afternoon with the scent of ripening fruit in the air.

Other good collections out of the West are H. L. Davis' Oregon stories, *Team Bells Woke Me* (1953), and *Love and Death* (1959) by Vardis Fisher. The latter includes the unforgettable "The Scarecrow" and other Idaho stories, which deserve to be better known. *The Big It* (1960) by A. B. Guthrie (1901–) contains deftly written tales, narrative sketches, and stories, some humorous and others serious, re-creating the American West from early in the nineteenth to the middle of our own century. The best stories of Edward Loomis' *Heroic Love* (1960), and *The Women on the Wall* (1950) and *The City of the Living* (1956) by Wallace Stegner (1909–) owe a good deal of their effectiveness to place and setting, as do the stories and personal reminiscences of Mormon life in Utah by Virginia Sorenson (1912–) in *Where Nothing Is Long Ago* (1963).

Important collections of short fiction from the Middle West include the quietly realistic and often deeply moving stories of rural and small-town life in Iowa by Ruth Suckow (1892–1960); they are characterized by unpretentious artistry and admirable understanding. Except for *Some Others and Myself* (1952), however, her short stories belong to the twenties and thirties. Many fine stories by Willa Cather (1837–1947), aside from *The Old Beauty and Others*, published posthumously in 1948, also belong to an earlier period (beginning with *The Troll Garden* [1905]). Missouri's Josephine Johnson (1910–), a 1935 Pulitzer Prize-winning novelist when she was only twenty-four, has two fine collections, *Winter Orchard* (1936) and *The Sorcerer's Son and Other Stories* (1965). Jessamyn West (1907–) has written deftly and sympathetically of an Indiana Quaker community in *The Friendly Persuasion* (1945) and equally effectively in *Love, Death, and the Ladies' Drill Team* (1955). *Wind-*

wagon Smith and Other Yarns (1947) by Wilbur Schramm (1907–) are tall tales filled with affection for the American frontier past and the fat dark earth of the Iowa farmlands. And prolific August Derleth (1909–) — he has published some eleven collections, to say nothing of about fifty novels — writes with similar distinction about his native Wisconsin.

R. V. Cassill (1913–) seems to me one of the best of the more recent writers from the Middle West. His short stories collected in *Fifteen by Three* (along with work by James B. Hall and Herbert Gold [1957]), *The Father* (1965), and *The Happy Marriage* (1965) are extremely varied in subject, mood, and setting, ranging from Iowa to New York City to New England. Among my favorites are "The Father," "The Biggest Band," and "The Prize," all set in Iowa and involving such subjects as a young boy's craving to catch a glimpse of fan-dancer Sally Rand at a fair and an unsentimentalized but affectionate family portrait involving another boy's efforts to win a contest during the early years of the Depression. *In the Heart of the Heart of the Country* (1968) by South Dakota's William H. Gass (1924–) captures the essence, it has been said, of various aspects of the life of the Middle West; in the title piece and "The Pederson Kid" region is not just setting but protagonist; Ohio's Jack Matthews' portrayals of mid-America, in *Bitter Knowledge* (1964), are equally effective. *The Angel and the Sailor* (1957) by Calvin Kentfield contains several good stories, including the title story, of life in small-town or rural Iowa; only "Windmills" and "Rose of Sharon" in his *The Great Wandering Goony Bird* (1963) have a specifically Middle Western setting. Evan S. Connell, Jr. (1924–), has two fine and varied collections, *The Anatomy Lesson and Other Stories* (1957) and *At the Crossroads* (1965); "The Beau Monde of Mrs. Bridge," from his earlier collection, introduces the heroine of his excellent novel, *Mrs. Bridge*. *Reapers of the Dust: A Prairie Chronicle* (1964) by Lois Phillips Hudson consists of effective low-keyed stories and sketches about South Dakota during what the author calls "our terrible 'Thirties and our terrible, heartbreaking migrations."

Nelson Algren (1909–) and James T. Farrell (1904–) are the

outstanding big-city spokesmen from the Middle West. The Chicago of Algren's *Neon Wilderness* (1948) and of Farrell's many collections have become so specifically their "country," particularly Farrell's, that today it is almost impossible to stop at the corner of Prairie Avenue and Fifty-eighth Street without thinking of Studs Lonigan and his disreputable peers, including the indefatigable Weary Reilly and the dogged Danny O'Neill.

The best and best known of Algren's individualistic stories of first- and second-generation Americans in the jungles of Chicago's west side include "A Bottle of Milk for Mother" and "How the Devil Came Down Division Street" and are close in spirit to the proletarian fiction of the thirties but far superior to the mass of "prole" literature; nothing in his second collection, *The Last Carousel* (1973), equals them and two or three other *Neon Wilderness* pieces in intensity and memorableness. Farrell, like Saroyan, has been around so long and has continued to be so prolific that one may underestimate the importance of his total contribution: fourteen volumes of stories, the most recent of which, *Judith* (1973), is considerably more varied than — and artistically superior to — some of his earliest collections.

Some of the best collections of stories from or about New England are the work of authors who have been discussed in previous chapters: Nancy Hale, John Cheever, and Louis Auchincloss, for example. The quietly effective Vermont stories by Dorothy Canfield Fisher (1879–1958) (in a preface to her most comprehensive collection she admits to *having* written a few set "outside of Vermont"), collected in *Four-Square* (1949) and *A Harvest of Stories from a Half Century of Writing* (1956), belong for the most part to an earlier period, as do the extremely competent and entertaining Maine stories by Ben Ames Williams (1889–1953) — he wrote almost a hundred of these and more than half originally appeared in the *Saturday Evening Post* — sixteen of which were collected in *Fraternity Village* (1949). Some of the best stories of *A High New House* (1963) by Thomas Williams (1926–) owe much of their impact to a skillfully drawn New Hampshire setting. Among uncollected stories, far and away the best I have read is Lawrence Sargent Hall's "The Ledge," a gripping, almost classic narrative of the destruction of a New England fisherman marooned with his son and nephew on a wind-swept, tide-threatened ledge.

Of the many collections with other than North American settings, one of the best and certainly the most interesting historically is *A Night Visitor and Other Stories* (1966) by B. Traven (1890–1969). For years a man of mystery who spent most of his life in Mexico, steadfastly refused interviews, and was internationally famous before being recognized in the States primarily for his early novel *The Treasure of the Sierra Madre* (via the film), Traven was at various times identified as the sister of Mexican President López Mateos, as an active Wobbly who was expelled from the United States in the 1918–19 witchhunts, as the German pamphleteer-philosopher Ret Marut, and so on. He was born Traven Torsvan in Chicago in 1890 of Norwegian-Swedish immigrant parents, and after experiences as a teen-aged cabin boy first visited Mexico in 1913. In 1920 he took up residence there and in the middle twenties began what was to become a distinguished literary career.

Mexico and her people, particularly the oppressed Indians, furnished subject and theme for Traven's many novels and short stories, several of which have not yet been published in the United States. If *A Night Visitor and Other Stories* is at all characteristic, Traven was one of the major short fiction writers of recent years. With its excellent introduction by Charles Miller, *A Night Visitor* is one of the books no one interested in short fiction should miss; particularly good are the title story, "The Cattle Drive," and "Conversion of Some Indians."

Other notable or representative collections include John Berry's *Flight of White Crows* (1961), stories and tales, all but one of which are set in India; Pearl Buck's *Far and Near: Stories of Japan, China, and America* (1947) and *Fourteen Stories* (1961); Paul Theroux's *Sinning with Annie* (1972), about wheelers and dealers in Africa, India, and Russia; Charles Edward Eaton's *Write Me from Rio* (1959) and *The Girl From Ipenema* (1973). Also of interest are Eugene Burdick's

The Blue of Capricorn (1961), a collection of stories and essays about people and places in the Pacific, as much ethnological, historical, and anthropological as fictional, as is James Michener's *Return to Paradise* (1951); Robin White's *Foreign Soil: Tales of South India* (1962); and Robert Murphy's *The Phantom Setter and Other Stories* (1966), particularly the Baffin Island pieces. The most important collections with the possible exception of *The Night Visitor* are Polish-born Jerzy Kosinski's powerful National Book Award winner *Steps* (1968), Vladmir Nabokov's *Nabokov's Dozen* (1968). ("I think of myself," Nabokov said in a 1966 interview, "as an American citizen who had once been a Russian one.") Massachusetts-born Mary Lavin's *Selected Stories* (1959) is one of her many collections concerned mostly with Ireland where she has lived, with only occasional exceptions, since childhood.

The quality of life in a small town, rural community, or country as opposed to the corrupting influence of metropolitan life is one of the most striking contrasts of much recent short fiction. In some stories, such as Oliver La Farge's "A Pause in the Desert" or Edward Loomis' "Mustangs," this contrast is specifically, almost didactically, spelled out, but for the most part the comparison is implicit in situation and character. This is not to suggest that the story set in small town, prairie, desert, hill or mountain country presents a rose-tinted picture of contemporary life. Tragedy and violence are as much a part of Eudora Welty's Mississippi as they are of Farrell's Chicago, but the deathly sickness of modern metropolitan life, which has engrossed so many major fiction writers since Joyce, has little counterpart in the writers who have fled or never lived in the New Yorks, Trentons, and Chicagos of America. The fiction of many of the big-city writers is essentially joyless; it shows life as meaningless, degrading, or both. Farrell's harlots, for example, drag their creaking bones wearily along dimly lit streets; sensitive youths dream in boyhood and are disillusioned in manhood; love turns to ashes and hope to gloom; and the individual disintegrates in an atmosphere of spiritual poverty and economic injustice. Or, as it is depicted by some of the most doleful of city prophets such as Leslie Fiedler, life itself has become a suppurating wound or an insult. By contrast, the work of writers like Saroyan or Faulkner or Clayton is full of fresh air and sunlight, quick with the challenge of life, whether that challenge end in triumph, disaster, or compromise. In the final analysis, such writers present a more true and, it seems to me, a more realistic picture of life than do their big city cousins. The feeling for place, the love of the land that gives a sense of permanence to life even in a dark age, is not rhetoric or boozy sentimentality or escapism. Anachronistic or unthinkable in the work of an Albert Maltz, it is a living truth in that of a Jesse Stuart:

> It is our land after all and you never hear one of us speak against it when we are away. We tell you that it is our land, that we are a part of it . . . the good clean wind of a Kentucky spring . . . the silking corn and . . . the cries of the wild birds . . . and we show you that we cannot escape it no matter how cruel or how kind it has been to us. How can we be contented among a multitude of strangers and many tongues?

III. Spaceships, Aliens, and Bug-Eyed Monsters

What some of its recent admirers have termed the Golden Age of science fiction began somewhere around 1940, for reasons that apparently even the experts are hard put to explain, although World War II unquestionably seems to have primed the pump. When almost every American family was in one way or another affected by the war, science fiction offered a ready avenue of escape from worry, stress, and tensions. At the same time, science fiction's blending of startling adventures and scientific or pseudo-scientific materials helped to satisfy a reading public whose appetites were being stimulated by daily newspaper and radio reports of almost unbelievable advances in science and technology.

Whatever the reasons for its rebirth, the short story of science fiction, and of its often degenerate cousin, fantasy, continues to be one of the most controversial fictional forms of recent years, a genre that almost inevitably evokes strongly partisan opinions. To criticize s.f. adversely is to elicit cries of "snob" or "square" from the faithful; to profess to admire it is to provoke head-shaking among most intellectuals. But if the science fiction of the last thirty years is not the treasure house created by master spirits that some of its admirers claim it to be (for example, Raymond H. Healy and J. Francis McComas' introduction to *Famous Science-Fiction Stories* [1957]), neither is it the subliterature that some of its critics have labeled it.

Following the era of the great pioneers, Jules Verne and H. G. Wells, and the brief revivals of the twenties and thirties, high-lighted by the founding of Hugo Gernsback's *Amazing Stories* in 1926 and John Campbell's *Astounding Stories* a little over a decade later, science fiction deteriorated in quantity and quality. By the end of the thirties, there were only five science-fiction magazines in America, as contrasted to more than four times that number three years later, and even the most dedicated admirers of spaceships, moon maids, and mad scientists were forced to admit that s.f. had become a combination of "science that was claptrap and fiction that was graceless and dull." After these doldrums, however, more recent or relatively recent writers of ability and in some cases genuine talent turned to science fiction; Anthony Boucher's *Fantasy and Science Fiction* and H. L. Gold's *Galaxy,* both founded in the early fifties, are said to have played influential roles in this new revival.

Since then s.f. has been booming, and though some critics like Arthur Jean Cox believe that it is on the verge of exhausting the limited number of possibilities remaining to be explored, its devotees feel that s.f. is only now about to seek and find its proper role in contemporary fiction. A knowledgeable buff and former student of mine, Creath Thorne, tells me that in the early sixties s.f. entered another "new and vigorous stage" marked by writers like Philip Dick, whose "remarkable books" examined the nature of reality, or Roger Zelazny and Samuel Delany, who emerged with "brilliant first stories." His comments are echoed by editors of various recent collections of the new science fiction. Among them is Robert Silverberg, who says in a good introduction to *New Dimensions I: Fourteen Original Science Fiction Stories* (1971): " . . . the past few years have been ones of unusual flux and ferment" for s.f., and a new generation is on the scene "whose tastes were formed not by *Thrilling Wonder Stories* but by Joyce, Fitzgerald, Hemingway, Kafka, and Mann."

I hope he is right, but I have yet to find a recent — say within the last decade — American writer of science fiction whose work approximates the likes of England's J. G. Ballard or that of several other younger English writers. I should pause here to say that I was an s.f. buff from the warm summer afternoons of a remote past when I and a couple of my boyhood friends argued the comparative merits of T. S. Stribling's "The Green Splotches" and Wells's "The Island of Dr. Moreau," and awaited the arrival of the new *Amazing Stories Annual* while loafing beneath the tall wild cherry trees bordering the kitchen-and-flower-gardens of my parents' place. I've logged in hundreds, perhaps thousands, of s.f. stories in my time, not a very remarkable feat when one realizes how alarmingly prolific most of the big names in s.f. are. But I began to lose interest in the form in the early sixties, so for the post-1960 period I have to rely primarily on the comments and generalizations of others, except to add that, although the magazines and periodicals devoted exclusively to s.f. have again dwindled as they did in the late thirties, the opposite certainly seems to be true of paperback and hard-cover originals and anthologies, which seem to be given more and more space in just about every bookstore or public library I have visited in the last five or six years, both in England and the United States. This, certainly, is a hopeful sign.

My own favorites — based for the most part on that relatively small pre-1965 sampling — are, I confess with sadness, conventional. They include, as might be expected, Ray Bradbury (1920–), the best known of all American writers in the field and, as far as I know, the only one to receive anything that approximates serious critical attention. Bradbury seems to me far and away the most consistently entertaining performer in the field, a formidable craftsman with a quick, alert mind and a sense of drama. Even Bradbury's less successful stories are usually free of the stylistic infelicities, the pseudoscientific or pseudotechnological jargon, and the stereotyped characters and situations of so much recent science fiction. Among the others Isaac Asimov seems both the most engaging and the most literate; like his British counterpart, Arthur C. Clarke, and like Bradbury, Asimov not only tells an engaging, frequently arresting story, but tells it well. Again like Clarke, he is a man of standing in his own professional field — he is a biochemist in the Boston University School of Medicine — and perhaps because of this his stories are not overburdened or clogged with the pseudoscientific-technological-sociological-historical flubdub and flummery, which is the hallmark of much second-rate s.f.

Then there are Robert Heinlein, considered by some the "greatest of the giants," whether writing under his own name or his pseudonym, Anson MacDonald; Robert Sheckley, s.f.'s "premier gadfly"; Frederik Pohl, who has been labeled the "most consistently able" recent writer of science fiction in America; and Clifford Simak, a "kind of science-fiction poet laureate of the countryside." Richard Matheson is a versatile performer and author of what seems to me the best recent American novel in the field, *I Am Legend;* he, Cyril Kornbluth, A. E. Van Vogt, Harlan Ellison, James Blish, Alfred Bester, Fredric Brown, Hal Clement, Avram Davidson, and Theodore Sturgeon possess individuality and insight and narrative skill, which sets them apart, as I read them, from the mass.

In spite of the s.f. writer's laments that his markets are drying up. or his groans at not receiving his just acclaim, he has really, it seems to me, had things pretty good during the last few years. But like the blind dog let loose in the butcher's shop, he has tried to gobble up too much too quickly, and in his own greediness has often perverted or debased what is potentially one of the most challenging and exciting literary forms of our times. The virtues inherent in s.f. are as conspicuous as the weaknesses of many of its practitioners, but s.f.'s shortcomings have been more widely commented upon than its strengths. One hardly need mention that the science fiction of yesterday has proved to be today's science; it seems reasonable to assume that some of today's science fiction is likely to be tomorrow's science. Quite apart from his ability to make, at times, almost uncanny prophecies or lucky guesses, the writer of s.f. possesses other very real assets, not the least of which is the fact that he is usually a cunning artisan who tells an engrossing story that quickly captures and maintains reader interest; his concerns are large, his subjects and themes often variations of universal or archetypal fictional materials. Space travel, for example, until recently the most popular and most frequently written about science-fiction subject but a virtual taboo since our lunar landing, has fascinated mankind since the Greeks. Similarly universal is the concept of the inspired, mad, or eccentric scientist or intellectual — Prometheus, Prospero, Faust — who with his beautiful daughter or fiancée or lab assistant appears in the s.f. or fantasy stories of the period. Equally appealing were the stories of the menace of "aliens" — the trade term for any reasoning individual or creature originating beyond the earth — or stories of cataclysmic threats to mankind in the form of monsters — B-E-M's (bug-eyed monsters) — or changes in the earth precipitated by threat from without or overzealous scientific experimentation from within. These and other favorite s.f. subjects and themes are in many ways the contemporary offspring of such diverse literary ancestors as the epic (one thinks, for example, of *Beowulf*, with its own brand of bug-eyed monsters, Grendel and his mother) or the fairy tale, preoccupied with the grotesque, the horrible, and the supernatural. Such materials, so important to science fiction, apparently will continue to appeal to any generation of readers able and willing to indulge, with Coleridge, in the luxurious necessity of the willing suspension of disbelief. At the same time, more recent practitioners have become increasingly taken with ideas — breakthroughs in genetics, for example, rather than the "old-fashioned stuff." Others produce a less desirable mingling of what is now standard X-rated movie porno with more conventional s.f., pure corn, and vulgar corn at that, if the few I have read are typical.

It is scarcely necessary to add that some of the progenitors of today's science fiction have found in the fantastic tale or the scientific spoof a vehicle for the most serious satire. Perhaps no body of contemporary literature is more concerned with the moral and practical dangers of overgrown technology than is science fiction. On the hide of an age in which technological progress has first overshadowed and ultimately threatened to engulf or destroy the individual, science fiction has been an angrily buzzing wasp. At its best, s.f.'s wide-eyed interest and often uncritical admiration for the scientist are capable of being illuminated by a genuine concern for individual man and the dangers that confront him when "progress" becomes more important than reason.

On the other hand, in spite of its potentialities, science fiction in recent years has stumbled as much as it has walked. Its most appalling defect, it seems to me, is its almost total lack of characterization. With very few exceptions, s.f.'s people, from the sub-human Yahoos of a story like Avram Davidson's "Now Let Us Sleep" to the hate-maddened monster of A. E. Van Vogt's "Black Destroyer" or the Chief of the Bureau of Robotics of Asimov's "Let's Get Together," are one-dimensional, lacking in individuality, almost completely devoid of complexity or even the illusion of complexity. Like the villains, heroes, and heroines of the old pulp Westerns, they exist on the surface only. Lacking depth and breadth, they lack reality; lacking reality, they fail to interest the adult reader, regardless of the author's ingenuity or the potential meaningfulness of his ideas.

Almost equally distressing is the preponderance of what can only be labeled the bad writing of much science fiction: slovenly writing, trite writing, stereotyped writing, florid writing overburdened with glittering adjectives and screaming adverbs. The frequently boozy or oversimplified metaphysics of science fiction, and its often labored passages of pseudoscience, pseudohistory, and pseudoeconomics are, in my opinion, far less reprehensible than this sophomoric writing. It remains to be seen whether the run-of-the-mill science-fiction writer will continue, as Kingsley Amis has observed in what still seems to be the best book on the subject (*New Maps of Hell: A Survey of Science Fiction* [1960]) to present "interesting ideas, and sometimes even original ones, in terms of electrifying banality." (Next to Amis' book, I enjoyed and profited most from

Brian W. Aldiss' *Billion Year Spree: The True History of Science Fiction*
[1973].) The achievement of some of the writers I have mentioned here suggests that though there will probably always be a
hack on the periphery of s.f. the genre will attract more good
writers in the future than it has in the past. Certainly the achievement of such novels as *Brave New World, Childhood's End,* and
Limbo — along with fascinating books that are difficult to classify,
like *Chariots of the Gods* — indicates the possibilities inherent in the
form.

IV. *"Fragments Are the Only Forms I Trust":* * *Barthelme and the Innovationists*

At recurring periods in literary history it has been fashionable to
announce the impending death of fiction or offer a requiem for its
eternal rest. As early as the fifties Alain Robbe-Grillet had announced that characters and incidents in fiction were both dis-
tasteful and dangerous; at the same time such major figures as
Beckett, Borges, and the leading practitioners of what was to become labeled as the theater of the absurd were altering and expanding the dimensions of imaginative literature. By the middle sixties
the rejection of conventional realism had become in some areas
almost a new religion. Realism, the innovationists and experimentalists declared, was dead, and with it linear, sequential fiction.
Reality itself was an illusion and God did not exist; the new journalism would wipe out the novel, to say nothing of the short story,
which was castigated as having been the most impervious to change
of all contemporary literary forms and therefore the one most
destined for oblivion. Many of America's major writers were being
attracted to nonfiction, which was outstripping fiction in popularity
and sales. The movies, television, spectator sports, and inflation
were killing off the fiction reading and buying public. Experiments in graphics and typography, nonstories, surfictions, antistories, neostories, breakthrough-fictions appeared with increasing

* Donald Barthelme, *"See the Moon,"* from *Unspeakable Practices, Unnatural Acts.*

frequency in periodicals ranging from the *New Yorker* to advance-guard limited-circulation little magazines; the first important anthology of innovative or experimental short fiction became an immediate best seller, the editor of another anthology of innovative fictions announced that language itself was not a necessary element in fiction, and one of the leading exponents of the new fiction stated that he considered the "true enemies" of fiction to be plot, character, setting, and theme. Meanwhile such diverse authors as Malcolm Cowley, Irwin Shaw, and Herbert Gold ("the storyteller must have a story to tell, not just some sweet prose to take out for a walk") rallied to the defense of character, situation, and place.

Of the innovationists, Donald Barthelme (1930–) was to become the most influential and most widely imitated American short fiction writer since Hemingway, as well as one of the most prolific: *Come Back, Dr. Caligari* (1964); *Unspeakable Practices, Unnatural Acts* (1968); *City Life* (1970); *Sadness* (1972); *Guilty Pleasures* (1974), called his first book of nonfiction but embodying techniques and methods similar to those of his short fictions and a 1975 National Book Award fiction nominee; his much-discussed short novel, *Snow White* (1967); a National Book Award-winning children's book; and miscellaneous *New Yorker* pieces published under the nom de plume Lily McNeil.

In a 1971 interview Barthelme was quoted as having said that "the principle of collage is the central principle of all art in the twentieth century in all media." Questioned about this in a 1972 interview, which was not published until late in 1974, he admitted to being "wrong, or too general," but went on to comment that "the point of collage is that unlike things are stuck together to make, in the best case, a new reality," which, in effect, restates what he had said in "Games," from his second book: "Chaos is tasty AND USEFUL TOO." Considered individually Barthelme's fictions are collages, from the rather obvious and dated experiments with design and typography ("The Glass Mountain" with its hundred numbered sentences or "The Explanation" with its black squares) to stories

like "Marie, Marie, Hold Me Tight," "Critique de la Vie Quoti-
dienne," "City Life," or "The Game," which employ relatively conventional fictional techniques and are among his best pieces. Somewhere between these extremes are such integrations of text and
graphics as "At the Tolstoy Museum," "Brain Damage," or "The
Flight of Pigeons from the Palace." In all of these, the kaleidoscopic bringing together of opposites, the fragmented union of the
meaningful and the meaningless, *works,* and in his best fictions the
chaos is as carefully charted as that of Joyce.

In a much broader sense Barthelme's work in toto is an enormous collage, embracing or including or touching upon most of
the directions and tendencies commented upon in the preceding
chapters: the concern with contemporary manners; the ability to
capture the fads, the mores, the absurdities, and the ambience of
the last decade; and the preoccupation with the bizarre, the sick,
the abnormal, and the grotesque, which often wanders into a surreal world or realm of fantasy that outblinks the fantasists.

Everyone who writes about Barthelme either begins or ends with
some comments about Borges. To this name we should add Dali
and Magritte, Walt Disney's world and that of Chester Gould and
Ingmar Bergman. Which is to suggest that Barthelme is a provocative but not a particularly original thinker, nor does he claim to be.
Instead he is endowed with a wondrous curiosity; he picks up facts
as a magnet picks up steel filings, and his work possesses, among
other things, the fascination of some treasure house of often unnec-
essary but delightful facts — a different kind of collage compounded of the Guinness *Book of World Records,* ancient encyclo-
pedias, almanacs, gift books, histories of art, Sears Roebuck cata-
logues, and last year's newspaper. Even when he is being didactic,
trivial, or self-imitative, Barthelme is fun to read; his relish for facts
is exceeded only by his verve, his gamesmanship, his style. And
such opening sentences! How can one put down stories that begin,
"Kellerman, gigantic with gin, runs through the park at noon with
his naked father slung under one arm" or "An aristocrat was riding
down the street in his carriage. He ran over my father" or "Hubert
gave Charles and Irene a nice baby for Christmas"?

Beneath the clowning and the cutting-and-pasting and the ransacking of archives, Barthelme is a conventional moralist, alternately attracted, amused, and appalled by what he sees as the sickness of his times, by its dullness and insipidity, by its indifference to art and things of the imagination, by its affronts to individual life and dignity. The comments of "Hiding Man" — from his first collection — are emblematic of his work in general and might well serve as his epitaph for his epoch:

> Most people haven't the wit to be afraid, most view television, smoke cigars, fondle wives, have children, vote, plant gladiolus, iris, phlox, never confront *Screaming Skull, Teenage Werewolf, Beast with a Thousand Eyes,* no conception of what lies beneath the surface, no faith in any manifestation not certified by hierarchy. Who is safe at home with *Teenage Werewolf* abroad . . .? People think these things are jokes, but they are wrong, it is dangerous to ignore a vision, consider Bane-Hipkiss, he has begun to bark.

So too might be the following from *Guilty Pleasures,* his most recent book: "We are adrift in a tense and joyless world that is falling apart at an accelerated rate."

John Barth (1930–) has been one of my favorite authors since a review copy of *The Floating Opera* turned up on my desk almost twenty years ago. He has wit, style, intelligence, seriousness of purpose, *and* (like Barthelme, but unlike some of his imitators) a sense of humor, along with a healthy skepticism and benign impatience for both the conventional for its own sake and the unconventional for *its* own sake: he can say with all seriousness that he tends to regard realism "as a kind of aberration in the history of literature" and admit in almost the same breath and with equal seriousness that he has never found the "modernist notion that plot is an anachronistic element in contemporary fiction [to be] a congenial notion." Such complexities animate the fictions in *Lost in the Funhouse* (1968) and the three novellas of his National Book Award-winning *Chimera* (1972).

As the subtitle (*Fiction for print, tape, live voice*) of *Lost in the Funhouse* suggests, the individual pieces vary enormously in subject matter, technique, and purpose in the same way that the volume as a whole differs from more conventional collections. This book, he says in his Author's Note, "is neither a collection nor a selection, but a series" and though some of the pieces were "composed expressly for print, others were not." "Glossalia," for example, "will make no sense unless heard in live or recorded voices . . . or read as if so heard"; the title story, on the other hand, would lose part of its point "in any except printed form"; "Night-Sea Journey" was intended either for "print or recorded authorial voice, but not for live or non-authorial voice." When this author's note was criticized by some reviewers as being pretentious, Barth added to a subsequent edition a comment, consisting of seven notes, maintaining that his "regnant idea" was the "unpretentious one of turning as many aspects of the fiction as possible . . . into dramatically relevant emblems of the theme."

The fourteen *Lost in the Funhouse* pieces constitute what has been termed a *künstlerroman* concerned with the search of the artist for a viable mode of fiction. "Ambrose His Mark," "Water-Message," and the title story are part narrative, part commentary, part esthetics, centering on the infancy, childhood, and adolescence of one Ambrose growing up on the Eastern shore of Maryland, where Barth was born and raised. At the other extreme are "Night-Sea Journey," a tour de force about the mock-heroic journey of sperm to egg, and "Frame Tale," the Moebius strip that opens the book. "Echo," "Menelaiad," and "Anonymiad" — with the Ambrose stories — are Barth at his best, bantering excursion-essays anticipating in his lavish playing with myth the "Dunyazadiad," "Bellerophoniad," and "Perseid" of the *Chimera* trilogy.

Throughout, Barth bullies, exhorts, and cajoles the reader:

> You, dogged, uninsultable, print-oriented bastard, it's you I'm addressing, who else, from inside this monstrous fiction. You've read me this far, then? Even this far? For what discreditable motive? How is it you don't go to a movie, watch TV, stare at a wall, play tennis with a friend, make amorous advances to the person who comes to your mind when I speak of amorous advances? Can nothing surfeit, saturate you, turn you off? Where's your shame?

Playing with words and ideas like the lapidary philosopher he is, hurdling the barriers of time, place, and situation, Barth in effect is looking through a dimensionless keyhole while someone else is looking at *him* through a keyhole at the same time that a big cosmic Eye in the cosmic sky (or a smaller less-cosmic contact lens) is looking at them both, neither approvingly nor disapprovingly. Just looking.

Much of this is not for the general reader, but Barth quite obviously couldn't care less, any more than did the poets and verse writers of the English Renaissance. More than any of the innovationists, it seems to me, his best work — the Ambrose and the myth fictions — has about it the ring and feel of permanence. If he has not attempted — wisely, in my opinion — to define the dimensions of the new fiction, his work suggests its *expandingness-ness* potential, and indicates at least one direction the fiction of the next decade may take. He has been quoted somewhere as saying he intends to abandon fiction; it is to be hoped that he may change his mind.

"I address these stories," Robert Coover (1932–) says in a preface to dedicated Cervantes — characteristically placed in the middle of *Pricksongs & Descants* (1969) — "to the need for new modes of perception and fictional forms able to encompass them." Like Cervantes, and in the tradition of the great fictional romancers or "irrealists" from Poe to Kafka to Nabokov to Borges, Coover is concerned with the problem of reality versus illusion; like them, he wrenches and distorts and fragments time; like them, he explores his scene from multiple points of view whether his substance consists of updated irreverent fairy tales and myths with their Red Riding Hoods and Hansels and Gretels, or of contemporary nightmares like "The Babysitter," "A Pedestrian Accident," or "The Elevator." Along with this, his work is kin to that of Ionesco, Beckett and the theater of the absurd, and the new grotesque. "Grotesque," shouts obscene, gross Charity Grundy of "A Pedestrian Accident"; "grotesque, perhaps, and yes, a bit awesome — but *absurd.*"

The terms are applicable to these engaging, disturbing, and varied fictions; "The Babysitter," Coover's most written about story, is not uncharacteristic. In a series of some hundred brief paragraphs, some of them similar to the "crots" of Richard Brautigan, Coover has created a kaleidoscope of contrasts. Point of view flashes, shifts, floats; the story has almost as many contrasts and angles of vision as Henry James's house of fiction has windows — from that of the babysitter to the children she is supposed to take care of to the pair of boys who are trying to make her to the parents of the children, particularly the father, Mr. Tucker, in whose garden the babysitter has the fairies set-a-dancing, even to the shifting television scenes the babysitter has been watching. And there are angles to the mood and "meaning': is the babysitter raped? or is a different babysitter raped? has the Tucker son been drowned? does Mr. Tucker enjoy the babysitter in the soapy waters? Or, indeed, does it all go back to the Golden Age and Calderon's *La Vida es Sueñō?*

Their voices are used now only to cry out in fear and hunger, and all their playing days are over, those days of careless pleasure that led them into the terrible woods. I fear that those poor lost dogs may be the shadow of a future journey if we don't watch out.

So speaks the voice of the Woodstock generation, Richard Brautigan (1935–) in "The View from the Dog Tower" from *Revenge of the Lawn* (1971). Like *Trout Fishing in America,* which is similar in mood and method but is classified as a novel, *Revenge of the Lawn* is a series of related or semirelated episodes, sketches, anecdotes, and stories. The title story, the first in the collection, concerns the narrator's grandmother — "a bootlegger in a little county up in the state of Washington" — and her husband, who had prophesied the exact date of the beginning of World War I and spent the rest of his life in an insane asylum as a result. The final piece, "The World War I Los Angeles Airplane," is a tribute in thirty-three numbered sentences and brief paragraphs to the narrator's father, who had "used the sweet wine in place of life because he didn't have any more life to lose." In between are some sixty pieces including one-

or-two-liners like "The Scarlatti Tilt": " 'It's very hard to live in a studio apartment in San Jose with a man who's learning to play the violin.' That's what she told the police when she handed them the empty revolver."

Brautigan, like Barthelme, has projected his own highly individ-ualistic vision of post-World War II America. Also like Barthelme, he has suffered from being widely imitated by a younger gener-ation of writers and pseudowriters who have aped his manner without being able to recapture his essence. Beneath his briskness, the light touch and the surface levity, the paradoxical juxtaposing of tone and mood, the absurd and the straight, the playful and the melancholy, *Revenge of the Lawn* is an elegy to the realization that the American dream is a fraud, living is losing; best to go under-ground, don't fight it, cool it, it's really no big thing either way. Muted words for a time when, as in the title story, only nature can fight back and the best mortals can do is suffer or withdraw in silence.

Like Barth and several of the writers roughly classified as innova-tive and experimental (not a group in any organized sense, of course, but they do tend to crop up again and again in each other's company, in articles, anthologies, interviews, and the like) some of the authors have done their best work in forms other than short fiction. Robert Creeley's poetry, for example, seems to me far more important than his short fiction. Thomas Pynchon, though some of his shorter work was subsequently incorporated in *V* and *Gravity's Rainbow,* is primarily a novelist. Kurt Vonnegut's *Welcome to the Monkey House* (1968), except for the title story and three or four other pieces, is considerably less important and "experimen-tal" than his novels. And the *Lunar Landscape* stories (1969) by John Hawkes (1925–), while they share in common with many of the innovationists the sense of anguish and the now-familiar love affair between myth and traditional reality, seem less important and far less experimental than his novels, a landscape of the mind peopled by shadows, dead creatures in a cold, usually sterile world.

William H. Gass's *In the Heart of the Heart of the Country* (1968), which I have commented on earlier, seems to have elicited more praise than it actually merited. His title story, "The Pederson Kid," and "Mrs. Mean" are notable for their perceptive characterization and evocation of place, and, with *Lunar Landscapes*, share the metaphysical anguish, free association of ideas, and existentialist position of so many of his peers, but are more conventional than experimental in method. (But since *Omensetter's Luck* [1966] was a long time in being recognized as the very important novel it is, perhaps some sort of retributive justice is at work here.) *Willie Masters' Lonesome Wife* (1971), however, is something else again. The text itself is hardly sensational: part allegory in which the lonesome wife — "I'm busty, passive, hairy, and will serve. Departure is my name. I travel, dream. I feel sometimes as if I *were* imagination (that spider goddess and thread-spinning muse — imagination imagining itself imagine" — is equated with poetry in search of or in need of the poet; a mixture of what a few years ago would have been called porno and conventional post-Joycean stream of consciousness. But the book itself, designed by Lawrence Levy, is a delight. The effective integration of different type faces, photographs of breastsbumandbelly, reversed pages, and the like suggest both the achievement and the potential in the blending of words, illustrations, type, and paper.

A bit too much, it seems to me, has been made of the importance and originality of the "new experimental fiction." Not by its major practitioners, but by their imitators and by the sometimes oversolemn pronouncements of editors or anthologists who have tended to equate resourcefulness or freakishness with talent, meaninglessness with profundity, and "experiments" with typography and graphics with originality. Or who have forgotten, for example, that Poe, like the contemporary fountainhead, Jorge Luis Borges, was at various times antirealist, irrealist, or surrealist rejecter of conventional fictional forms and modes. Such "breakthroughs," along with fragmentation or the exploration of reality versus illusion from multiple points of view, are hardly a unique manifestation of the sixties. At its best, however, the work of such innovationists and experimentalists as those discussed above is a fresh, vigorous, and exciting indication of the health of the short story at a time when prose fiction in general is fighting for its life. At its least successful, it is unashamedly imitative, flagrantly self-congratulatory or pretentious, and possesses little more artistic merit than the weather drawings by school children that accompany the nightly weather reports of our local television channel in Boone County, Missouri.

Various good anthologies are available, among them *Anti-Story: An Anthology of Experimental Fiction,* edited by Philip Stevick (1971); *New American Story,* edited by Donald M. Allen and Robert Creeley (1965); *Innovative Fiction: Stories for the Seventies,* edited by Jerome Klinkowitz and John Somer (1972); *Stories from the Sixties,* edited by Stanley Elkin (1971); *12 from the Sixties,* edited by Richard Kostelanetz (1967); and *Ongoing American Fiction,* (*Tri-Quarterly #26,* Winter 1973), edited by Charles Newman. Interesting and informative interviews with Barth, Barthelme, Hawkes, and others are collected in *The New Fiction: Interviews with Innovative American Writers,* edited by Joe David Bellamy (1974). Additional individual collections include Stanley Berne, *The Multiple Gods and Other Stories* (1964); Ethel Broner, *Journal/Nocturnal and Seven Stories* (1968); Marvin Cohen, *The Monday Rhetoric of the Love Club and Other Parables* (1973); Richard Farina's *Been Down So Long It Looks Like Up to Me* (1966); Robert Creeley, *The Gold-Digger and Other Stories* (1965); John Gardner, *The King's Indian: Stories and Tales* (1974); George Garrett, *The Magic Striptease* (1973); Richard Stern, *Teeth, Dying, and Other Matters* (1964) and *1968: A Short Novel, an Urban Idyll, Five Stories and Two Trade Notes* (1970); Ronald Sukenik, *The Death of the Novel and Other Stories* (1969); and Curtis Zahn, *American Contemporary* (1963).

Chapter 9

Some Concluding Remarks and an Informal Postscript

In the preceding chapters I have tried to indicate what seem to me the major tendencies and achievements of American short fiction since around 1940. Some of the authors I have discussed are now recognized as masters of the genre, some have been recognized by their peers but not by the general public, a few are virtually unknown. In spite of mass audience indifference, the writer of short fiction has gradually emerged from obscurity. Publishers continue to be reluctant to publish collections of stories by new or little known authors, but the old taboos no longer exist. Not only do more good volumes of short fiction get into print but increasingly they achieve considerable popularity or critical recognition or both. J. D. Salinger's *Franny and Zooey* and *Raise High the Roof Beam, Carpenters,* for example, were best sellers; Jean Stafford's *Collected Stories* won the Pulitzer Prize; recent National Book Award winners include Bernard Malamud's *The Magic Barrel;* Philip Roth's *Goodbye, Columbus;* Katherine Anne Porter's *Collected Stories;* and, in 1974, I. B. Singer's *A Crown of Feathers* (that same year four of the eleven fiction nominees were collections of short fiction: the others were Doris Betts's *Beasts of the Southern Wild,* John Cheever's *The World of Apples,* and Stanley Elkin's *Searches and Seizures*).

Vigor, variety, technical and artistic expertise: these seem to me the hallmarks of the recent American short story. Whether short fiction is the most important native form of the last three and a half decades is something for subsequent literary historians and critics to assess, but it seems to me that it is. Meanwhile this study will serve my purpose if it does nothing more than lead a new generation of readers to "discover" some of the writers who have contributed to what I find to be the most exciting and substantial fictional achievement of recent years.

What directions will tomorrow's short fiction writers take? Who will they be and what kind of fictions will they make? Will past achievements be equalled or surpassed? Obviously such questions are easier to ask than answer, but it seems reasonable to assume that the genre will flourish in the face of mounting difficulties. The influence of the innovationists is likely to grow; the form, at least in one main line of development, will be more concerned with ideas and experiments with graphics, collages, and other visual media than with story as such; more private, more varied and flexible, more concerned with gamesmanship, private or peer-group communication. On the other hand the concept of fiction as not necessarily concerned with people and incidents and place and ideas may seem as dated in a few years as the fiction of the 1890s; the concept of the Jamesian window on life rather than fiction as found object will thrive in the midst of adversity. Stories by and about American blacks are likely to grow both in number and quality and, having gone through the inevitable stage of journalism and sociology, become art. In general the short story will continue to attract the young writer and challenge the resources of the professional. One thing is certain: there will be hard times ahead for both. At no time in the twentieth century has the economy and its effect upon the serious writer been more threatening. As of early 1975 the future of the National Book Awards, the most prestigious literary prizes in the United States, is uncertain; the major book publishers are reducing or planning to reduce both their staffs and their lists, and are concentrating on fewer, more-likely-to-be-financially-successful titles; the textbook industry and the paperback trade, long-time shock absorbers and steady moneymakers, are becoming shaky. The short story, along with poetry, is the genre most likely to suffer from such conditions, conditions that will probably get considerably worse before they get much better: the only possible ray of light on the immediate horizon is the growing interest in short fiction displayed by the university presses.

In spite of all this, perhaps to a degree because of it, short fiction will continue to be perhaps the most vital of contemporary fictional forms.

The short fiction writers discussed in the preceding pages, for all their differences in subject matter and method, have much in common. James Purdy, John Cheever, and Donald Barthelme share a similar interest in their concern for the problems of individual and societal idiocy; Truman Capote and I. B. Singer are alike in their preoccupation with the contrast between the real and the illusory and in the hallucinated dreamlike quality that makes their best work so memorable. Disenchantment with the quality of contemporary life in America, anger or distrust with the present and uncertainty concerning the future, the search for identity and self-realization, the striving for meaning in a dark time — these and similar concerns appear and reappear in the diverse short fiction of the last three and a half decades. In spite of enormous differences within this body of literature, at its center is twentieth-century man, whose problems are not very different from those of his predecessors. Recent short fiction reminds us anew of the validity of Goethe's observation: "If you inquire what the people are like here, I must answer 'The same as everywhere.' "

Chekhov once commented, partly facetiously, I suppose, that there were only two kinds of literary works, those he liked and those he didn't like. Henry James, on the other hand, stated that the only distinction that had any meaning to him was that there are "bad" stories and "good ones." My approach lies somewhere between those extremes. In the preceding pages I've tried to comment on all of the writers of short fiction since around 1940 who have seemed to me the most important or the most representative of certain trends; at the same time, I have included some authors who are among my own personal favorites. The number and the variety and the achievement of such writers has forced me to make some rather arbitrary classifications and to indulge in the dubious luxury of categorizing — the short fiction of manners, the black writers, the regionalists, and so on.* But as much as possible, I have tried to avoid overrigidity or overcomplexity, and whenever possible I've not commented on an individual author in more than one chapter unless I felt that the nature of his work necessitated it.

The short story, as I've mentioned once or twice, is an extremely personal literary form as well as a very varied one. What one reader admires greatly may leave another indifferent or irritated. As the amiable and knowledgeable Herschel Brickell, who edited the annual *O. Henry* collections for a good many years, used to say, the short story is a "perfect subject for argument and honest difference of opinion" — which I soon learned was an understatement when I first started writing about short stories. I hope I haven't bypassed anybody's favorites, but as I said earlier my purpose was not to compile a small encyclopedia but to suggest the richness, diversity, and major tendencies of short fiction during the last three and a half decades. If by omission or commission I have upset any aficionado — even the kind who tossed and gored me slightly for not commenting on one or two authors whose stories had not been published in book form at the time the earlier version of my study went to press — may I make a suggestion?

I have a good friend at Newberry College in South Carolina who edits one of the best specialized quarterly magazines in the country, *Studies in Short Fiction.* His name is Frank Hoskins, and he and his staff are deluged with articles about major figures — Poe and Joyce and Faulkner and Hemingway and Flannery O'Connor and people like that — but they don't get much about the lesser figures. Professor Hoskins would be very happy, I'm sure, to receive manuscripts

---

* Flannery O'Connor, for example, might have been discussed in Chapter Eight rather than Chapter Five; Hortense Calisher in Chapter Six rather than Chapter Four.

about some of the lesser known, less written about, less appreciated good writers like many of those I've discussed in this book or for one reason or another haven't commented on.

That way all of us — authors and readers, publishers and editors — would be the gainers.

Appendix. One Hundred-Plus Notable or Representative American Short Story Writers, 1940–1975

I have not included in this checklist some very notable authors who did most of their work prior to 1940 even though, as with William Carlos Williams, their collected stories appeared after 1940, or, as is the case with Kay Boyle, they published individual volumes of short fiction during the period. A list of such authors appears after the main checklist. Although the major emphasis is on what I consider the importance of the authors included in the main list, I have also tried to indicate the variety of the short fiction since 1940. In a few cases, birth dates have not been obtainable.

Part 1

ALGREN, NELSON (1909–). *The Neon Wilderness.* New York: Doubleday, 1948. *The Last Carousel.* New York: Putnam's, 1973.

AUCHINCLOSS, LOUIS (1917–). *The Injustice Collectors.* Boston: Houghton Mifflin, 1950. *The Romantic Egoists; A Reflection in Eight Minutes.* Boston: Houghton Mifflin, 1954. *Powers of Attorney.* Boston: Houghton Mifflin, 1963. *Tales of Manhattan.* Boston: Houghton Mifflin, 1967. *Second Chance: Tales of Two Generations.* Boston: Houghton Mifflin, 1970. *The Partners.* Boston: Houghton Mifflin, 1974.

BALDWIN, JAMES (1924–). *Going to Meet the Man.* New York: Dial, 1965.

BARTH, JOHN (1930–). *Lost in the Funhouse: Fiction for print, tape, live voice.* New York: Doubleday, 1968. *Chimera* (three novellas). New York: Random House, 1972.

BARTHELME, DONALD (1930–). *Come Back, Dr. Caligari.* Boston: Little Brown, 1964. *Unspeakable Practices, Unnatural Acts.* New York: Farrar,

Straus & Giroux, 1968. *City Life.* New York: Farrar, Straus & Giroux, 1970. *Sadness.* New York: Farrar, Straus & Giroux, 1972. *Guilty Pleasures.* New York: Farrar, Straus & Giroux, 1974.

BECK, WARREN. *The Blue Sash and Other Stories.* Yellow Springs, Ohio: Antioch Press, 1941. *The First Fish and Other Stories.* Yellow Springs, Ohio: Antioch Press, 1947. *The Far Whistle and Other Stories.* Yellow Springs, Ohio: Antioch Press, 1951. *The Rest is Silence and Other Stories.* Denver: Alan Swallow, 1963.

BELLOW, SAUL (1915–). *Seize the Day: With Three Short Stories and a Play.* New York: Viking, 1956. *Mosby's Memoirs and Other Stories.* New York: Viking, 1968.

BETTS, DORIS (1932–). *The Gentle Insurrection and Other Stories.* New York: Putnam's, 1954. *The Astronomer & Other Stories.* New York: Harper & Row, 1965. *Beasts of the Southern Wild and Other Stories.* New York: Harper & Row, 1973.

BEMELMANS, LUDWIG (1898–1962). *I Love You, I Love You, I Love You.* New York: Viking, 1942. *Hotel Bemelmans.* New York: Viking, 1946.

BINGHAM, SALLIE (1937–). *The Touching Hand and Six Short Stories.* Boston: Houghton Mifflin, 1967. *The Way It Is Now.* New York: Viking, 1972.

BOWLES, PAUL (1911–). *The Delicate Prey and Other Stories.* New York: Random House, 1950. *A Hundred Camels in the Courtyard.* San Francisco: City Lights Press, 1962. *The Time of Friendship: A Volume of Short Stories.* New York: Holt, Rinehart & Winston, 1967.

BRADBURY, RAY (1920–). *Dark Carnival.* Sauk City, Wisconsin: Arkham House, 1947. *The Martian Chronicles.* New York: Doubleday, 1950. *The Illustrated Man.* New York: Doubleday, 1951. *The Golden Apples of the Sun.* New York: Doubleday, 1953. *Fahrenheit 451* (three novellas). New York: Ballantine, 1953. *The October Country.* New York: Ballantine, 1955. *A Medicine for Melancholy.* New York: Doubleday, 1959. *The Machineries of Joy.* New York: Simon & Schuster, 1964. *The Vintage Bradbury.* New York: Random House, 1965. *The Autumn People.* New York: Ballantine, 1965. *Tomorrow Midnight.* New York: Ballantine, 1966. *I Sing the Body Electric.* New York: Ballantine, 1969.

BULLINS, ED (1935–). *The Hungered One.* New York: Morrow, 1971.

BURNS, JOHN HORNE (1916–1953). *The Gallery.* New York: Harper & Brothers, 1947.

CALISHER, HORTENSE (1911–). *In the Absence of Angels.* Boston: Little, Brown, 1951. *Tale for the Mirror and Other Stories.* Boston: Little, Brown, 1962. *Extreme Magic: A Novella and Other Stories.* Boston: Little, Brown, 1964. *The Railway Police and the Last Trolley Ride* (novellas). Boston: Little, Brown, 1966.

CAPOTE, TRUMAN (1924–). *A Tree of Night and Other Stories.* New York: Random House, 1949. *Breakfast at Tiffany's: A Short Novel and Three Stories.* New York: Random House, 1958.

CASSILL, R. V. (1919–). *The Father and Other Stories.* New York: Simon & Schuster, 1965. *The Happy Marriage and Other Stories.* Evanston, Indiana: Purdue University Press, 1956. Five of R. V. Cassill's stories are included in *Fifteen by Three* (Norfolk, Connecticut: New Directions, 1957).

CHEEVER, JOHN (1912–). *The Way Some People Live: A Book of Stories.* New York: Random House, 1943. *The Enormous Radio and Other Stories.* New York: Funk & Wagnalls, 1958. *The Housebreaker of Shady Hill and Other Stories.* New York: Harper & Brothers, 1958. *Some People, Places, and Things That Will Not Appear in My Next Novel.* New York: Harper & Brothers, 1961. *The Brigadier and the Golf Widow.* New York: Harper & Row, 1964. *The World of Apples.* New York: Knopf, 1973.

CLARK, WALTER VANTILBURG (1909–1971). *The Watchful Gods and Other Stories.* New York: Random House, 1950.

CLAYTON, JOHN BELL (1906–1955). *The Strangers Were There: Selected Stories.* New York: Macmillan, 1957.

COATES, ROBERT M. (1897–). *All the Year Round: A Book of Stories.* New York: Harcourt, Brace, 1943. *The Hour After Westerly and Other Stories.* New York: Harcourt, Brace, 1957. *The Man Just Ahead of You.* New York: W. Sloane, 1964.

COLLIER, JOHN (1901–). *Presenting Moonshine.* New York: Viking, 1941. *A Touch of Nutmeg.* New York: The Press of the Readers Club, 1943. *Fancies and Goodnights.* New York: Doubleday, 1951.

CONNELL, Evan S. (1924–). *The Anatomy Lesson and Other Stories.* New York: Viking, 1957. *At the Crossroads: Stories.* New York: Simon & Schuster, 1965.

COOVER, ROBERT (1932–). *Pricksongs & Descants.* New York: Dutton, 1969.

CULLINAN, ELIZABETH (1933–). *The Time of Adam: Stories.* Boston: Houghton Mifflin, 1971.

DORRANCE, Ward (1904–). *The White Hound: Stories by Ward Dorrance and Thomas Mabry.* Columbia: Univ. of Missouri Press, 1959. *The Man of the House* (novella). Columbia: Univ. of Missouri Press, 1972.

ELKIN, STANLEY (1930–). *Criers and Kibitzers, Kibitzers and Criers.* New York: Random House, 1965. *Snatches and Seizures.* New York: Random House, 1973.

ELLIOTT, GEORGE P. (1918–). *Among the Dangs: Ten Short Stories.* New York: Holt, Rinehart & Winston, 1961. *An Hour of Last Things and Other Stories.* New York: Harper & Row, 1968.

ELLISON, HARLAN. *From the Land of Fear*. New York: Belmont Tower Books, 1973. *Ellison Wonderland*. New York: New American Library, 1974. *The Beast That Shouted Love at the Heart of the World*. New York: New American Library, 1974. *Deathbed Stories*. New York: Harper & Row, 1975.

ENRIGHT, ELIZABETH (1909–1968). *Borrowed Summer and Other Stories*. New York: Rinehart, 1946. *The Moment Before the Rain*. New York: Harcourt, Brace, 1955. *The Riddle of the Fly and Other Stories*. New York: Harcourt, Brace, 1959.

FARRELL, JAMES T. (1909–). *When Boyhood Dreams Come True*. New York: Vanguard, 1946. *The Life Adventurous and Other Stories*. New York: Vanguard, 1947. *French Girls Are Vicious and Other Stories*. New York: Vanguard, 1955. *A Dangerous Woman and Other Stories*. New York: Vanguard, 1957. *Judith and Other Stories*. New York: Doubleday, 1973. Earlier collections of Farrell's short stories include *Calico Shoes and Other Stories* (1934), *Guillotine Party and Other Stories* (1935), and *Can All This Grandeur Perish and Other Stories* (1937), all published by Vanguard.

FAUST, IRVIN (1924–). *Roar Lion Roar and Other Stories*. New York: Random House, 1965.

FRIEDMAN, BRUCE JAY (1930–). *Far from the City of Class*. New York: Frommer-Pasmantier, 1963. *Black Angels*. New York: Simon & Schuster, 1966.

GAINES, ERNEST J. (1933–). *Bloodlines*. New York: Dial, 1968.

GARRETT, GEORGE P. (1929–). *King of the Mountain*. New York: Scribner, 1957. *In the Briar Patch: A Book of Stories*. Austin: Univ. of Texas Press, 1961. *Cold Ground Was My Bed Last Night*. Columbia: Univ. of Missouri Press, 1964. *The Magic Striptease* (novellas), New York: Doubleday, 1973.

GASS, WILLIAM (1924–). *In the Heart of the Heart of the Country and Other Stories*. New York: Harper & Row, 1968. *Willie Masters' Lonesome Wife*. New York: Knopf, 1971.

GELLHORN, MARTHA (1908–). *The Honeyed Peace*. New York: Doubleday, 1953. *Two by Two*. New York: Simon & Schuster 1958. *Pretty Tales for Tired People*. New York: Simon & Schuster, 1965.

GILL, BRENDAN (1914–). *Ways of Loving*. New York: Harcourt, Brace & Jovanovich, 1974.

GOLD, HERBERT (1929–). *Love and Like*. New York: Dial, 1960. *The Magic Will: Stories and Essays of a Decade*. New York: Random House, 1971. Several of his stories are included in *Fifteen by Three* (see CASSILL).

GORDON, CAROLINE (1895–). *The Forest of the South*. New York: Scribner, 1945. *Old Red and Other Stories*. New York: Scribner, 1963.

GOYEN, WILLIAM (1915–). *Ghost and Flesh: Stories and Tales*. New York: Random House, 1952. *The Faces of Blood Kindred: A Novella and Ten*

Stories. New York: Random House, 1960. *Collected Stories.* New York: Doubleday, 1975.

GRAU, SHIRLEY ANN (1929–). *The Black Prince and Other Stories.* New York: Knopf, 1954. *The Wind Shifting West.* New York: Knopf, 1973.

HALE, NANCY (1908–). *Between the Dark and the Daylight.* New York: Scribner, 1943. *The Empress's Ring.* New York: Scribner, 1955. *Heaven and Hardpan Farm.* New York: Scribner, 1957. *A New England Girlhood.* Boston: Little, Brown, 1958. *The Pattern of Perfection.* Boston: Little, Brown, 1960. Nancy Hale's earliest collection is *The Earliest Dreams* (New York: Scribner, 1936).

HAWKES, JOHN (1925–). *Lunar Landscapes.* New York: New Directions, 1969.

HORGAN, PAUL (1903–). *The Peachstone: Stories from Four Decades.* New York: Farrar, Straus & Giroux, 1967.

HUGHES, LANGSTON (1902–1967). *Laughing to Keep from Crying.* New York: Holt, 1952. *Something In Common and Other Stories.* New York: Hill & Wang, 1963. Langston Hughes's earliest collection is *The Ways of White Folks,* 1934.

HUMPHREY, WILLIAM (1925–). *The Last Husband and Other Stories.* New York: Morrow, 1953. *A Time and a Place: Stories of the Red River Country.* New York: Knopf, 1965.

JACKSON, CHARLES (1903–). *The Sunnier Side: Twelve Arcadian Tales.* New York: Farrar, Straus, 1950. *Earthly Creatures: Ten Stories.* New York: Farrar, Straus & Young, 1953.

JACKSON, SHIRLEY (1919–1964). *The Lottery, or the Adventures of James Harris.* New York: Farrar, Straus, 1949. *The Magic of Shirley Jackson.* New York: Farrar, Straus & Giroux, 1966 (contains three novels and eleven short stories).

JOHNSON, JOSEPHINE (1910–). *The Sorcerer's Son and Other Stories.* New York: Simon & Schuster, 1965. An earlier collection, *Winter Orchard,* was published in 1936.

JUST, WARD (1925–). *The Congressman Who Loved Flaubert and Other Washington Stories.* Boston: Atlantic Monthly Press–Little, Brown, 1973.

KENTFIELD, CALVIN (1925–). *The Angel and the Sailor: A Novella and Nine Stories.* New York: McGraw-Hill, 1957. *The Great Wandering Goony Bird.* New York: Random House, 1963.

KNOWLES, JOHN (1926–). *Phineas: 6 Stories.* New York: Random House, 1968.

KOSINSKI, JERZY (1933–). *Steps.* New York: Random House, 1968.

LA FARGE, CHRISTOPHER (1897–1956). *The Wilsons.* New York: Coward-McCann, 1941. *East by Southwest.* New York: Coward-McCann, 1944. *All Sorts and Kinds.* New York: Coward-McCann, 1949.

LA FARGE, OLIVER (1901–1963). *A Pause in the Desert and Other Stories.* Boston: Houghton Mifflin, 1957. *The Door in the Wall.* Boston: Houghton Mifflin, 1965. La Farge has an earlier collection, *All the Young Men* (Boston: Houghton Mifflin, 1935).

LOWRY, ROBERT (1919–). *The Wolf That Fed Us.* New York: Doubleday, 1949. *Happy New Year, Kamerades!* New York: Doubleday, 1954. *The Last Party.* New York: Popular Library, 1956. *New York Call Girl.* New York: Doubleday, 1958. *Party of Dreamers.* New York: Fleet, 1962.

MCCARTHY, MARY (1912–). *The Company She Keeps.* New York: Simon & Schuster, 1942. *Cast a Cold Eye.* New York: Harcourt, Brace, 1950.

MCCULLERS, CARSON (1917–1967). *The Ballad of the Sad Café.* Boston: Houghton Mifflin, 1951. *The Mortgaged Heart.* Boston: Houghton Mifflin, 1971 (contains seven previously uncollected early stories, four later ones, and miscellaneous materials).

MCKINLEY, GEORGIA. *The Mighty Distance.* Boston: Houghton Mifflin, 1965.

MCNULTY, JOHN (1895–1956). *Third Avenue, New York.* Boston: Little, Brown, 1946. *A Man Gets Around.* Boston: Little, Brown, 1951. *My Son Johnny.* New York: Simon & Schuster, 1955. *The World of John McNulty.* New York: Doubleday, 1957 (contains selections from the above, plus twenty previously uncollected stories).

MALAMUD, BERNARD (1914–). *The Magic Barrel.* New York: Farrar, Straus & Cudahy, 1958. *Idiots First.* New York: Farrar, Straus, 1963. *Pictures of Fidelman: An Exhibition.* New York: Farrar, Straus, & Giroux, 1969. *Rembrandt's Hat.* New York: Farrar, Straus & Giroux, 1973. *A Malamud Reader* (Farrar, Straus & Giroux, 1967) contains ten stories from *The Magic Barrel* and *Idiots First,* along with *The Assistant* and selections from other novels.

MICHAELS, LEONARD (1933–). *Going Places.* New York: Farrar, Straus & Giroux, 1969. *I Would Have Saved Them If I Could.* New York: Farrar, Straus & Giroux, 1975.

MICHENER, JAMES (1907–). *Tales of the South Pacific.* New York: Macmillan, 1947. *Return to Paradise.* New York: Random House, 1951.

MORGAN, BERRY. *The Mystic Adventures of Roxie Stoner.* Boston: Houghton Mifflin, 1974.

NABOKOV, VLADIMIR (1899–). *Nine Stories.* Norfolk, Conn.: New Directions, 1947. *Nabokov's Dozen: A Collection of Thirteen Stories.* New York: Doubleday, 1958. *Nabokov's Quartet.* New York: Phaedra, 1966. *Nabokov's Congeries: An Anthology.* New York: Viking, 1968. *A Russian Beauty and Other Stories.* New York: McGraw-Hill, 1973. *Tyrants Destroyed and Other Stories.* New York: McGraw-Hill, 1975.

NEUGEBOREN, JAY (1938–). *Corky's Brother.* New York: Farrar, Straus & Giroux, 1969.

NEWHOUSE, EDWARD (1911–). *Anything Can Happen.* New York: Harcourt, Brace, 1941. *The Iron Chain.* New York: Harcourt, Brace, 1946. *Many Are Called: Forty-Two Short Stories.* New York: Sloane, 1951.

NISSENSON, HUGH (1933–). *A Pile of Stones.* New York: Scribner, 1965. *In the Reign of Peace.* New York: Farrar, Straus & Giroux, 1972.

OATES, JOYCE CAROL (1938–). *By the North Gate.* New York: Vanguard, 1963. *Upon the Sweeping Flood and Other Stories.* New York: Vanguard, 1966. *The Wheel of Love and Other Stories.* New York: Vanguard, 1970. *Marriages and Infidelities.* New York: Vanguard, 1972. *The Hungry Ghosts: Seven Allusive Comedies.* Los Angeles: Black Sparrow Press, 1974. *The Goddess and Other Women.* New York: Vanguard, 1974.

O'CONNOR, FLANNERY (1925–1964). *A Good Man Is Hard to Find and Other Stories.* New York: Harcourt, Brace, 1955. *Everything That Rises Must Converge.* New York: Farrar, Straus & Giroux, 1965. *The Complete Stories.* New York: Farrar, Straus & Giroux, 1971.

O'HARA, JOHN (1905–1970). *Pal Joey.* New York: Duell, Sloan & Pearce, 1940. *Pipe Night.* New York: Duell, Sloan & Pearce, 1945. *Hellbox.* New York: Random House, 1947. *Assembly.* New York: Random House, 1961. *The Cape Cod Lighter.* New York: Random House, 1962. *The Hat on the Bed.* New York: Random House, 1963. *The Horse Knows the Way.* New York: Random House, 1964. *Waiting for Winter.* New York: Random House, 1966. *And Other Stories.* New York: Random House, 1969. *The Time Element and Other Stories.* New York: Random House, 1972. *The O'Hara Generation* (New York: Random House, 1969) contains twenty-two stories, from 1935–1966. O'Hara's pre-1940 collections are *The Doctor's Son and Other Stories* (New York: Duell, Sloan & Pearce, 1935) and *Files on Parade* (New York: Harcourt, Brace, 1939).

OLSEN, TILLIE (1913–). *Tell Me a Riddle.* Philadelphia: Lippincott, 1961.

OZICK, CYNTHIA. *The Pagan Rabbi and Other Stories.* New York: Knopf, 1971.

PALEY, GRACE (1922–). *The Little Disturbances of Man.* New York: Doubleday, 1959; reissued by Viking, 1968. *Enormous Changes at the Last Minute.* New York: Farrar, Straus & Giroux, 1974.

PETRY, ANN (1911–). *Miss Muriel and Other Stories.* Boston: Houghton Mifflin, 1971.

POWERS, J. E. (1917–). *Prince of Darkness.* New York: Doubleday, 1947. *The Presence of Grace.* New York: Doubleday, 1956.

PRICE, REYNOLDS (1933–). *The Names and Faces of Heroes.* New York: Atheneum, 1963. *Permanent Errors.* New York: Atheneum, 1970.

PURDY, JAMES (1923–). *Color of Darkness: Eleven Stories and a Novella.* Norfolk, Conn.: New Directions, 1957. *Children Is All.* Norfolk, Conn.: New Directions, 1962.

ROGIN, GILBERT (1929–). *The Fencing Master and Other Stories.* New York: Random House, 1965. *What Happens Next.* New York: Random House, 1971.

ROSTEN, LEO [Leonard Q. Ross] (1908–). *The Return of H*Y*M*A*N K*A*P*L*A*N.* New York: Harper & Brothers, 1959. An earlier collection, *The Education of H*Y*M*A*N K*A*P*L*A*N,* was published in 1937 by Harcourt, Brace.

ROTH, PHILIP (1933–). *Goodbye, Columbus and Five Short Stories.* Boston: Houghton Mifflin, 1959. *My Life as a Man* (two short stories and a novella). New York: Holt, Rinehart & Winston, 1974.

SALINGER, J. D. (1919–). *Nine Stories.* Boston: Little, Brown, 1953. *Franny and Zooey.* Boston: Little, Brown, 1961. *Raise High the Roof Beam, Carpenters* and *Seymour An Introduction.* Boston: Little, Brown, 1963.

SAROYAN, WILLIAM (1908–). *My Name is Aram.* New York: Harcourt, Brace, 1940. *Dear Baby.* New York: Harcourt, Brace, 1945. *The Assyrian and Other Stories.* New York: Harcourt, Brace, 1950. *Love.* New York: Lion books, 1955. *The Whole Voyald and Other Stories.* Boston: Little, Brown, 1956. *My Kind of Crazy, Wonderful People: Seventeen Stories and a Play.* New York: Harcourt, Brace & World, 1966. *The Man with the Heart in the Highlands and Other Stories.* New York: Dell, 1968. *The Daring Young Man on the Flying Trapeze and Other Stories,* published by Random House in 1934, made Saroyan a literary sensation.

SCHORER, MARK (1908–). *The State of Mind.* Boston: Houghton Mifflin, 1947.

SCHWARTZ, DELMORE (1913–1966). *The World is a Wedding.* Norfolk, Conn.: New Directions, 1948. *Successful Love and Other Stories.* New York: Corinth Books, 1961.

SELBY, HUBERT (1928–). *Last Exit to Brooklyn.* New York: Grove, 1964.

SHAW, IRWIN (1913–). *Welcome to the City and Other Stories.* New York: Random House, 1942. *Act of Faith and Other Stories.* New York: Random House, 1946. *Mixed Company: Collected Short Stories.* New York: Random House, 1950. *Tip on a Dead Jockey and Other Stories.* New York: Random House, 1957. *Love on a Dark Street and Other Stories.* New York: Delacorte, 1965. *Short Stories.* New York: Random House, 1966. *God Was Here But He Left Early: Short Fiction.* New York: Arbor House, 1972.

SINGER, ISAAC BASHEVIS (1909–). *Gimpel the Fool and Other Stories.* New York: Noonday, 1957. *The Spinoza of Market Street.* New York: Farrar, Straus & Cudahy, 1961. *Short Friday and Other Stories.* New York: Farrar, Straus & Giroux, 1964. *Zlatch the Goat and Other Stories.* New York: Harper & Row, 1966. *The Séance and Other Stories.* New York: Farrar, Straus & Giroux, 1968. *When Schlemiel Went to Warsaw and Other Stories.*

New York: Farrar, Straus & Giroux, 1968. *A Day of Pleasure: Stories of a Boy Growing Up in Warsaw.* New York: Farrar, Straus & Giroux, 1969. *A Friend of Kafka and Other Stories.* New York: Farrar, Straus & Giroux, 1970. *An Isaac Bashevis Singer Reader.* New York: Farrar, Straus & Giroux, 1971. *A Crown of Feathers and Other Stories.* New York: Farrar, Straus & Giroux, 1973.

STAFFORD, JEAN (1915–). *Children Are Bored on Sunday.* New York: Harcourt, Brace, 1953. *Bad Characters.* New York: Farrar, Straus, 1964. *The Collected Stories of Jean Stafford.* New York: Farrar, Straus & Giroux, 1969. Four additional and previously uncollected stories by Jean Stafford are included in *Stories: Jean Stafford, John Cheever, Daniel Fuchs, William Maxwell* (New York: Farrar, Straus & Cudahy, 1956).

STEGNER, WALLACE (1909–). *The Women on the Wall.* Boston: Houghton Mifflin, 1949. *The City of the Living.* Boston: Houghton Mifflin, 1956.

STUART, JESSE (1907–). *Men of the Mountain.* New York: Dutton, 1941. *Tales from the Plum Grove Hills.* New York: Dutton, 1946. *Clearing in the Sky and Other Stories.* New York: McGraw-Hill, 1950. *Plowshare in Heaven: Stories.* New York: McGraw-Hill, 1958. *Stories and Poems.* New York: McGraw-Hill, 1963. *Save Every Lamb.* New York: McGraw-Hill, 1964. *A Jesse Stuart Harvest.* New York: Dell, 1965. *My Land Has a Voice.* New York: McGraw-Hill, 1966. *Come, Gentle Spring.* New York: McGraw-Hill, 1969. *Dawn of Remembered Spring.* New York: McGraw-Hill, 1972. Stuart's first volume of short stories is *Head of W—— Hollow* (New York: Dutton, 1936).

STYRON, WILLIAM (1925–). *The Long March.* New York: Random House, 1956.

TAYLOR, PETER (1917–). *A Long Fourth and Other Stories.* New York: Harcourt, Brace, 1948. *The Widows of Thornton.* New York: Harcourt, Brace, 1954. *Happy Families Are All Alike: A Collection of Stories.* New York: McDowell, Obolensky, 1959. *Miss Leonora When Last Seen and Fifteen Other Stories.* New York: Obolensky, 1963. *The Collected Stories of Peter Taylor.* New York: Farrar, Straus & Giroux, 1969.

TRAVEN, B. (1890?–1969). *The Night Visitor and Other Stories.* New York: Hill & Wang, 1967.

UPDIKE, JOHN (1932–). *The Same Door: Short Stories.* New York: Knopf, 1959. *Pigeon Feathers.* New York: Knopf, 1962. *Olinger Stories: A Selection.* New York: Vintage Books, 1964. *The Music School: Short Stories.* New York: Knopf, 1966. *Bech: A Book.* New York: Knopf, 1970. *Museums and Women and Other Stories.* New York: Knopf, 1972.

VAN DOREN, MARK (1894–1972). *The Witch of Ramoth and Other Tales.* York, Pa.: Maple Press, 1950. *Short Stories of Mark Van Doren.* New

York: Abelard, 1950. *Nobody Said a Word and Other Stories.* New York: Holt, 1953. *Home with Hazel and Other Stories.* New York: Harcourt, Brace, 1957. *Collected Stories.* New York: Hill & Wang, 1962.

WARREN, ROBERT PENN (1905–). *The Circus in the Attic and Other Stories.* New York: Harcourt, Brace, 1948.

VONNEGUT, KURT (1922–). *Welcome to the Monkey House.* New York: Delacorte, 1968.

WALKER, ALICE (1944–). *In Love and Trouble: Stories of Black Women.* New York: Harcourt, Brace & Jovanovich, 1973.

WEIDMAN, JEROME (1913–). *The Captain's Tiger.* New York: Reynal & Hitchcock, 1947. *A Dime a Throw.* New York: Doubleday, 1957. *My Father Sits in the Dark and Other Stories.* New York: Random House, 1961. *Back Talk.* New York: Random House, 1963.

WELTY, EUDORA (1909–). *A Curtain of Green.* New York: Harcourt, Brace, 1941. *The Wide Net.* New York: Harcourt Brace, 1943. *The Golden Apples.* New York: Harcourt, Brace, 1949. *The Ponder Heart.* New York: Harcourt, Brace, 1954. *The Bride of the Innisfallen and Other Stories.* New York: Harcourt, Brace, 1955.

WEST, JESSAMYN (1907–). *The Friendly Persuasion.* New York: Harcourt, Brace, 1945. *Love, Death, and the Ladies' Drill Team.* New York: Harcourt, Brace, 1955.

WILLIAMS, TENNESSEE (1914–). *One Arm and Other Stories.* Norfolk, Conn.: New Directions, 1948, 1954. *Hard Candy: A Book of Stories.* Norfolk, Conn.: New Directions, 1954. *The Knightly Quest: A Novella and Four Stories.* New York: New Directions, 1967. *Eight Mortal Ladies Possessed: A Book of Stories.* New York: New Directions, 1974.

WILSON, EDMUND (1895–1972). *Memoirs of Hecate County.* New York: Doubleday, 1946. Rev. ed., New York: L.C. Page, 1959.

WRIGHT, RICHARD (1908–1960). *Uncle Tom's Children.* New York: Harper & Brothers, 1940. *Eight Men.* World, 1961.

YATES, RICHARD (1926–). *Eleven Kinds of Loneliness.* Boston: Little, Brown, 1962.

Part 2

AIKEN, CONRAD (1889–1973). *Collected Short Stories.* Cleveland: World, 1960. This contains forty-one of Aiken's stories, several previously uncollected pieces, and some pieces from his previous collections: *Bring! Bring! and Other Stories* (New York: Boni & Liveright, 1925), *Costumes by Eros* (New York: Scribner, 1928), and *Among the Lost People* (New York:

Scribner, 1934). An earlier collected edition, *The Short Stories of Conrad Aiken*, was published by Duell, Sloan & Pearce in 1940.

BEER, THOMAS (1888–1940). Wilson Follett, ed. *Mrs. Egg and Other Americans: Collected Stories.* New York: Knopf, 1947. This is the first and thus far the last volume of a projected complete edition of the more than 150 stories Thomas Beer published during his lifetime; it consists of twenty-nine stories, three of which were previously unpublished. Only one volume of Beer's stories appeared during his lifetime, *Mrs. Egg and Other Barbarians* (New York: Knopf, 1933).

BENÉT, STEPHEN VINCENT (1898–1943). *Twenty-Five Short Stories.* New York: Doubleday, 1943. *The Last Circle.* New York: Farrar & Rinehart, 1946. *Twenty-Five Short Stories* contains stories from Benét's previous collections, *Thirteen O'Clock: Stories of Several Worlds* (New York: Farrar & Rinehart, 1937) and *Tales Before Midnight* (New York: Farrar & Rinehart, 1939). *The Last Circle* contains fifteen stories and several poems, most of them written during Benét's last years.

BOYLE, KAY (1903–). *Thirty Stories.* New York: Simon & Schuster, 1946. *The Smoking Mountain: Stories of Postwar Germany.* New York: McGraw-Hill, 1951. *Thirty Stories* contains stories from Boyle's previous collections — *Wedding Day and Other Stories* (New York: Cape & Smith, 1930), *The First Lover and Other Stories* (New York: Smith and Haas, 1933), and *The White Horses of Vienna and Other Stories* (New York: Harcourt, Brace, 1936) — along with previously uncollected stories, including thirteen published in or after 1940. *Nothing Ever Breaks Except the Heart* (New York: Doubleday, 1966) contains stories written between 1939 and 1950.

CALDWELL, ERSKINE (1903–). *Jackpot.* New York: Duell, Sloan & Pearce, 1940. Carvel Collins, ed. *Men and Women: Twenty-Two Stories.* Boston: Little, Brown, 1961. *Jackpot* contains seventy-five stories, nine of them hitherto uncollected, from Caldwell's several previous volumes, including *American Earth* (New York: Scribner, 1931), *We Are the Living* (1933), *Kneel to the Rising Sun and Other Stories* (1935), and *Southways* (1938), all published by Viking. *Erskine Caldwell's Men and Women* contains twenty-one stories selected from Caldwell's some hundred and fifty; the subject matter is arranged from childhood to death.

FAULKNER, WILLIAM (1897–1962). *Go Down, Moses and Other Stories.* New York: Random House, 1942. *Knight's Gambit.* New York: Random House, 1949. *Collected Stories.* New York: Random House, 1950. In addition to previously uncollected Faulkner stories, this last book contains stories from *These Thirteen* (New York: Cape & Smith, 1931), *Doctor Martino and Other Stories* (New York: Smith & Haas, 1934), and *Go Down, Moses and Other Stories.*

MARCH, WILLIAM (1893–1954). *Trial Balance: Collected Short Stories* (New York: Harcourt, Brace, 1945) contains stories from *The Little Wife and Other Stories* (New York: Harrison Smith, 1935), *Some Like Them Short* (Boston: Little, Brown, 1939), and ten uncollected stories published after 1940. *Company K,* sometimes classified as a novel, is in effect a series of vignettes and narrative sketches with unified subject, theme, and structure; it is a much-neglected classic of the fiction growing out of World War I (New York: Smith & Haas, 1933).

PORTER, KATHERINE ANNE (1890–). *The Leaning Tower and Other Stories.* New York: Harcourt, Brace, 1944. Except for *The Leaning Tower,* Porter's stories are essentially products of the twenties and thirties. *Flowering Judas* was first published in a limited edition in 1930 and in a trade edition, which included four additional stories, by Harcourt, Brace in 1935. *Pale Horse, Pale Rider,* a collection of three novellas one of which was originally published by itself, appeared in 1939, from Harcourt, Brace. Her *Collected Stories,* published in 1965 by Harcourt, Brace & World, won the National Book Award.

STEELE, WILBUR DANIEL (1886–1970). *The Best Stories of Wilbur Daniel Steele.* New York: Doubleday, 1946. *Full Cargo: More Stories.* New York: Doubleday, 1951. These collections are from stories originally published in *Land's End and Other Stories* (1918), *The Shame Dance and Other Stories* (1923), *The Man Who Saw Through Heaven and Other Stories* (1927), and *Tower of Sand and Other Stories* (1929), all published by Harper, and *Urkey Island* (1926), published by Harcourt, Brace.

THURBER, JAMES (1894–1961). *My World — and Welcome to It.* New York: Harcourt, Brace, 1942. *The Thurber Carnival.* New York: Harper, 1945. In addition to six previously uncollected pieces, *The Thurber Carnival* contains stories from *My Life and Hard Times* (1933), *The Middle-Aged Man on the Flying Trapeze: A Collection of Short Pieces* (1935), and *Let Your Mind Alone: and Other More or Less Inspirational Pieces* (1937), all published by Harper, and *My World — and Welcome to It.*

WILLIAMS, WILLIAM CARLOS (1883–1963). *Make Light of It: Collected Stories.* New York: Random House, 1950. *Make Light of It* contains stories from *The Knife of the Times* (Ithaca, New York: Dragon Press, 1932) and *Life Along the Passaic River* (New York: New Directions, 1938), together with twenty-one previously uncollected stories, thirteen of them published for the first time. *The Farmers' Daughters: The Collected Stories of William Carlos Williams* (Norfolk: Conn.: New Directions, 1961) is identical to *Make Light of It,* except for the title piece and a brief introduction by Van Wyck Brooks.

Index